Ethnic Conflict

RELIGION, IDENTITY, AND POLITICS

Edited by

S. A. GIANNAKOS

Ohio University Center for International Studies
Research in International Studies
Global and Comparative Studies Series No. 1

Ohio University Press
Athens

© 2002 by the Center for International Studies
Ohio University
Printed in the United States of America
All rights reserved

The books in the Ohio University Research in International Studies series
are printed on acid-free paper ⊗ ™

10 09 08 07 06 05 04 03 02   5 4 3 2 1

Library of Congress Cataloging-in-Publication Data

Ethnic conflict : religion, identity, and politics / edited by S.A. Giannakos.
    p. cm. -- (Research in international studies. Global and comparative studies se-
    ries ; no. 1)
  Includes bibligraphical references and index.
  ISBN 0-89680-222-1 (pbk. : alk. paper)
    1. Ethnic conflict. I. Giannakos, S. A. (Symeon A.), 1957 - II. Series.

  HM 121 .E74 2001
  305.8--dc21

Contents

Acknowledgments   vii

CHAPTER ONE
Introduction   1
S. A. Giannakos

CHAPTER TWO
A Primer for Analyzing Ethnonational Conflict   21
Walker Connor

CHAPTER THREE
Violent Conflict and Patterns of Geopolitical Interaction
in Southeastern Europe   43
S. A. Giannakos

CHAPTER FOUR
Changes and Opportunities Wrought by Exile and Repatriation:
New Identities among Guatemalan Refugee Women   67
Paula Worby

CHAPTER FIVE
Religion and National Identity in Stalin's USSR:
Implications for Post-Soviet Politics   93
Steven Miner

CHAPTER SIX

Ethnic Conflict in Georgia   108

Neil MacFarlane, with George Khutsishvili

CHAPTER SEVEN

Democratic Governance and the Roots of Conflict in Africa   139

Muna Ndulo

CHAPTER EIGHT

Political Centralization and Social Conflict in Indonesia   170

Michael Malley

CHAPTER NINE

Sources of and Responses to Violent Conflict in South Asia   190

Chetan Kumar

CHAPTER TEN

International Organizations and the Prevention of Ethnic
Conflicts: Searching for an Effective Formula   216

Albrecht Schnabel

Contributors   237

Index   241

Acknowledgments

This edited volume is the result of a conference titled Interethnic and Religious Conflicts in Cross-Cultural Perspective that took place at Ohio University, Athens, in May 2000. The conference was primarily sponsored by the Center for International Studies, with substantial contributions from the Kennedy Lecture Fund, the Department of Political Science, African Studies, the Institute for Applied and Professional Ethics, Latin American Studies, Communication and Development Studies, Southeast Asian Studies, International Development Studies, and the Contemporary History Institute. The participants, whose varied backgrounds reflected the conference's interdisciplinary and cross-regional focus, made the conference a most pleasant and educational experience.

In addition to the participants who have contributed their conference papers to this volume, Robert Hayden and Diane Nelson participated and contributed to both the learning and enjoyable atmosphere of the conference. Harold Molineu, William Liddle, David Williams, Ann Freter, Steve Rubenstein, and Okon Akiba graciously served as discussants. Polly Sandenburgh, while awaiting the arrival of baby Claire, handled the logistics of the conference with patience and dexterity.

The conference itself would not have been possible without the unconditional support of Elizabeth Collins. Gillian Berchowitz selflessly contributed her time and ideas. Without her commitment from the very beginning this project would not have materialized.

I also acknowledge the students in my fall 2000 course on nationalism and ethnic conflict. They diligently read a number of chapters and provided useful comments.

My personal thanks go to Michael Mumper, who is primarily responsible for my involvement in this project.

Ethnic Conflict

1

Introduction

S. A. Giannakos

THE LAST DECADE of the second millennium was especially characterized by multiple and devastating violent conflicts along apparent religious and ethnic lines. This book seeks to expand the understanding
of the fundamental underpinnings of inter- and intragroup conflict
through a comparative interdisciplinary and interregional analytical
approach that proves the existence of common causal denominators
in the outbreak of violent conflicts across the globe. The existence of
common causal factors, independent of group identity, undermine the
often held assumption that violent conflict can be solely explained
away on identity incompatibility between groups. It is the book's contention that the understanding of the fundamental roots of violent
conflict is directly related to our ability to manage, resolve, and prevent conflicts.

Any analysis that seeks to understand the relationship between
group identity and violent conflict must begin with an attempt at
clarifying the concept of group identity. In trying to define national
or ethnic identity, scholars tend to focus on identity either as an end in
itself or as a means to an end, but hardly ever on both. Those who
focus on identity as an end tend to explain collective identity in

terms of assumed racial/genetic characteristics or presumed cultural/ linguistic uniqueness. Usually this line of thinking is associated with Johann Gottfried von Herder and his description of German nationalism.[1] An example of a more explicit and more contemporary work is that of Clifford Geertz, who emphasizes the concept of "primordial attachments," based on "given" independent variables such as "immediate contiguity and kin connection" and "being born into a particular religious community, speaking a particular language, or even a dialect of a language, and following particular social practices."[2] Anthony D. Smith also leans toward this interpretation by emphasizing the mythological origins of a group as the most important differentiating element of that group's ethnic or national identity.[3] The general thrust in this line of thinking is that culture-based identity must be retained and preserved and that its subscribers will and do take pride in its uniqueness.

The criticism often leveled against this school of thought is the same as Aristotle's criticism of the Platonic forms. Engaging in discovering the forms pleases the senses and the intellect a great deal, but what practical benefits does one derive from it? What are the practical applications of the forms? Is there a tangible practical benefit in philosophizing for the sake of philosophizing? Similarly, other than being proud of one's collective identity, what are the tangible benefits of this identity and do people really try to preserve it regardless of the cost associated with the effort of preservation? If collective identity is conceived only as an end, this would certainly contradict the concept of humans being rational and purposeful creatures. In his *National Identity*, Anthony D. Smith never even speculates as to what would happen to the identity of a group if that group actually came to realize that the mythological bases of its uniqueness are just that: mythological. Does the group then stop being the group and dissolve into oblivion? If not, then there must be other reasons that keep the group in existence.

The above realization provides the conceptual basis of the second school of thought, which views identity as a means to a specific end. Among many, the most prominent representatives of this school are Ernest Gellner, Benedict Anderson, Eric Hobsbawm, and Karl Deutsch.

In general terms, they tend to view collective identity as the instrument by which institutions, such as a state or a national state, become legitimate in the eyes of its citizens and the world, or a group of citizens (or potential citizens) becomes sovereign over a specific territory (the right to national self-determination). Again, collective identity in this context becomes the means by which certain institutions become or attempt to become legitimate. The creating of collective identity therefore is attributed to a process in which the role of the individual is strictly passive—collective identity is imposed on the group by realities beyond the individual's realm, such as systemic economic and political ones. Examples of this sort of manufactured identity vary across the spectrum, from the purely Marxist point of view, in which economic goals and relations define identity, to a more subtle Deutschian view that communication patterns create identity in the framework of progress. Gellner points out that "at the base of the modern social order stands not the executioner but the professor. Not the guillotine, but the (aptly named) *doctorat d'etat* is the main tool and symbol of state power."[4]

Explicit in Gellner's view is the notion that the institutions that control education and its content control collective identity. Since education in modern times is the function of the state, whoever is in control of the state controls education and, by extension, collective identity. In this context, collective identity serves specific purposes within the context of modernization,[5] which brought into the forefront such dilemmas as political legitimacy, centralization of political power, mass political participation, institutionalization of power sharing and distribution of resources, and self- and group awareness through education. In the fast-paced, unpredictable environment of modernity, identity became a remedy for the above dilemmas. In summary, the implication here is that the group and the group's identity are not produced by nature but by the social environment for specific social purposes.

Although the latter school of thought seems to be more popular than the former, it nonetheless suffers from certain inconsistencies. The tendency of the second school has been to use identity and the environment interchangeably or overlapping one another. If we take the analogy of a chameleon, this school of thought seems to argue that the immediate environment (the color of the rock or the color of the tree) transfers its characteristics to the chameleon rather than the chameleon assuming different colors, instinctively or otherwise. To take the analogy one step further, in this school's thinking, the chameleon's essence is reduced to its appearance, whichever one an observer witnesses at a specific time and under specific circumstances. Subsequently, there are as many definitions of collective identity as there are authors. For example: John Breuilly defines nationalism as a political ideology; Ernest Gellner, as a sentiment and "a political principle, which holds that the political and the national unit should be congruent"; Benedict Anderson, as the act of imagining a community; and Eric Hobsbawm, as an invented tradition (the color of the chameleon is an invention). It is this reality that has prompted Walker Connor to argue that "a nation is a nation, is a state, is an ethnic group, is a . . ."[6]

The above analysis delineates the general differences between the two schools of thought, which often are referred to, respectively, as primordialists and modernists, ethnonationalists and civic nationalists, or even nationalizers and Europeanizers.[7] As different as the two schools appear to be, they can still be the subjects of a single criticism. Whether they examine collective identity either as a means or as an end, they tend to examine collective identity in isolation from other collective identities, which might coexist or be in mutual conflict in the minds of individuals making up a group. They treat collective identity as if it is a monolith when in reality it contains elements of both schools of thought. For the proponents of civil nationalism, this oversight amounts to the situation in which they criticize the advocates of ethnic nationalism of irrational myth making and self-deception (it is unnatural for a chameleon to claim to have a single primordial and favorite color). For that reason, they end up suggesting a change of perception from ethnic nationalism to civic nationalism. In this regard, the modernists' recommendation for conflict resolution or prevention for ethnic conflicts rests entirely with convincing elites and peoples to change their primordial perceptions of collective identity.

To the primordialists, however, the above suggestion appears to be contradictory on two accounts. It seems that in their analytical approach the civic nationalists argue that it is the social and economic environment that dictates collective identity, but in their prescriptive approach they seem to argue that elites and people are the ones that really matter. This is especially intriguing in those cases in which decision making seeks to contain ethnic nationalism through economic sanctions, which tend to undermine economic development and political change (Serbian ethnic nationalism and Western economic sanctions in the 1990s come to mind here). On the second account, ethnic nationalists can make a case by arguing that groups or states claiming to be basing their identity on civic nationalism are in reality basing their identity on ethnic nationalism. The United States, for example, was developed as a state on the basis of an Anglo-Saxon ethnic identity—Mediterranean refugees, fleeing violence in Asia Minor in the 1920s, were refused entrance to the United States on the basis that they did not meet ethnic qualifications. The same could apply to Great Britain and the English or to France and the French, and certainly Germany and the Germans. In this climate of argumentation between the two schools of thought, the ongoing debate about what is ethnic and what is national identity and how they relate to conflict becomes part of the problem rather than part of the solution. This lack of clarity certainly corrupted policy in the case of Somalia, Rwanda, and Yugoslavia: the Somali conflict was considered malleable due to a perceived ethnic homogeneity of the Somalis; the Rwandan case, most intractable due to a perceived ethnic heterogeneity of the Rwandans; and the Yugoslav case, most confused due to the impossibility to fit into any specific category for any specific period of time.

Conceptualizing Group Identity

This section will attempt to undermine the tendency to view collective identity as a means or only as an end. It will establish a correlation between the individual's natural propensity to identify with something and the environmental stimuli that interact with human factors to produce multiple and multidimensional identities. This section will also argue that although the propensity to identify has been a permanent feature of human existence, the scope and content of identity has always been in flux and never a constant feature of an individual or a group. This notion will explain the inability to define and codify identity, thus signifying the need to shift the research focus to the purposes served by a specific identity rather than its nature. Thus it is the contention of this section that group identity can be better understood through the functional utilities it provides to its subscribers and which utilities are molded by time and space (where time correlates to knowledge and understanding, and space correlates to resources), and projected to a given political realm, which then filters and facilitates the manifestation of the identity. By clarifying the purpose and functions of identity, analysts will be able to calibrate the relation between identity and conflict, develop a more reliable diagnostic method about conflict causation, and produce more effective political and economic responses to dealing with conflict. For example, it is perplexing to be constantly exposed to the notion that certain conflicts are based on ancient hatred or that certain conflicts are based on religious differences. The conflict in Northern Ireland can be illustrative of this tendency. More often than not, and as Walker Connor demonstrates in this volume, this particular conflict is referred to as a religious one. In reality, all parties to the conflict are of the same religion. Religiously, therefore, they are more similar than they are different. In such cases, the questions that need to be asked and answered are, What causes the participants in such a conflict to produce religious differences? and Why do they then focus on the few differences rather than the vast similarities?

An instrumental analysis of an identity can begin with a reference to the second book of the *Republic,* where Plato begins his quest to define justice. He connects justice to one of three categories into which all things can be classified. He points out that there are things that people wish to possess for their own sake and not for any effects that might be entailed in them. There are things that people desire for both their own sake and for subsequent benefits that they will accrue.

And, there are things that are not by themselves desired, but are sought out only for the benefits they will accrue. Accordingly, Plato concludes that justice belongs to the second and fairest category, which a human seeks both for its own sake and for its beneficial consequences—while justice is considered to be a noble thing in itself, its practice also guarantees happiness to its practitioner.

What Plato said about justice can also be said of identity. Just as people value themselves or others for being just and take pride in being just, they also value having a social identity and taking pride in that identity. In this regard, identity can be viewed as an end only. But identity is also valued for the benefits it is thought to bring to its bearer. Often a person presumed to have no identity or negative identity (which is not actually possible since everyone has an identity) is ignored or considered a liability. On the other hand, a person considered to have an identity is either respected or despised (or feared), depending on the content of that person's identity. In this regard, identity can be thought of as a means to an end. This means identity is used toward winning recognition and acceptance from others. Subsequently, a social identity is both an end and a means to an end.

A metaphor taken from the world of chameleons again can be instrumental in conceptualizing which ends a social identity serves. Since it cannot become invisible, the chameleon must content itself with a qualified or limited ability to evade predators and stay alive while searching for the sources that will sustain existence. In its attempt to stay alive, the chameleon changes its color to avoid detection by predators. Color changing then becomes a defense mechanism in the pursuit of security (avoidance of bodily harm or death). In this regard, security or existence is an end in itself, while the defense mechanism based on color changing is the means to that end.

As far as existence goes, what applies to chameleons also applies to humans—the difference being that whereas the chameleon relies on color changing for defense, humans rely on numbers or on social structures. But just as the chameleon relies on a specific color at a specific time and place for defense, humans, at specific times and places, rely on specific social structures for defense against threats to individual existence. Although a particular society can be viewed as an end (since we all take pleasure in gossiping, the act of socializing is, in a sense, clearly pleasurable in itself), in reality a society is far more of a means to an end than just an end. Primarily then, a social structure can be viewed as the individual's shelter against threats to life. A social structure for a human being is what a school of fish is to a fish or a flock of birds is to a bird. Therefore, existence, which is an end in itself, dictates that humans live in social structures and adopt themselves to them just as a chameleon manifests colors to blend into a given environment. Identifying, then, with a social structure becomes a natural extension of human needs and desires, whether these are cognitive or instinctive. In this regard, a social identity is like clothing. Just as the natural and social environment dictates the need, availability, and properties of the garment(s), the natural and social environment also dictates the need, spectrum, and property characteristics of identity(ies)—in addition to the fact that people take pride in their clothing. This realization means that in the context of time and space, needs can be prioritized in terms of importance, and that the degree to which they can be satisfied relates to the availability of structures, tools, and tactics. The dependence of need satisfaction on structures, tools, and tactics manifests itself in terms of identity; see Paula Worby's chapter in this volume regarding identity manifestations among refugees of the Guatemalan civil war.

Just as needs and desires can be haphazardly prioritized, so can social identities. As humans go, different social structures provide different degrees of security against threats to existence. Hence, individuals primarily identify with those societal structures that appear to provide greater degrees of security and identify less with those that provide lower degrees of security. Since people tend to identity more with social structures that provide greater degrees of security and identify less with those that provide lesser degrees of security, social structures can also be prioritized. The availability of social structures varies from time to time and from place to place depending on the availability or feasibility of those tools and tactics that go into creating and maintaining social structures. Different times and resources allow the production or abandonment (or both) of different tools and tactics people deploy in pursuing the universal ends of humans, such as physical security (health included), economic security (maintaining a sustainable degree of affordability and well-being), individual accomplishment, social recognition, and contribution and usefulness, along with enjoying life's simple pleasures.

An attempt to prioritize needs within a political realm can be borrowed from Hedley Bull's approach. Keeping in mind that a society is more of a means to an end and not just an end, it is useful to note that in his *Anarchical Society,* Bull writes that "all societies seek to ensure that life will be in some measure secure against violence resulting in death or bodily harm."[8] This means that the primary and elementary goal (end) of any human being, and therefore of a social structure or a society, is the physical security of the society's individual members. Without the existence of relative security (a general perception that existence is conditionally guaranteed), an individual cannot be as mindful of the other primary, and certainly secondary, goals. This concept can be illustrated by the fact that when one is confronted by the dilemma of surrendering one's life or one's possessions, one clearly prefers to dispense of one's possessions, unless the surrendering of possessions means absolute physical insecurity.

By extension, the identity related to the need for physical security is clearly the most important primary identity, which means that an individual develops loyalty to the social structure that provides him or her with physical security. A primary and elementary collective identity, thus, can be conceptualized in terms of its shape and in terms of its substance. A collective identity's shape is associated with the characteristics of various social structures. It manifests itself in terms of individuals identifying with family, clan, tribe, nation, humanity, or neighborhood, village, city, state, or even the globe. Thus both the shape and the characteristics of the social structure are dependent on time and space—different times and different spaces produce different structures or different structural characteristics. On the other hand, the substance of any identity is based on the reality that individual security can only be attained in a societal setting in which the security of one individual depends on the association with others. Since there can be no society with one person, there can be no security for the individual who stands alone.

The above realization means that the substance of the most important primary collective identity is communicative along horizontal and vertical lines (between individuals and between generations), metaphysically (toward the dead and the yet to be born), as well as existentially and spatially (between human existence and the environment). This demonstrates that collective identity is not only multiple but multidimensional as well. It needs to be analyzed, conceived, and prioritized on two different levels (the individual and the group) in two dimensions (the physical and the metaphysical) and in two parameters (time and space). Recognizing the existence of identity at different levels, at different dimensions, and at different times and places will help in prioritizing between simultaneously existing identities within the same individual and the same group and, of course, between different groups. Sophocles has presented the best example demonstrating this reality in his tragedy *Antigone,* where the multiple and multidimensional aspects of identity come into an irreconcilable focus.

By conceptualizing collective identity along the lines above, one will be able to make sensible comparisons between similar manifestations of identity at different spaces and times; to distinguish between a collective identity's shape and its substance (patriotism and nationalism?), and to avoid falling into the fallacy of comparing the shape and substance of different identity manifestation, when in essence one is actually comparing different times and places. This leads to the position in which one can distinguish between dominant collective identities and subdominant ones, thus demonstrating that through time and space dominant identities can become subdominant and vice-versa. For example, a feudal identity might give priority to regionalism, patriotism, or nepotism, while an imperial identity might give priority to a national identity, which in turn might give way to a supranational identity, which eventually might become a national identity in a different context.

The chameleon and many sea creatures can change colors. Humans can change identities based on the purpose(s) each of them serves. It is not an automatic process. Rather it is the result of a prolonged and deliberate communicative process in which the individual makes a series of conscious decisions. No individual will willingly abandon an ethnic identity as long as that identity serves certain purposes for that individual and its group. Similarly, no force is capable of infusing a certain degree of civic identity to an individual if the individual does not see a certain purpose in adopting that identity. Thus it is not easy to get people to go along with replacing their loyalty to a state with loyalty to an empire, or loyalty to a local community with loyalty to a national community—with the reverse being the case as well.

In trying to prioritize manifestations of collective identity, one can begin by separating individual manifestations at the level of an individual's domain, and group identity manifestations at the social domain. As the above analysis regarding security indicates, an individual's social identity manifestations supersede individual manifestations. This is not because the group is considered more important than the individual, but because individuals invest their existence in group existence. Thus individual existence relies primarily on group existence, where the group is the investment individuals make in order to safeguard the sanctity of individual existence. This relationship is predictable enough so as to state that the greater the threat to individual existence, the higher the individual's identity with a group and the more the individual becomes willing to undertake risks on behalf of the group (in economic terms this is like protecting one's investments). This concept not only explains the existence of gangs in inner cities in the United States, where policing is weak, but also group identity in the Balkans, where security institutions are also weak. When individual and group physical security is relatively high, individual identity manifestations tend to be more pronounced. This explains such common stereotypes and comparisons as those pertaining to American individualism versus European or Japanese socialism, or American civic nationalism against Balkan ethnic nationalism. In reality the difference between the two identities is a difference in degree of group security resulting from the existence of strong policing and military institutions in the United States along with the absence of direct external threats, but increasingly weakening or disappearing ones in what used to be Yugoslavia—in other words, differences in time and space.

The reality that individual existence relies on group security also manifests itself in relation to the security of past and future generations. Sacrifices by individuals in the past command respect and reverence and obligates individuals of the present generation to preserve a degree of security for future generations. In this context, identity transcends time and generation gaps (often this sense of obligation is metaphorically referred to as collective memory or common historical experience). Individuals who are assumed to have sacrificed themselves for group security (in essence they sacrifice themselves to the sanctity of individual existence) become modal personalities, which in turn demand respect and recognition—that they did not die in vain. Here again, the lower that degree of individual and group security, the more respected the hero personalities become. The opposite clearly applies as well. On the other hand, when the waging of war becomes potentially detrimental to the sanctity of individual security, war heroes cease being modal personalities and attention then shifts to antiwar heroes or pacifists. This notion is illustrated best by public attitudes regarding the Vietnam War. On the other hand, struggles for political liberation, which also requires self-sacrifice, is among other causes justified on the rationalization that the sacrifice will allow future generations to live in peace. American involvement in World War I was in part portrayed as an investment necessary to end all wars. On the other side of the equation in the notion analyzed here are traitors and cowards, who are commonly despised.

Concern for individual and group security—for past, present, and future generations—achieves metaphysical connotations in the extent to which the sanctity of individual existence transcends a believed boundary separating the living and the dead. Socrates, who is little known for having repeatedly fought to defend Athens in war, is a well-known historical personality who opted for death in order to maintain his spiritual integrity and, presumably, existence. Also little known is the fact that once he refused an order by the tyrannical and oligarchic authorities of Athens to arrest a member of the democratic opposition. Among other things, his example clearly illustrates that the metaphysical qualities of identity, connected to security, manifest themselves in religious terms. Thus individuals tend to identify with religious beliefs or spiritual security structures the same way they identify with social security structures. Parallel to a social identity an individual maintains a spiritual identity and, as a result, the individual is constantly struggling to reconcile the two—physical needs and spiritual needs are not always compatible and threats to one are not necessarily threats to the other.

Next to identifying with a social and spiritual entity, individuals will identify with the environment on which the social entity relies for both physical security (the environment might be providing natural defenses against security threats), and economic security, which is intertwined with the group's physical security. Here again, the greater the degree of security provided to an individual by the environment, the higher the degree to which the individual tends to identify with the environment. Since security is not absolute but relative, individuals tend to identify with the broadest environment possible. Identifying with the river, the sea, the mountain, or the valley comes before identifying with the canoe, the boat, the cabin, or the field. Identities at this level target a wide spectrum: from a child's favorite hiding spot (one of a child's manifestations of patriotism), to the earth as a whole (earth images from space have changed the way people feel about their identity with the environment). The determining factor in establishing the scope of environmental identity is provided by time—the greater the ability to organize more efficient and more secure social units, the larger the scope of environmental identity by the individual. An example of this is individual identity with a country whose geographical scope varies from time to time.

Moving down the priority list of needs, collective identity can be connected to subsocial and subterritorial units that also provide important functions to secondary needs of human existence. Here individuals identify with employment organizations and structures or whatever individuals will end up doing to generate their living. Thus we end up with economic functional identities such as castes, clubs, occupational associations, class identity, or party affiliation. The intensity of identity manifestations at this level is analogous to the value of rewards perceived by the individual. An identity at this level can be easily transferable based on the availability of employment opportunities, advancement, self-fulfillment, and functional recognition. Along these lines, individuals identify with the educational practices or institution, which they may have relied on to acquire the skills or knowledge to enhance their existence and human potential. Educational experiences are directly connected to the form of individual identity mentioned earlier in the analysis. Education, whether it is formal or informal, traditional or modern, is the key link between the shape and substance of identity—it helps people prioritize social structure through an evaluation of the security functions they provide. In conclusion, while the substance of collective identity is always constant, the shape is not.

Functional Dependence and Change

It is argued so far that identity can be conceptualized in its multiple and multidimensional manifestations in terms of the purposes it serves for an individual. Human identity is connected to human needs and human needs are connected to functions designed to satisfy them. Identity, thus, can be understood though its functional base. Once the practicality of a function is proven through trial and error, individuals tend to adopt it. Unless an individual or a group perceives no alternative but change, there is always a great reluctance to abandon established functions. This is mainly due to an omnipresent uncertainty about the effectiveness and efficiency of untried functions and about the perceived ability by the would-be practitioners to perform these functions. Drastic and abrupt shifts in time and space (political change) produce the need for social adaptation. In turn, political change is characterized by insecurity due to competition between functions associated with security opportunities and functions associated with security risks. Unregulated competition between functions—for example, those related to security risks and those related to security opportunities—produces conflict between individuals connected with the respective functions. A number of similarly affected individuals (a social force) will organize themselves into a political force poised to promote or defend certain functions. The larger the magnitude and scope by which individuals are affected by abrupt and drastic political change, the larger will be those affected, and the larger will be the scope of opportunities and risks. Failure or inability to reconcile risks and opportunities results in the failure to address the security concerns of groups at the earliest possible stage of their development. This failure invariably results in devastating consequences. Individuals and groups gradually and systematically see their security structures being steadily undermined until all they are left with is a psychological inclination toward a social structure (shape) that is no longer functional. At such a point, collective identity is reduced to its substance and is treated exclusively as an end—to be defended at all costs and by all means. As violent, large-scale conflict erupts, its psychological dimension becomes most difficult to comprehend and confusion and stubbornness undermine logic. Violence becomes the instrument of the strategy by which the termination of the conflict is sought through forced identity modification—each of the embattled groups becomes involved in a mutually futile attempt to modify the other side's perception. This approach—along with the attempt by outsiders to also change identity perceptions as a way of managing and possibly resolving the conflict—often reinforces each group's tendency to perceive identity as an end only.

When the above occurs, it appears that groups, formed on a functional platform, are defending or promoting an identity, when in essence they are supposed to be defending or promoting a common function and only by extension the identity associated with that function. Unfortunately, all rational evaluation of security costs, risks, and opportunities tends to become inert in such situations. The best description of such a situation can be found in Thucydides' description of civil war in Corcyra in the *History of the Peloponnesian War*. To understand conflict that enters that extreme psychological state one needs to understand both the characteristics of a group's identity and also the purposes which the identity serves. Similarly, to take action toward changing an identity is not the same as addressing the causes of a seeming identity conflict. In the first instance, one tries to treat the symptoms. In the second instance, one tries to change the symptoms. Neither is an effective mechanism for reconciling functions through the art of compromising, commonly referred to as politics. The chapters in this volume are illustrative of the reality explained above.

Walker Connor demonstrates the psychological need for security and belonging as it manifests itself in the framework of the state system. He points out that although nation-states (each defined national group having its own state) might be ideal structures for group security, they are not always possible because states and groups do not coincide. For that reason, individuals and groups must reconcile their loyalty to the group with loyalty or disloyalty to the state they live in. He argues that more often than not the two loyalties are compatible and the identities (nationalism and patriotism) can be reconciled. However, governments need to be sensitive to this possibility and be constantly working to reconcile the different loyalties and identities. Connor also provides vivid illustrations of the multidimensional qualities of group identity which transcend time (generations) and space. Thus, he warns scholars and officials that perceptions are part of reality and should take seriously the fact that all national identities contain elements of primordial ties. He concludes by saying that as powerful as the national psychological bond is, it is not always the primary cause for conflict; it tends to become untamed once conflict reaches the level at which people are targeted because of their group identity.

S.A. Giannakos demonstrates the environment's role in group formation and group identity. By using the Balkan region as an example, he demonstrates that static environmental conditions over many centuries created entrenched group identities that manifest themselves in nearly exclusive primordial aspects. As such, they can be utilized as powerful devices for justifying political action regardless of whether these actions are compatible with the security interests of the groups involved in the actions. He also shows that the tendency to explain conflict exclusively in terms of the primordial manifestations of group identity results in the misdiagnosing of the causes of violent conflict. As a result, applied solutions end up becoming causes. Any accurate diagnosis must take into consideration all dimensions of collective identity.

Paula Worby's chapter on women's identity and political fortunes in conflict-torn Guatemala reveals three important realities about violent conflicts. The first is the degree and scope of devastation that conflict inflicts on all segments of society, regardless of age or gender, but, most significant, to those most vulnerable and least responsible for the outbreak of conflict. The individual pain and suffering remains always unaccountable. The second reality is the demonstration of how political change—unfortunately, that which produces the greatest degree of insecurity—becomes the impetus for politicization and identity construction by combining human potential and political parameters. Worby demonstrates how women in refugee camps took control of their destiny, organized themselves with the help of United Nations organizations, and converted themselves into a political force effectively demanding the recognition by the Guatemalan authorities of both their political and economic rights. Ironically, the third realization is that positive identity changes, when not facilitated or at least accommodated by a reciprocal political and economic change, lead to frustration. Women refugees returning to Guatemala found that their political gains had been sacrificed for the sake of reestablishing a seemingly stable social order that, in terms of gender relations, reduced women to their prewar social subordination.

Steven Miner, writing on religion in the Soviet Union, demonstrates that because of the metaphysical qualities of both national and religious identities, and because of the fact that individuals have multiple and multidimensional identities, a religious identity and a national identity tend to connect when a government (the Soviet government) fails to reconcile itself with the metaphysical, but indispensable, qualities of religious identity. Misplaced policies tend to alienate religious institutions, thus creating or reinforcing disloyalty to the government and loyalty to the opposition (dissenting national and religious movements).

Neil MacFarlane and George Khutsishvili's chapter on ethnic conflict in Georgia demonstrates the long-term counterproductive effects that Soviet national policies have had on the evolutionary dynamics of politics in the Caucasus region. The chapter shows that Soviet attempts to create, from above, security structures for the people of the Caucasus (like autonomous oblasts and regions, primarily to facilitate Soviet security concerns and control), created regional institutional interests which manifested themselves along ethnic lines when central power weakened in Moscow. Regional elites, which had been willingly co-opted into the Soviet order, were anxious to create their own security structures once the diminishing trend of Soviet authority became a reality. At the same time, subregional elites like those in Abkhazia, sought to utilize their connections with Moscow in order to prevent being co-opted by larger regional elites and political institutions like those of Georgia. Overall, the chapter demonstrates the extent to which ethnic identities are constructed in reaction to political risks and opportunities and in accordance with security concerns.

Muna Ndulo explains the role that governance has on the outbreak of violent conflicts in Africa. He points out that the lack of developed constitutional and institutional political mechanisms, suitable to the particular circumstances confronting the people in Africa, leads to the situation in which people's concerns and problems tend to be ignored, thus leading to repeated intrastate violent conflicts. By extension, Ndulo suggests that good governance would not only ameliorate the negative political and economic predicaments of the continent, but also provide a platform for viable political interaction between different groups forced into one state by historical circumstances associated with colonialism.

Michael Malley's chapter on Indonesia reaffirms the findings of the previous chapters. In addition, it draws attention to the correlation between the political causes of violent intrastate conflicts and the ethnic identity overtones that might come to characterize such conflicts. It is such a correlation that makes these conflicts intractable to rational and systematic analysis. Malley opens the way to the realization that created political disputes can gradually intensify into violent conflicts, which can intertwine with the psychological aspects of group identity, gain their own rationale, and achieve their own momentum. At this stage, groups tend to target each other's identity, and of course the carriers of that identity, with little logical and calculated thinking about the extent to which their actions are compatible with their political goals. Instead, the elimination of an identity is perceived to be the same as eliminating a problem, even though problems exist apart from identity.

Chetan Kumar examines conflict in South Asia and demonstrates not only the political roots of conflict, but also the tendency for local and regional conflicts to become mutually reinforcing, producing a degree of intractability that makes violent conflicts nearly impossible to resolve and most difficult to manage or prevent from becoming violent interstate conflicts. Kumar's chapter is a stern reminder that it is far easier and less expensive to prevent conflicts from intertwining to intractable levels than to allocate time and resources in trying to manage and resolve them.

Finally, Albrecht Schnabel demonstrates that conflict prevention (an attempt to ameliorate the social, economic, and political conditions that produce violence), albeit most difficult, should receive priority in the agenda of local, regional, and international agents (both governmental and nongovernmental). The various agents that are responsible for dispensing assistance should find ways to cooperate toward developing and administering prevention assistance and resources. The chapter takes into consideration the reality that the fact that something is sensible and desirable but not evidently possible should not deter us from exploring it. The alternative of simply reacting to situations, often too late and with too little, is certainly far more costly to humanity.

Notes

1. See Johann Gottfried von Herder, *Outlines of a Philosophy of the History of Man* (London: printed for J. Johnson by L. Hansard, 1800).

2. Clifford Geertz, "The Integrative Revolution: Primordial Sentiments and Civil Politics in the New States," in *Old Societies and New States: The Quest for Modernity in Asia and Africa,* ed. Clifford Geertz (New York: Free Press, 1963); quoted in J. Hutchinson and A. D. Smith, *Nationalism* (Oxford: Oxford University Press, 1994).

3. See Anthony D. Smith, *National Identity* (Reno: University of Nevada Press, 1991).

4. Ernest Gellner, *Nations and Nationalism* (Ithaca, N.Y.: Cornell University Press, 1983), 34.

5. James Coleman defines modernization as the stage of human development characterized by the following: a degree of self-sustaining growth in the economy; a measure of public participation in the polity; an increment of mobility in the society; and a corresponding transformation in the modal personality of individuals. See James S. Coleman, "Modernization: Political Aspects," in *International Encyclopedia of the Social Sciences,* ed. David Sills, 17 vols. (New York: Macmillan, 1968), 10: 400.

6. Walker Connor, "A Nation Is a Nation, Is a State, Is an Ethnic Group, Is a . . . ," *Ethnic and Racial Studies* 1 (4) (1978): 379–88.

7. See Ulf Hedetoft, ed., *Political Symbols, Symbolic Politics: European Identities in Transformation* (Brookfield, Vt.: Ashgate Publishing, 1998).

8. Hedley Bull, *The Anarchical Society* (New York: Columbia University Press, 1983), 4–5. On the spectrum of existence, insecurity is at the negative end, denoting imminent termination of existence. At the other end, security signifies a conditional guarantee that existence is safeguarded. In this context, security is always relative. Absolute security, in which existence is unconditionally guaranteed, is not feasible in our time.

2

A Primer for Analyzing Ethnonational Conflict

Walker Connor

THE STUDY OF ethnonational conflict is marked by profound confusion and disagreement. To substantiate this disarray, one need only review U.S. policy toward pre-1991 Yugoslavia and its successor states.

Following World War I, Woodrow Wilson had paradoxically promoted the creation of this multinational entity (originally named the Kingdom of the Serbs, Croats, and Slovenes) under the banner of self-determination of nations. The country was plagued by ethnonational tensions from the beginning,[1] a vulnerability effectively exploited by Nazi Germany and Fascist Italy during World War II. Throughout Yugoslavia's entire history—notions of national self-determination to the contrary—the United States remained a staunch supporter of Yugoslav unity, particularly following Tito's break with Stalin in 1948. After Tito's death, ethnic antagonisms became more conspicuous, but the Reagan administration viewed this unrest as driven primarily by economic factors (inflation, unemployment, and the like), although comparative data establish that economic concerns are seldom primary.[2] Lending a note of scientific certitude to this thesis of economic causation, one otherwise unidentified "senior Administration official" stated that the national outbursts were "70 percent economic" in origin.[3] No perceptible change in policy occurred during the Bush administration. Practically on the eve of the country's breakup, Secretary of State Baker publicly stated that Yugoslavia should remain "one nation," a statement broadly viewed as giving Serbian Slobodan Milosevic carte blanche to use force against Croatian separatists.[4]

Although the Clinton administration's perspectives on ethnic conflict in the region departed from the emphasis on economic explanations, they swung between two extremes. At first, Clinton was heavily influenced by Robert Kaplan's best-seller *Balkan Ghosts: A Journey Through History* (1993). Kaplan's thesis was that the peoples of the area were driven by historic, unchanging hatreds. Years later, now under the influence of Noel Malcolm's *Bosnia: A Short History* (1994), the president would tell the cadets at the Air Force Academy that it is "simply not true, as some have alleged, [that the peoples of the region] are genetically predisposed" to ethnic hatreds; Malcolm's thesis was that the ethnic strife was due to manipulation by elites, most notably Slobodan Milosevic.[5] That two popular writers should have exerted greater influence on U.S. foreign policy than did the State Department, the National Security Council, and the Intelligence agencies is truly remarkable, but it might be noted that the State Department and the CIA had an extremely poor record of recognizing and comprehending ethnonational unrest within the former Soviet Union and elsewhere.[6]

Perceptions of the nature of ethnonational conflict necessarily lead to the selection of specific means for managing the conflict. If the root cause is viewed as economic, the solution, as adopted by the Reagan administration, is to alter the mix of economic forces through an infusion of economic aid. If immutable hatreds are the cause, a do-nothing policy, such as that which characterized the early Clinton presidency, is logical. If manipulation by elites is the cause, the answer is simply to get rid of the Milosevices, a policy still in place at this writing. None of these policies worked because they were all predicated upon a flawed understanding of ethnonationalism.

What follows then are six suggested guidelines for the student of ethnonational conflict. They are treated under the headings: (1) What

Makes Ethnonational Movements Different, (2) The Role of Homelands and Homeland Psychology, (3) Are Homeland Peoples Intent on Independence, (4) Problems Associated with Autonomy, (5) The Need to Concentrate on Evidence of What the People Think and Feel Rather Than on What Elites Claim They Do, and (6) The Need to Respect the Distinction between Fact and Perceptions of Fact.

What Makes Ethnonational Movements Different?

To answer this, we must first ask, What is ethnonationalism and how does it differ from just plain nationalism? The answer is that there is no difference if *nationalism* is used in its proper sense. Unfortunately, this is rarely the case. The comparative study of nationalism has been plagued by improper and inconsistent terminology. Particularly troublesome has been the slipshod use of the two most central terms: *nations* and *nationalism.*

Although often so used, *nation* is *not* a proper synonym for either a state or for the entire population of a state without regard to its ethnic composition. In its pristine sense, *nation* refers to a group of people who believe they are ancestrally related. It is the largest group that can be aroused, stimulated to action, by appeals to common ancestors and to a blood bond. It is, in this sense, the fully extended family. The term *American nation,* whether used in reference to the United States or to its citizens, is therefore a misnomer.

Nationalism, as properly used, does *not* connote loyalty to the state; that loyalty is properly termed patriotism. Nationalism should connote loyalty to one's nation, to one's extended family. One can therefore speak of English or Welsh nationalism but not of British nationalism, the latter being a case of patriotism. This is not a matter of semantic nit-picking, for it is essential that the vital difference between the two loyalties never be blurred. As reflected in many of the chapters in this volume, conflicts involving loyalty to state (patriotism) and loyalty to national group (nationalism) speckle the globe from Tibet to Kashmir to Kurdistan to Chechnya to Transylvania to Kosovo to the Basque country to Shan state to Rwanda to Chiapas to Quebec.

The most current vogue among writers on nationalism is to refer to loyalty to the state as civic nationalism and loyalty to the nation as ethnic nationalism. But this only tends to propagate the misconception that we are dealing with two variants of the same phenomenon. If writers prefer to use *civic identity* or *civic loyalty* in preference to *patriotism*—fine. But the fundamental dissimilarities between state loyalty and nationalism should not be glossed over by employing the noun *nationalism* to refer to two quite different phenomena.

The two loyalties represent two very different orders of things. Loyalty to the state is sociopolitical in nature, and is based in large part on rational self-interest. Loyalty to the nation is intuitive rather than rational, and is predicated upon a sense of consanguinity. When the two are viewed as being in irreconcilable conflict, loyalty to the nation customarily proves the more powerful.

The term *ethnonationalism* therefore contains an inner redundancy. If nationalism were consistently employed to refer to the nation or *ethnos* (the Greek equivalent for nation), then ethnonationalism would be a one-word tautology (*i.e.*, "national nationalism"). It is used simply to make certain that others are aware that what is being referred to is not loyalty to the state but loyalty to the extended family.

Ethnonational movements, then, are movements conducted in the name of the national group. Their leaders employ familial words and metaphors in their call to arms. The people are quite commonly addressed as "Brothers and Sisters" and common ancestry is stressed. Listen, for example to Mao Tse-tung in 1939:

> Fathers, brothers, aunts, and sisters throughout the country: we know that in order to transform this glorious future into a new China, independent, free, and happy, all our fellow countrymen, every single zealous descendent of Huang-ti [the legendary first emperor of China] must determinedly and relentlessly participate in the concerted struggle.[7]

And here is Ho Chi Minh in 1946:

> Compatriots in the South and Southern part of Central Viet-Nam! The North, Center, and South are part and parcel of Viet-Nam! . . . We have the same ancestors, we are of the same family, we are all brothers

and sisters. . . . No one can divide the children of the same family. Likewise, no one can divide Viet-Nam.[8]

The use of these communist examples is a reminder that leaders of the most diverse ideological inclinations, even ideologies that are ostensibly opposed to nationalism, resort to playing the ethnonational card when trying to mobilize a people.

Examples of such speeches could be multiplied many times over. A more contemporary illustration is offered by Slobodan Milosevic, whose 1987 speech to Serbs in Kosovo served as a major catalyst for subsequent Serbian behavior: "This is your land. These are your houses. Your meadows and gardens. Your memories. You shouldn't abandon your land just because it's difficult to live, because you are pressured by injustice and degradation. It was never part of the Serbian . . . character to give up in the face of obstacles, to demobilize when it's time to fight. . . . You should stay here for the sake of your ancestors and descendants. Otherwise your ancestors would be defiled and descendants disappointed."[9]

For some time now, I have been collecting the speeches of nationalist leaders and the proclamations and programs of national movements. What impresses is their striking similarities. The near universality with which certain images and phrases appear—blood, family, ancestors, mother (as in motherland and mother tongue), father (as in *fatherland* and *forefathers*), brothers, sisters, home, hearth, cradle land—and the proven success of such invocations in eliciting massive popular responses—tell us much about the nature of national identity and ethnonational movements.

Ethnonational movements are not always recognized as such. Perhaps this is most common where a religious or denominational cleft closely corresponds with an ethnonational division. For example, the protracted struggle in Northern Ireland—although often described as a religious issue—is better understood as a competition between those who consider themselves ethnically Irish and those who do not. The non-Irish are mostly descendants of seventeenth-century settlers from lowland Scotland. In the nineteenth century, Joseph Chamberlain, in his resistance to home rule for all of Ireland, made much of this by urging the people of lowland Scotland to stick by their kin. He reminded them that the people of Ulster were "bone of your bone, flesh of your flesh" and that "blood is thicker than water."[10] Note the absence of a reference to the common religion. The relative unimportance of religion to the conflict was manifest in a poll conducted in 1990. Asked to list what they perceived as the causes of the conflict, only 13 percent of those described as Protestants and 12 percent of those described as Catholic listed religion as a factor.[11]

A somewhat similar case in Egypt is currently in the news. One of the many periodic outbreaks of violence involving the Coptic minority has, as usual, been described solely as a conflict between Muslims and the Coptic Christians. But religious preference in what is termed the Arab World is often an indicator of national identity. Within Egypt, two identities have long competed: the concept of Egyptian, with roots going back to Pharaonic times, and the concept of being part of the Arab nation. The Coptic Church was prominent within Egypt long before Islam was brought by Arabs from the Arabian Peninsula and the word Copt means Egyptian. To both its members and its enemies, the Coptic religion is therefore a symbol of a pre-Islamic but also a pre-Arab identity.

A potent illustration of a person failing to recognize an ethnonational struggle for what it is is offered by Carlos Westendorp, the former high representative of the United Nations charged with carrying out the Bosnian Peace Agreement. In an interview, Mr. Westendorp maintained that the conflict is simply a religious one, noting, "The Bosnians are all the same people. They are all Slavs."[12] Well, yes. But so are the Poles and the Russians, who are not noted for sharing a sense of common identity. And so too are the Czechs and Slovaks— now living apart despite both common Slavness and common Catholicism.

As earlier noted, when nationalism and patriotism are perceived to be in conflict, it is nationalism that customarily proves the more powerful allegiance. This is not to deny that patriotism can be a very powerful sentiment. The state has many effective means for inculcating love of country and love of political institutions—what social scientists collectively term political socialization. Not the least effective of these is control of public education, and particularly control over the content of history courses. But despite the many advantages that the state has for politically socializing its citizens in patriotic values, patriotism, as evident from the multitude of separatist movements pockmarking the globe, cannot muster the level of emotional commitment that nationalism can. Perhaps the most instructive recent case is that of the former Soviet Union, wherein a most comprehensive, intensive, and multigenerational program to exorcise nationalism and to exalt what was quite correctly called "Soviet patriotism" proved remarkably ineffective.

The impact of nationalism on yesterday's political map has been enormous. The dismemberment of the former Soviet Union and the Federal Republic of Yugoslavia and the independence of East Timor are only the most recent manifestations of the challenge that ethnonationalism poses to the survival of the multinational state. At the bottom of all this unrest is a concept of political legitimacy that makes ethnicity the ultimate standard for judging legitimacy. It holds that a national group—just because it considers itself to be a separate nation—has the right, if it so desires, to its own state. At first untitled, later referred to as "the principle of nationalities," and more recently as "national self-determination," this concept of political legitimacy now manifests itself throughout the globe in antistate movements.

Despite the history of national self-determination, the continuing lack of coincidence between ethnic and political borders is glaring. Of the more than 190 contemporary states, probably not more than fifteen could qualify as essentially homogeneous: Japan, Iceland, the two Koreas, Portugal, and a very few others. Moreover, we have entered a period of unprecedented migrations, which are currently altering the homogeneity of a number of these exceptions. The multiethnic state is therefore easily the most common form of country. It contains at least two significant groups. In 40 percent of all states there are five or more such groups. Some states contain more than one hundred groups. Perhaps the most startling statistic is that in nearly one-third of all states (31 percent), the largest national group is not even a majority. This is true of newly independent Kazakhstan and nearly true of newly independent Latvia. Ethnic heterogeneity, and not homogeneity, therefore characterizes the typical state.

The Role of Homelands and Homeland Psychology

Most states are not just multiethnic but multihomeland as well. With the principal exception of a few immigrant societies such as Argentina, Australia, and the United States, the landmasses of the world are divided into ethnic homelands, territories whose names reflect a particular people. Catalonia, Croatia, England (from Engla land: land of the Angles), Euzkadi (lit., Basque Homeland) Finland, Iboland, Ireland, Kurdistan (lit., land of the Kurds), Mongolia, Nagaland, Pakhtunistan, Poland, Scotland, Swaziland, Sweden, Tibet, and Uzbekistan constitute but a small sampling.

To the people who have lent their name to the area, the homeland is much more than territory. The emotional attachment is reflected in such widely used descriptions as the native land, the fatherland, this sacred soil, the ancestral land, this hallowed place, the motherland, land of our fathers, and, not least, the homeland. In the case of a homeland, territory becomes intermeshed with notions of ancestry and family. This is how Sir Walter Scott expressed it in the eighteenth century:

> Breathes there the man, with soul so dead,
> Who never to himself hath said,
> This is my own, my native land!
>
> . . .
>
> Land of my sires! what mortal hand
> Can e'er untie the filial band
> That knits me to thy rugged strand.[13]

The invulnerability of such sentiments to time, place, and culture is suggested by the works of a contemporary Uzbek poet whose homeland is in Muslim Central Asia, part of the former Soviet Union:

> So that my generation would comprehend the Homeland's worth,
> Men were always transformed to dust it seems.
> The Homeland is the remains of our forefathers
> Who turned into dust for this precious soil.[14]

Poets, of course, are not the only ones to invoke the homeland. Listen to the words of Stefan Cardinal Wyszynski, who, more than anyone else, could claim to speak for the Polish nation in the post–World War II era: "Next to God, our love is Poland. After God, one must above all remain faithful to our homeland, to the Polish national culture."[15] That is to say, one must love the homeland ahead of self, ahead of family, ahead of everything but God. Yet more recently, in his outgoing speech as Israel's prime minister, Yitzhak Shamir said, "Eretz Yisra'el is not only another piece of land, it is not just a place to live. Above all, Eretz Yisra'el is a value; it is holy. Any conscientious Jew aware of his roots will never be able to treat Eretz Yisra'el as a commodity. . . . [A]nd just as there is a single Eretz Yisra'el, there is only one nation of Israel."[16]

This emotional attachment to the homeland derives from perceptions of it as the cultural hearth and, very often, as the geographic cradle of the ethnonational group. In Bismarckian terminology, blood and soil (Blut und Boden!) have become mixed. The emotionally pregnant concept of "my roots" implies soil. The psychological associations thus made between homeland and one's people are the more—not the less—intense for being emotional and resisting exposition in rational terms.

The important point is that the populated world is subdivided into a series of perceived homelands to which, in each case, the indigenous ethnonational group is convinced it has a profound and proprietary claim. Again, the particular words used to describe homelands are instructive. Who but the Scots could have plenary claim to Scotland, who but the Kashmiri to Kashmir, the Flemish to Flanders, Corsicans to Corsica, Basques to Euzkadi, or Welsh to Wales?

Given that the land masses of the world are divided into some three thousand homelands over which the political borders of something less than two hundred countries have been superimposed, it is hardly surprising that most states are not just multinational but also multihomeland. This is of the greatest significance when assessing the probable political instability of tomorrow's world, for the demands of ethnonational movements tend to be coterminous with their homeland. In terms of geography, it is for the homeland that ethnonational groups demand greater autonomy or full independence. For example, in the last stages of the Soviet Union, it was precisely over their homeland—over mother Armenia, Estonia, Georgia, Latvia, Lithuania, and so on—that the non-Russian peoples demanded of Gorbachev greater control. It is over Euszkadi, Corsica, Kashmir, Nagaland, and Tibet that the Basques, the Corsicans, the Kashmiris, the Nagas, and the Tibetans demand greater control. The principal slogan of the Québécois, "*Maîtres Chez Nous*"—captures this attitude nicely. The Québécois must be masters in our home—meaning the homeland of Québec.

It is possible, of course, that an autonomy or independence movement may be based on regionalism rather than on an ethnic homeland. This is true of the movement which recently separated Eritrea from Ethiopia and is also true of a much weaker and nonviolent movement to separate British Columbia and other western provinces from Canada. But the great numbers of autonomy and secessionist movements that pockmark the globe are being waged by homeland peoples. It is the multihomeland state that is the target of ethnonational demands for autonomy or independence (or both).

A number of states are essentially unihomeland, a characterization often reflected in the name of the state (e.g., Bulgaria, Deutschland [Germany], Estonia, Ireland, Nippon [Japan], and the like). A unihomeland state may contain large numbers of ethnic minorities because of past migration, but the aspirations of such minorities, denied as they are of a homeland base and usually being rather geographically diffuse, are customarily directed to equal treatment and improved status within the society rather than to autonomy or secession. In such states, homeland psychology may be a major factor leading to violence, demands for ethnic cleansing, and the like. But only the homeland psychology of the state's dominant group is involved. There are usually no demands for autonomy or for the state's dismemberment on the part of minorities.

In addition to unihomeland states, there are, as earlier noted, a small number of immigrant states which are essentially nonhomeland states. Behavior patterns, as reflected in much higher intergroup marriage rates, language acculturation rates, and assimilation rates, are very different within immigrant and nonimmigrant states. As we are all aware, the United States—that immigrant state par excellence—is certainly not free of ethnic problems. But, as in the case of unihomeland states, it is equal rights and opportunities, not questions of autonomy or separatism, that dominate minority-majority relations there. Questions concerning autonomy arise within the United States only in relation to its relatively few homeland peoples: Hawaiians, those Amerindian peoples who have elected to remain on "reserved" Indian lands, and those Eskimos or Inuits living in settled communities within Alaska. The point is that it is the integrity of the multihomeland state that is challenged by ethnonationally inspired movements and that analogies should not be drawn between their problems and the experiences of unihomeland or nonhomeland states.

Are Homeland Minority People Intent on Separation?

Noting that homeland-dwelling minorities aspire to greater independence from the state is not to imply that they seek independence. The essence of the national self-determination imperative is choice, not result. As mentioned, it holds that a national group has the right to secede and form its own state *if it so desires*. But in the overwhelming number of cases for which we have data, a majority—usually a substantial majority—are often prepared to settle for something less than independence. Attitudinal data on the Basques indicate that the percentage of those strongly committed to separatism peaked in the late 1970s at about 36 percent.[17] A survey conducted in Scotland in 1995 indicates that two-thirds of the populace did not favor independence.[18] A mid-1996 poll indicates that 86 percent of the Corsican population is opposed to separation from France.[19] And although the Slovaks were given their independence from Czechoslovakia in the early 1990s, this had not been the goal of most Slovaks; a 1990 poll, for example, indicated that only 8 percent of Slovakia's population desired it.[20] In the case of the Québécois, the data suggest that pro-separatists never surpassed 20 percent of the Franco-Canadian community prior to 1990.[21]

While separatists were a minority in these cases, a preponderant percentage of those same groups did favor major alterations in their country's power structure—that is to say, they desired a much greater measure of meaningful autonomy. In a 1968 poll of Franco-Canadian youth (seventeen to nineteen years of age), for example, while only 13 percent favored separatism, 68 percent favored greater autonomy for Québec, and only 8 percent preferred no change in Québec's status.[22] While, as mentioned, polls in Scotland show only a minority prefer total separation, a strong majority has regularly indicated a preference for greater autonomy. In 1997, some three-fourths (74.3 percent) of the Scottish electorate voted affirmatively in a referendum offering greater autonomy to Scotland. A similar offer of autonomy was made to the Welsh at about the same time, and much was made of the fact that only a slight majority voted in favor. However, approximately 40 percent of all people living in Wales are of English descent, so it may well be that the number of ethnically Welsh people indicating an interest in greater autonomy exceeded 80 percent.

There are numerous other illustrations of a people broadly prepared to settle for something less than independence. A 1996 poll of Okinawan opinion, conducted by the University of the Ryukyus, demonstrated a similar pattern. While only 3.3 percent preferred independence, 13.2 percent desired homeland control over all powers other than foreign policy and defense, and 38.4 percent desired authority over budgetary and legal matters.[23] On the ethnically Swedish Åland Islands, which are owned by Finland, only 17 percent favor separation, a result of an unusually high degree of autonomy enjoyed by islanders.[24] Similarly, in the above-mentioned poll of Slovaks, while only 8 percent desired independence, 71 percent desired a major decentralization of political power, and only 16 percent favored no major changes. Moreover, in a number of situations for which we have no attitudinal data, the same willingness to settle for something less than separatism is often evident. Thus, a letter to the editor of the *New York Times* (February 10, 1996) from the president of the Association of Tamils of Sri Lanka in the United States read in part: "The Tamils want a space of their own where their physical security, economic welfare, and ethnic and cultural identity can be assured. All

Tamil parties, including the Liberation Tigers of Tamil Eelam, are agreed on this demand. They also agree it is possible to find a solution within a united but not unitary Sri Lanka."[25]

There are numerous reasons why most members of a national group may be prepared to settle for autonomy rather than independence. A major factor often accounting for a willingness to settle for something less than total independence—at least in the democratic states of Western Europe and Canada—is that the state frequently enjoys a reservoir of good will. Members of national groups, even groups who are not dominant in the state, do not necessarily perceive loyalty to national group and loyalty to country as incompatible. Thus, while the Québécois express a greater affinity toward Québec than toward Canada, they nonetheless express a powerful sense of affection toward Canada.[26] Similarly, although the Basques have good reasons historically to distrust the Spanish state (most recently their experiences during the Franco regime), some 10 percent of respondents to a poll chose to identify themselves as "more Basque than Spanish" in preference to the more limited category of "Basque."[27] At least to this 10 percent, "Basque," while being considered the more important identity, was not perceived as excluding a significant measure of affinity for the Spanish state. In like manner, in a 1992 poll only 19 percent of Scots elected to describe themselves as "Scottish not British," while 40 percent selected "more Scottish than British" and 33 percent selected "equally Scottish and British."[28]

There are, of course, peoples who strongly desire independence. In sharp contrast with Canada, the United Kingdom, Spain, and other states, opinion polls conducted within the Soviet Union during its last years starkly underline the lack of affection for that state on the part of non-Russians. A poll conducted in October 1990, for example, indicated that 91 percent of the three Baltic nations and 92 percent of all Georgians favored secession.[29] And in September 1999, 78.5 percent of those East Timorese who risked physical harm to vote, voted for independence.

Such high levels of pro-separatist sentiment reflect a startling level of anti-state sentiment, for even if the state is viewed with only marginal fondness, it is not incongruous that most members of a national minority are prepared to settle for autonomy. Autonomy has the potential for satisfying the principal aspirations of the group. Devolution—the decentralization of political decision making—has the potential for elevating a national group to the status of masters in their own home. And this may be quite enough. Ethnonational aspirations, by their very nature, are driven more by the dream of *freedom from*—freedom from domination by outsiders—than *freedom to*—freedom to conduct relations with states. Ethnocracy need not presume independence, but it must presume *meaningful* autonomy at the minimum. As earlier noted, the conviction that the nation must exert control over its own destiny is reflected in the chief slogan of the Québécois, *Maîtres Chez Nous*. The Québécois must be masters in their own home, meaning the homeland of Québec. They are convinced that within their homeland they must have the ultimate power of decision making over those matters most affecting ethnonational sensibilities and nation maintenance.

Unfortunately, central authorities have tended to perceive any demand for a significant increase in autonomy as tantamount to, or an important step toward, secession. Governments have been inclined to guard their prerogatives zealously and to resist any move toward decentralization. In doing so, they often further the very result that they ostensibly wish to avoid, for there is an inverse relationship between a government's willingness to grant meaningful autonomy and the level of separatist sentiment. For example, when the Spanish government first granted an autonomy statute to the Basques in 1979, the proportion of Basques desiring independence dropped from 36 per cent to 12 per cent.[30] Recent events in Canada illustrate this same phenomenon in reverse. Denied in 1990 a request that the constitution be so worded as to recognize the French-speaking people of Québec as "a distinct society," those Québécois in favor of separation rose dramatically from less than 20 percent to well over 50 percent.

The message therefore is clear: governments of multinational states refuse to countenance demands for decentralization at the peril of increasing separatist sentiment and increasing the likelihood of violence.

Switzerland, while certainly not immune to ethnically inspired dissension, demonstrates that a multinational democracy can survive for centuries if the political system is sufficiently decentralized. The confederal, cantonal structure of the country, combined with its ethnic map, minimizes the possibility of domination or even the *perception* of domination by the numerically predominant Germanic element. In the case of the Jura region in the canton of Bern, within which a sizable French-speaking minority was dominated by the Germanic element, the Francophones waged a successful secession movement during the 1970s. But, most instructively, the secessionists aspired to secede only from the German-dominated canton of Bern, not from Switzerland. Given their own ethnocracy (the Jura canton), they considered their right to national self-determination fulfilled. Following, if somewhat haltingly, this same path, a number of Western democracies, most notably Belgium, Britain, Canada, Italy, and Spain, have at least partially assuaged ethnonational aspirations through the recent granting of substantial autonomy to ethnonational groups.

Problems Associated with Autonomy

Why has autonomy often only assuaged rather than satisfied? It was earlier noted that most members of a national minority are prepared to settle for *meaningful* autonomy. But autonomy is an amorphous concept meaning quite different things to different people. It may refer to very limited home rule or to regional control over everything other than foreign policy, that is to say, it can depict any situation on the continuum between total subordination to the center and total independence.

A rational first step for those hoping to negotiate an agreement for peacefully accommodating ethnonational aspirations is to ascertain (through referenda, attitudinal surveys, and the like) the full spectrum of popular sentiments among the homeland people concerning minimally acceptable changes in the distribution of powers. What percentage is prepared to settle for the status quo, or for this or that or the other, all the way across the spectrum to those who will settle for nothing less than independence. Also ascertained should be the maximal levels of concessions to autonomy that are acceptable to various segments of the state's wider population. Such data often discredit extremist positions held by those claiming to speak for the entire homeland people or by those claiming to speak for the entire population of the state living outside the homeland, thereby relieving negotiators on both sides from unhelpful pressures.

Agreements concerning the division of powers between homelands and the central state are difficult to achieve and, once achieved, to maintain. Peace accords between independent states can endure because the parties can subsequently each go their own way—that is to say—states occupy separate spheres. But homelands and states do not occupy separate spheres—they overlap. And many of the prerogatives inherent in the homeland peoples' demand to be "Masters in Our Home" naturally conflict with prerogatives adhering to state sovereignty.

Consider just the issue of the movement of peoples. Central governments not only control the movement of people across the state's borders (immigration/emigration) but also the movement of people within the country. Democratic governments customarily insist that all legal residents have the right to live wherever they choose. Typical is the wording of Article 19 of the Indian constitution, which stipulates that all citizens "shall have the right to move freely throughout the territory [and] to reside and settle in any part of the territory of India." On the other hand, few if any matters will be deemed a more exclusive prerogative by a homeland people than the issue of who is to be permitted to live within the nation's home. An influx of significant numbers of nonmembers of the nation can be expected to trigger resentment and a rise in separatist sentiments. And indeed, such an influx undergirds much of the violence and separatist sentiment throughout the homelands that comprise northeastern India.

Any agreement reached concerning migration cannot eradicate the natural tension between the notion of, let us say, Corsica for the Corsicans and the notion of the free movement of citizens within the state. An autonomy agreement may coat over but cannot eradicate such underlying contradictions. An agreement should therefore not be viewed as permanently ensuring a nonviolent relationship. The price of an enduring peaceful relationship is apt to be permanent renegotiation. Working, enduring autonomy will require periodic adjustments in the interrelationship of the homeland and the center in response to changing circumstances and perceptions.

The Need to Concentrate on Evidence of What the People Think and Feel Rather Than on What Elites Claim They Do

Nationalism is a mass, not an elite, phenomenon, and the gap between popular attitudes and the manner in which those attitudes are described by elites is often very large. Consider the case of East and West Germany. The East German authorities had for some time maintained that the difference in socioeconomic forces within East and West had given rise to a separate national identity on the part of East Germans. It was perhaps not too surprising that many American academics bought this. But so too did the academicians in West Germany. By the mid-1970s there was a general consensus among German intellectuals that the Germans of the two states had come to develop two totally distinct national identities. There were now two families, so talk of reunification of the family had no relevance. How wrong they were! Ethnic identity proved far more durable and powerful than the intellectuals could appreciate. Recall the events of 1989, when even those who suggested that reunion be carried out by stages proved no match for Helmut Kohl, who, under his seductive banner *Wir Sind Ein Volk!* (We are one nation!), called for immediate union.

On the fifth anniversary of reunification, an editorial in a Frankfurt newspaper had this to say of those intellectuals who had closed their eyes to a great many indications of the continuing vitality of a single German consciousness:

> How . . . was it possible that a large number of . . . luminaries spoke about unity ambivalently or reluctantly? Representatives of intellectual Germany solemnly declared that they had no use for the notion of bringing together Germans in one state. This, they said, was also the feeling of the German people, which [as it turned out] was better than

its reputation. After unification, no one in western Germany gave up his/her position or responsibilities on account of such foolishness and lack of character. . . . Should someone who, in freedom and prosperity, turned on his/her own people remain uncensored, indeed stand there blameless?[31]

The writer of this editorial clearly wants revenge on those scholars—fellow ethnics—who failed to appreciate the power of ethnonational identity. As I read the piece, I could not help but think that were such draconian measures applied to all the Soviet and East European specialists throughout Europe and North America who had ignored or misunderstood the significance of ethnonationalism, as well as all the authorities in international relations and security studies who had suffered from the same blindness, we would be facing a purge of truly Stalinesque proportions. Similarly, in the period leading up to the ratification of the Maastricht Treaty, the political, industrial, financial, labor, religious, academic, and media elites represented popular opinion throughout all of Western Europe as favoring a trend toward regional political integration, despite massive displeasure with such eventuality.[32] The movement toward this political integration of Western Europe has been elite driven and should not be perceived—as many intellectuals have insisted—as evidence of the erosion of nationalism within the region.

Analysts should therefore key on evidence of popular attitudes: mass movements, level of support for the most unequivocally nationalist leaders, and the like. Despite obvious shortcomings, attitudinal polls, when intelligently analyzed, are far preferable to the assertions of elites or to analyses offering no firm evidence of popular sentiments. Polls of young children are often particularly valuable because they reflect what elders are saying within the relative security of the home. Overall, as we are reminded by the decades of conventional and imperfect analyses of the Soviet Union, the view from the palace and the capitol should not blind the analysts to the far more perfect view from the streets and the hinterland.

The Need to Respect the Distinction between Fact and Perceptions of Fact

The analysis of ethnonational conflict deals with the latter. Not with facts, but with perceptions of fact. Not with chronological history, but with sentient, or felt, history. Pointing out, for example, that the Croats and the Serbs are descended from the same ancestors will not alter the intuitive conviction that each group tends to harbor concerning its own ethnic purity. Historical facts and current incidents are internalized through ethnic filters. Objective reality and ethnically processed reality are not the same.

In the fall of 1994, the North Atlantic Council sponsored a meeting in Romania that brought together an impressively large number of relatively young members of the business, educational, financial, labor, media, military, and political elites of Western Europe, East Asia, North America, and the former Soviet Union. The purpose was to discuss ethnic and sectarian conflict. Participants were often drawn from bitterly opposed groups. Here is the conclusion from the final report on the conference:

> Ethnic conflicts cannot be entirely reduced to arguments over resources. . . . Often, ethnic aims are pursued at the expense of other issues because they come from a subjective, emotional commitment the other side finds difficult to understand in objective terms. . . . This theme echoed throughout almost every discussion, leading participants to one of the most simple but profound conclusions of the conference: perceptions are as important or more so than reality when it comes to ethnic issues and must be addressed before discussion can move forward.[33]

In sum, realistic attempts to peacefully resolve ethnic conflicts necessitate an appreciation of the emotional and illusory nature of ethnic identity and homeland psychology. Probing these matters requires a knowledge not of "facts" but of commonly held perceptions of facts. Facts perceived through Israeli eyes are markedly different than are those facts when filtered through Palestinian eyes. The same holds true for Russian-processed versus Chechen-processed facts, Irish versus Ulsterman facts, Xhosa versus Zulu facts. This duality helps to explain why fact-finding commissions and mediators whose past experience is limited to nonethnic disputes have not achieved notable successes in resolving ethnic conflicts.

Conclusion

The quest for formulae to accommodate peacefully ethnic heterogeneity need not be a quixotic one. The principle of national self-determination need not presume a world in which each nation possesses its own state. A realistic attempt to arrive at a formula for the peaceful accommodation of heterogeneity should consider the following:

1. The segment of a homeland-dwelling people who will not be content with anything less than independence often represents a minority of that people.
2. However, a large majority typically desires significant changes in the distribution of powers between the center and the homeland.
3. The specific goals of those favoring greater autonomy can range over a broad spectrum from very limited home rule to homeland control over everything other than foreign policy.
4. Ascertaining the attitudes of the homeland and state-wide peoples toward specific grants of autonomy should be a primary goal of negotiators.
5. Both center and homeland leaders are typically under intense pressure to maximize/minimize concessions.
6. Because of the antithetical nature of state supremacy and autonomy, the specifics of any agreement concerning autonomy will be subject to periodic pressures for change.
7. Analysts should concentrate on the attitudes and feelings of the people, not on what elites say they are.
8. A formidable handicap in seeking a formula for peacefully accommodating the aspirations of an ethnonational minority is that it is not reality, but reality filtered through different ethnic prisms, that influences attitudes and behavior.

Notes

1. See Walker Connor, *The National Question in Marxist-Leninist Theory and Strategy* (Princeton, N.J.: Princeton University Press, 1984), 128–71, 222–31, 266–67, 286–88, 295–97, 329–37, 430–44, 516–17, 536–39, 550, 555–57.

2. See, for example, Walker Connor, "The Seductive Lure of Economic Explanation," in *Ethnonationalism: The Quest for Understanding* (Princeton, N.J.: Princeton University Press, 1994), 144–64.

3. *New York Times,* October 12, 1988.

4. *New York Times,* March 10, 1998.

5. For an account of Kaplan's and Malcolm's influence on Clinton's perspectives, see David Remnick, "The Back Page," *New Yorker,* June 14, 1999.

6. See, for example, Daniel Patrick Moynihan, *Pandaemonium: Ethnicity in International Politics* (Oxford: Oxford University Press, 1993), 49, 167.

7. Conrad Brandt, Benjamin Schwartz, and John K. Fairbank, *A Documentary History of Chinese Communism* (London: G. Allen and Unwin, 1952), 245.

8. Ho Chi Minh, *On Revolution: Selected Writings 1920–1966,* ed. Bernard Fall (New York: New American Library, 1967), 158.

9. Laura Silber and Allan Little, *Yugoslavia: Death of a Nation* (New York: Penguin, 1996), 38.

10. James Loughlin, "Joseph Chamberlain, English Nationalism and the Ulster Question," *History* 77 (June 1992): 215.

11. John McGarry and Brendan O'Leary, *Explaining Northern Ireland* (Oxford: Oxford University Press, 1995), 195.

12. *New York Times,* April 10, 1998.

13. Sir Walter Scott, *The Lay of the Last Minstrel,* canto 6, stanza 1, 2.

14. Cited in Walker Connor, "The Impact of Homelands upon Diasporas," in *Modern Diasporas in International Politics,* ed. Gabriel Sheffer (London: Croom Helm, 1985), 17.

15. Nearly the same words were voiced by Bishop Lech Kaczmarek of the Gdansk Diocese: "May we give our lives for Him Our Lord Jesus Christ and for our Homeland, as it is our sacred duty to cherish her immediately after God." *Slowo powszechne* (Warsaw), no. 272 (December 17, 1980).

16. Foreign Broadcast Information Service, FBIS-NES-922–135 (July 14, 1992), 28.

17. Robert Clark, *The Basque Insurgents: ETA, 1952–1980* (Madison: University of Wisconsin Press, 1984), 171–5. This figure would be substantially higher, however, if restricted to those of ethnically Basque background.

18. The survey is reproduced in Lynn Bennie, Jack Brand, and James

Mitchell, *How Scotland Votes: Scottish Parties and Elections* (Manchester: Manchester University Press, 1997), 155. There was remarkably little change in separatist sentiment between 1982 and 1992. See the survey reported in the *New York Times*, March 24, 1982.

19. *International Herald Tribune,* June 6, 1996.

20. See, for example, Vladimir Kusin, "Czechs and Slovaks: The Road to the Current Debate," *Report on Eastern Europe* 1 (October 5, 1990): 6.

21. The reason for the abrupt change in 1990 is discussed below. For an analysis of earlier separatist sentiment in Québec, see Richard Hamilton and Maurice Pinard, "The Bases of Parti Quebecois Support in Recent Quebec Elections," *Canadian Journal of Political Science* 11 (1976): 1–26.

22. H. D. Forbes, *Nationalism, Ethnocentrism, and Personality: Social Science and Critical Theory* (Chicago: Chicago University Press, 1985), 200–201.

23. *Weekly News* (Okinawa), February 26, 1996.

24. *Insular Regions and European Integration: Corsica and the Åland Islands Compared,* report no. 5 of the European Centre for Minority Issues (November 1999), 27.

25. *New York Times,* February 10, 1996.

26. See, for example, the results of a poll in Lawrence LeDuc, "Canadian Attitudes towards Quebec Independence," *Public Opinion Quarterly* (Fall 1977), esp. 352–53. Canada, however, was held in lower esteem within Québec than it was in the other provinces.

27. Richard Gunther, *A Comparative Study of Regionalism in Spain* (Toronto: Toronto University Press, 1981). See also the table in Goldie Shabad and Richard Gunther, "Language, Nationalism, and Political Conflict in Spain," *Comparative Politics* (July 1982): 449.

28. Bennie, Brand, and Mitchell, *How Scotland Votes,* 155.

29. See Vera Tolz, "The USSR This Week," *Report on the USSR,* October 26, 1990, 30

30. Clark, *Basque Insurgents,* 172.

31. *Frankfurter Allgemeine Zeitung,* October 4, 1994. Reprinted in *The Week in Germany,* October 7, 1994.

32. For the details, see Walker Connor, "From a Theory of Relative Economic Deprivation toward a Theory of Relative Political Deprivation," in *Minority Nationalism in a Changing World,* ed. Michael Keating and John McGarry (Oxford: Oxford University Press, 2000).

33. Author's notes, 1994.

3

Violent Conflict and Patterns of Geopolitical Interaction in Southeastern Europe

S. A. Giannakos

ALTHOUGH VIOLENT CONFLICT in the Balkans was mostly absent for the duration of the Cold War, the outbreak of such conflicts was readily attributed to the explosive nature of historical memories, ancient hatreds, and religious incompatibilities. It is true that both Herodotus and Thucydides documented violent conflict in the region, but hardly anyone argues that those conflicts were based on ethnic and religious differences. Political squabbles and local patriotism appear to have been far more important causal factors than ethnicity and religion. Although the Trojan War could be explained on the basis of ethnonationalism (the Trojans insulted the Greek ethnos by stealing Helen) such an approach would be as unbelievable as the legend regarding Helen itself.

But even when modern writers assume that ancient conflicts were based on ethnicity, they make no effort to explain the ways in which ancient hatreds trigger group violence in our day. How does the collective memory of past conflicts survive long periods of inactivity and inertia to suddenly emerge, becoming the single most important motivating factor of group behavior? After all, the Athenians and the Spartans are no longer fighting each other. More important, there has been no effort to explain the root cause of historical animosities and the reasons for their emergence. Instead, historical animosities are taken for granted and are treated as causes rather than symptoms.

It can be argued, however, that repeated regional conflicts are testimonies of a pattern of international interaction that was gradually established in the region over centuries, but was overshadowed by the fixity of the geopolitical boundaries of the post-WWII bipolar system and the security priorities of its primary actors. The end of that bipolar system allowed this geopolitical pattern to resume its functioning and it has become once again a living testimony of the political realities which have been characterizing international relations in southeastern Europe for centuries. Indeed there is a discernible pattern, which is derivative of enduring geopolitical idiosyncrasies, whose understanding and abandonment might be indispensable to breaking the vicious circle of repeated regional warfare it produces. All attempts to promote regional cooperation need to take into consideration and deal with the enduring geopolitical realities of the region. This chapter charts these enduring realities (by way of charting a specific pattern they conform to), examines the sources and the parameters of that pattern, traces its historical development, reveals its political implications in terms of regional instability, and then suggests ways to break out and away from it and from its perpetual cycle of violence.

The Geopolitical Pattern of the Balkans

The pattern I have described can be visualized as two overlapping and geopolitically incompatible triangles defined by a number of points corresponding to specific geographical features in the region (see diagram on page 45). The Belgrade-Bucharest-Athens (BBA) triangle with its base on the Danubian planes and its tip on the Mediterranean Sea is split by the Zagreb-Tiranë-Istanbul (ZTI) triangle, which connects the Adriatic coast with the straits of the Bosporus and the Dardanelles. The dichotomies of the two triangles create one vertical and one horizontal axis whose interaction has been historically competitive and adversarial. These axes can be referred to as the north-south axis and the east-west axis. An examination of the BBA triangle reveals a degree of geopolitical compatibility. In historical terms, authorities and institutions based on common geopolitical interests have dominated the defining points of this triangle and the relations between them have been characterized by the general absence of enmity and a tendency toward amity. It can be said that relations between them have been stable and predictable. Exceptions to this pattern have been isolated incidents imposed by extraregional factors and circumstances to be discussed later in the chapter. Furthermore, the corner represented now by Bucharest often has the tendency to vacillate away from southeastern Europe because its regional considerations must be balanced by interests connected to central European and Eurasian realities (Transylvania and Moldova being the regions of most immediate concern).

The corners of the ZTI triangle have been dominated by institutions and authorities whose base is politically complex, whose interests tend to be the subject of political dichotomies and controversies, whose relations are generally unpredictable, and whose cooperation historically is the result of uneasy compromises and seasonal political expediencies to be explained later in the chapter. Looking at the

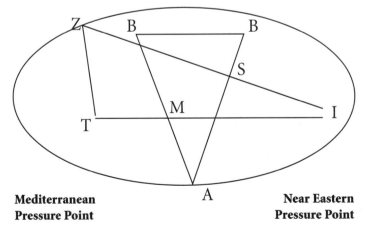

relations between the two triangles, one sees a pattern of adversity that either involves specific points on each triangle or is all encompassing. Historically, the interaction between the two triangles has, more often than not, been characterized by extreme enmity. Spells of cooperation and accommodation have traditionally not lasted long and have been rather limited in scope. They were quickly succeeded by resumed adversity and were never utilized as the basis of building confidence and trust.

The Extraregional Geopolitical Pattern

To a great extent the substance of the relations between the two triangles has been influenced by four extraregional pressure points that can be visualized as points on a circle surrounding the two overlapping triangles mentioned above. The first can be referred to as the Near Eastern pressure point. Its roots are in the Middle East and its front spreads along the continental demarcation line between Europe and Asia or, more precisely, from the Bosporus and the Dardanelles, down the coast of Asia Minor, and as far as Cyprus. The second is the Mediterranean pressure point. It originates in the western part of the Mediterranean and its area of contention runs across the western and southwestern coast of southeastern Europe. The third pressure point originates in Eurasia and its area of contention runs along the western coast of the Black Sea. The fourth originates in central Europe and its area of contention is along the northwestern periphery of the Balkan peninsula.

The historical relationship between the four extraregional pressure points, as these relations pertain to their objectives towards the Balkan region, ranges from outright incompatibility to complete compatibility. The Near Eastern pressure point, for example, has hardly ever been compatible with the Eurasian point. The Mediterranean one and the central European one have been incompatible only under specific circumstances, and certainly never completely incompatible. Similarly, the Mediterranean pressure point has always been incompatible with the Eurasian one, while its relation with the

Near Eastern one carries shades of compatibility and incompatibility of different tones and proportions. Also the relationship between the central European point and the Eurasian one has been complex. The two points tend to be incompatible except when and to the extent that the central European point becomes incompatible with the Near Eastern point. Also, the focal point of both triangles and the circle that surrounds them is in the center representing what is commonly referred to as the Macedonian question.

Regional and Extraregional Actors

The relationship between the extraregional pressure points and the two triangles has been somewhat complex, but a recurring general pattern can be charted. The Near Eastern pressure point has been generally incompatible with the BBA triangle. The Eurasian pressure point, however, which is incompatible with the Near Eastern one, has been compatible with the BBA triangle and incompatible with the ZTI triangle. The Mediterranean pressure point has been balancing between its compatibility with both triangles and its incompatibility with the Eurasian pressure point. When the compatibility between the Eurasian point and the BBA triangle is active, then the relationship between the Mediterranean pressure point and the BBA triangle becomes incompatible. When the Mediterranean pressure point becomes actively compatible with BBA triangle the relationship between that and the Eurasian pressure point becomes incompatible. Both the central European and the Mediterranean pressure points have the same relationship with the two triangles unless the central European point happens to be incompatible with the Mediterranean point, in which case the central European point becomes incompatible with triangle BBA. The operative aspects of this pattern can be charted around the geostrategic importance of the Balkan peninsula, about which much has been written (and which I will only summarize here).

The Geophysical Basis of the Geopolitical Pattern

Both Ferdinand Schevill and Leften Stavrianos argue that the Balkan peninsula has been a traditional battleground of peoples, empires, and cultures because of its unusual topography.[1] Like Schevill, Stavrianos points out that the peninsula lacks natural barriers to incursions from the north. The Danubian plains, far from providing a shelter from Central Europe, "serve as a highway." The Italian boot to the west is a mere fifty miles away from the Albanian coast. To the south, the island of Crete is a "natural stepping-stone" to the peninsula, and to the east the Aegean islands perform the same function. At the same time, mountain ranges and rivers create natural pockets of geographical isolation within the peninsula. According to Stavrianos, the "rugged and complex topography [of the region] has prevented unification and encouraged isolations and particularism. Thus, the normal political state of the Balkan Peninsula has been fragmentation. Unity in the past has not risen from within, but has been forced from without by foreign conquerors."[2] What both Schevill and Stavrianos do not mention is that interregional quarrels have provided the opportunity for outside forces to be invited into the region. Once invited in by one faction or another, they have been in a position to take advantage of political fragmentation and dominate the region by force. Once the power of the dominant outside forces gradually declined, the region reverted to particularism and fragmentation.

Empirical Manifestations of Geopolitical Interests

In the *History of the Peloponnesian War,* Thucydides provides a realistic account of the establishment of permanent settlements in the Balkan peninsula. Referring specifically to the southern part of the peninsula, he notes that there was

> no settled population . . . ; instead there was a series of migrations, as the various tribes, being under the constant pressure of invaders who were stronger than they were, were always prepared to abandon their

own territory. There was no commerce, and no safe communication either by land or sea; the use they made of their land was limited to the production of necessities; they had no surplus left over for capital, and no regular system of agriculture, since they lacked the protection of fortifications and at any moment an invader might appear and take their land away from them. Thus, in the belief that the day-to-day necessities of life could be secured just as well in one place as in another, they showed no reluctance in moving from their homes, and therefore built no cities of any size or strength, nor acquired any important resources. Where the soil was most fertile there were the most frequent changes of population.[3]

He mentions that robbery was prevalent through out the land and since communications were unsafe, "it was the normal thing to carry arms on all occasions, a custom still practiced by foreigners." Sea communications were easier but "piracy became a common profession both among the Hellenes and among the barbarians who lived on the coast and in the islands." He mentions that the first to organize a navy and create colonies was the Cretan King Minos, who "it is reasonable to suppose that he did his best to put down piracy in order to secure his own revenues." Subsequently, Minos improved sea communications and created colonies and "drove out the notorious pirates, with the result that those who lived on the sea-coasts were now in a position to acquire wealth and live a more settled life. Some of them, on the strength of their new riches, built walls for their cities. The weaker, because of the general desire to make profits, were content to put up with being governed by the stronger."[4] In his attempt to write a book that would "last for ever," Thucydides explained in great detail the competition not only between opposing oligarch and democratic factions in specific localities, but between various regions that formed into defensive and offensive alliances based on capabilities and interests. Such is the detail and depth of analysis Thucydides employed to explain the wars between the various city-states that one would never consider single-cause explanations; any attempt to explain the conflict exclusively in terms of Ionian Athenians fighting against the Dorian Spartans would sound absurd. Far from it, Thucydides account reveals the high degree of political fragmentation established in the region due to the topography.

More than two thousand years after Thucydides, Rebecca West, referring to the political realities of interwar Yugoslavia, wrote that the Uskoks of the Dalmatian coast had "developed all the characteristics of gunmen: a loyalty that went unbroken to the death, unsurpassable courage, brutality, greed, and, oddly enough thriftlessness."[5] To be certain, the Romans had eradicated piracy throughout the region, but the political decline of the Romans and the Byzantines who replaced them resurrected it. The difference between the post-Roman pirates and the pre-Minoan ones was that the earlier pirates took pride in their profession, which was considered both resourceful and honorable, but under Christianity and the emergence of power centers, piracy lost its pagan glory, and pirates had to justify their actions on the basis of life's cruel necessities and stay in business by playing one power center against the other. West suggests that the Uskoks survived as pirates in the sixteenth century by bribing Austrian officials, who often sold the looted goods to Venetian officials, who in turn "marketed them at a profit in Venice."[6]

In order to connect Thucydides' accounts with those of Rebecca West and follow the development of a pattern, we must start with the Athenians, who took over from the Cretans the responsibility of managing sea communications. The Athenian consolidation of regional power was tested in two ways: they were put into contrast with the emerging Near Eastern pressure point exercised by the Persians and in direct confrontation with the Spartans—the other emerging regional contender to the southern corner in the geopolitical triangle BBA mentioned above. The outcome of this developing scenario is all too familiar. By building a stronger and faster naval vessel, the trireme, the Athenians stood up to the Near Eastern pressure point in the Persian wars only to be defeated by the Spartans in the Peloponnesian War. The weakening of both Athens and Sparta in their competition to control the southern corner of triangle BBA allowed the Macedonians to end up the winners. Political fragmentation was undermined, and regional political unification allowed the southern corner to not only stand up to the Near Eastern pressure point, but to defeat it as well. But regional disagreements reemerged immediately after Alexander's death.

With the Near Eastern pressure point neutralized effectively for years to come, the ensuing regional fragmentation would probably have gone unnoticed if it were not for the emerging Mediterranean pressure point. Taking advantage of Macedonian disputes against the Aetolian League (now central Greece), and having been invited by the latter for assistance against the Macedonians, the Romans became the new political and military arbitrators of regional fragmentation. Invited by the Aetolian League, the Romans defeated the Macedonians at Cynoscephalae in 197 B.C. and "liberated" the Greek city-states from Macedonian control. This is how Will Durant describes the effects of this "liberation."

> Rome had freed the Greeks, but on condition that both war and class war should end. Freedom without war was a novel and irksome life for the city-states that made up Hellas; the upper classes yearned to play power politics against neighboring cities, and the poor complained that Rome everywhere buttressed the rich against the poor.
>
> The rival cities, factions, and classes of Hellas appealed to the Senate for support, and gave cause for interferences that made Greece actually subject though nominally free. The partisans of the Scipios in the Senate were overruled by realists who felt that there would be no lasting peace or order in Greece until it was completely under Roman rule. In 146 the cities of the Achaean League, while Rome was in conflict with Carthage and Spain, announced a war of liberation. Leaders of the poor seized control of the movement, freed and armed the slaves, declared a moratorium on debts, promised a redistribution of land, and added revolution to war. When the Romans . . . entered Greece they found a divided people and easily overcame the undisciplined Greek troops . . . burned Corinth, slew its males, sold its women and children into bondage. . . . Greece disappeared from political history for two thousand years.[7]

The lamenting associated with Greece disappearing from political history needs to be juxtaposed with the end of particularism that also coincided with the Roman domination of the peninsula. Not only did the Romans forbid city-sates in the region to wage foreign and class wars, but they also defied regional geography by creating a vast network of highways that cut right through the mountains, interconnecting hitherto isolated geographical pockets and valleys. The murders Agatha Christie describes in *Murder in the Orient Express* would never have taken place if the Romans had not built these highways, the most famous being Via Egnatia, which traversed the peninsula from west to east and created connections with the north and south. The project resulted in the thorough Romanization of the region, as exemplified by the Aromanians, or Vlachs, who live throughout the peninsula and still speak a language derived from Latin.

Rome's control of the peninsula ended in A.D. 351, when the eastern Roman emperor, Constantius, defeated the usurper, the western emperor Magnus Magnentius. Because of the ensuing political separation, the sacking of Rome in 410 by Alaric's Visigoths did not have much of a military effect on the peninsula. Although Alaric defeated the Romans in Adrianople (present-day Edirne) in 378, Constantinople, the newly declared Roman capital, was unaffected; it survived as the capital of the eastern part of what became the Byzantine Empire, which lasted until the Ottoman conquest in 1453. Politically, the establishment of Byzantium on the peninsula can be viewed as the reestablishment of the Macedonian Empire mainly due to the decline of the West (the Mediterranean pressure point). The analogy is more sensible considering that the Byzantines were confronted right away by a rejuvenated Persian Empire under the Sassanids, to be followed by the Arabs and eventually by the Seljuk Turks.

Like the Macedonians, who had to confront the Illyrians (by now thoroughly Romanized and Christianized, and thus Byzantinized), the Byzantines faced the infusion of the Germanic people known as Visigoths and Ostrogoths. Having been defeated by the Visigoths in 378, the Byzantines made concession to them as well to the Ostrogoths that followed them. According to George Ostrogorsky, "the Ostrogoths were to settle in Pannonia, [and] the Visigoths in the northern districts of the diocese of Thrace—both strategically important areas in the region. They were granted complete autonomy, exemption from taxation and a high rate of pay for their military services."[8] In specific localities like Thessaloniki and elsewhere, the Byzantines had to face the dilemma of consolidating power against religious heresies such as Arianism or the new version of the old democratic-oligarchic political struggles between the commercial and landowning classes referred to as Greens and Blues because of their preferred colors in the hippodrome.

The eventual departure of most of the Germanic tribes from the peninsula did not change the political situation; their departure opened the way for Avars and Slavs to move into the Danubian plains. By the end of the sixth century, groups of Slavs had begun moving into the peninsula. Unlike the German groups, who moved on, the Slavs stayed permanently. The eventual Christianization of the Slavs by the Byzantines reestablished social homogeneity existing during the Roman times, but political stability remained an elusive reality, especially because the constant pressure from east and west prevented the Byzantines from maintaining control. Subsequently, regionalism and particularism reemerged in the peninsula—not along city-state lines, but along regional lines, as geographically homogeneous regions begun gravitating toward emerging power centers. In the northeast of the peninsula, the Slavs would be organized under the feudal control of Bulgarian kings while the western part came under the feudal control of Serbian kings. In the west, through its naval strength, Venice gradually and steadily expanded her trade routes into the Balkan shores of the Adriatic and the eastern Mediterranean. At the same time, the Hungarian land forces were pressuring the Danubian territories in the northwest. Frank and Norman forces followed subsequent Venetian and Hungarian infusions.

Venetian or papal involvement was characterized by a dual policy comprising attempts to maintain and enhance papal influence in the Balkans and to prevent or resist Frankish, Norman, or Hungarian influence by helping the Byzantines. This broader competition for power and influence was accompanied by regional power struggles, illustrated by a Byzantine pattern of alignments, sometimes with the

Hungarian kings against the Serbian monarchs, sometimes with the Bulgarians against the Serbians, and other times with the Serbians against the Hungarians. At still other times, the Serbian and the Bulgarian kings would find themselves allied with the Germanic people against the Hungarians and the Byzantines, with the emerging Seljuk Turks against either one of the above. In addition, slowly but steadily Russian influence was also making its presence felt in the Balkans, even though it was not yet strong enough to balance either Western or Ottoman influence. Thus, by the time of the crusades the geopolitical pattern of interaction in the peninsula was in place. Since then, the main characteristic of this pattern has been the competition between the extraregional pressure points—exercised initially by the Romans and the Venetians, and later by Great Britain, France, or the United States (the Mediterranean pressure point), by the Germanic and Hungarian peoples (the central European pressure point), by the Russians (the Eurasian pressure point), and by the Ottomans or Turks (the Near Eastern pressure point)—for either expansion, influence projection, or mutual containment (or all three).

This pattern of interaction emerged primarily because of the region's strategic importance. It is here that East comes into contact with West (Asia with Europe), North with South (Eurasia with Africa and the Middle East), Christianity with Islam and Judaism, Indo-Europeans with Turks and Arabs, continental climates with Mediterranean ones, European rationalism with Mediterranean spontaneity, secularism with religiosity and faith, and science and empiricism with superstition and mythology. The peninsula has been the geographic key to three continents, all wetting their shores in the Mediterranean.

To some extent, the Balkan peninsula can be considered a political microcosm where one can witness any conceivable political and social scenario. Along with the constant competition among the extraregional pressure points, history has witnessed the constant competition among the regional power centers along communication patterns established since the building of the Roman highways. These centers correspond to specific geographical features, such as the Drava and Sava Rivers in the northwest, which lead out to central

Europe and northern Italy (Peartree Pass); the Morava Valley (separated from the east by the Iron Gate); the Danubian plains in the northeast, which lead out to the Prut and Dniester Rivers; the Maritsa Valley, between the Balkan Mountains and the Rhodope Mountains (separated in the north and the northwest by the Shipka and the Dragoman Passes respectively); the straits of the Bosporus and the Dardanelles (separating the peninsula from Asia); the southern coastal outlets to the Aegean and the Mediterranean; and the Dalmatian coastal outlets to the Adriatic in the west of the Dinaric Alps. This is the typical situation in which mountains and rivers create isolated geographical pockets. Illustrative is the recent failure of the Romanian and Bulgarian governments to negotiate the construction of a second bridge over the Danube. Clearly, the Roman highway system undermined the isolating features of the peninsula's unique geography, which had encouraged the development of the city-state.

Once Roman power declined, however, and the highway system was neglected, particularism reemerged around the isolated pockets described above. Towns and cities, built in important communications and trade spots, began spiraling their influence outward and coming into competition with nearby town and cities—just as before the Peloponnesian War, but now including the surrounding region. Under feudalism, conflicts between city-states were transformed into regional conflicts, and then, upon the advent of the nation-state, into national conflicts, in which particular cities tried to justify their outward-spiraling expansion into the countryside through nationalism. Communism transformed these conflicts once again, but once that ideology was bankrupt, the region went back to manifestations of national and ethnic conflicts. Since regional communications have remained more or less the same up to the advent of the European Union (EU), the regional pattern of interaction has remained unaltered. This often misperceived reality gives grounds to the attempt to explain the region's conflicts in terms of repeated ancestral ethnic hatreds, when in fact it is local geopolitical interests that drive the conflicts. These interests have not changed over the centuries, and neither have the conflicts.

Understanding the politics of the region, therefore, necessitates the understanding of three interacting realities: the interaction of the regional power centers along lines of political interest, dictated initially by geography; the interaction among the extraregional pressure points, representing global geopolitical trends; and the interaction between the regional power centers and the extraregional pressure points. Clearly, if the interests of all points were compatible, the political landscape of the region would not be as ragged as the geographical landscape. Furthermore, due to the multiplicity of actors corresponding to the multiple points, and due to the complex interaction of all points, politics in the region remain generally unpredictable. What follows is an attempt to demonstrate empirically the results of the general interaction of the pattern and suggest ways to alter it.

Geopolitical Conflicts as Ethnic Articulations

The battles of Marathon, Thermopylae, and Salamis are well-known manifestations of the influence of the Near Eastern pressure point. They have earned a place in history as occasions where democratic principles overcame the incursion of Near Eastern absolutism. Yet these battles must be juxtaposed against the little-advertised Battle of Manzikert, near Lake Van, where the Seljuk Turks defeated the Byzantine armies in 1071. The Byzantine Empire never quite recovered from the effect of this battle—it lost to the Seljuks the ability to influence the Asia Minor provinces, an ability which the city-states and the earlier Byzantines had maintained successfully against numerous Persian and Arab attempts to control them. The loss of the provinces of Asia Minor meant the inevitable downfall of Constantinople. Steadily pressured from Asia, Byzantium became desperate for Western assistance, but remained unwilling to resubordinate itself politically to the West (the Eastern Orthodox Church still refuses to mend its break with the Catholic Church, which became permanent in 1054). Thus, intra-European conflicts, mainly Franco-Hungarian or Franco-German, combined with Byzantine religious stubbornness against a rapprochement with the Vatican, gave the Ottomans the opportunity to infiltrate the region in support of one or another warring faction, gradually overrun Byzantium, and replace it.

To be certain, the Seljuk Turks were invited in by the warring feudal elements organized along geographical points corresponding to the corners of the ZTI and BBA triangles. Since the emergence of the modern state system in the region in the nineteenth century, these struggles have been projected by nationalistic historiographies as national or ethnic conflicts. Thus, it has been depicted that Byzantine Greeks were fighting Bulgarians or Serbians or both, and Bulgarians fighting Serbians and vice versa. In essence, these conflicts were similar to the pre-Roman conflicts in the region. The most striking difference between earlier and later conflicts is that the former were carried out within a pagan cultural domain, the latter a Christian religious-cultural domain where there was no concept of national or ethnic allegiance. For example, Simeon, who consolidated his position between the Balkan and the Rhodope Mountains, had received a Christian education in Constantinople and aspired to become a Byzantine emperor and be recognized as such by the Orthodox religious authorities. The same is true of Stephan Dushan, who declared himself emperor (tsar) in 1346 just like Simeon had more than three centuries before. Characteristically, both political entities set up corresponding religious centers (patriarchates) mirroring the religious and political institutional arrangements of Constantinople.

More often than not, all these political entities are presented today as national entities. In essence they were nothing more than feudal political ambitions at a time when the same institutions in Europe had started to become obsolete, being slowly replaced by modern state institutions that would gradually begin the process of creating national sentiments among their subjects. Short of labels referring to groups of powerful land-owning political elites, there is no other evidence to substantiate any claims to ethnic or national allegiances among the people, some of whom begun seeing the rising Seljuk Turks as a remedy, not only to the increasing feudalization of the region, but to the resurfacing endless fragmentation as well. Longing for both political stability and land possession, the people of the region became willing to shift their allegiance to the newcomers, who would not only put an end to the fragmentation, but engaged in massive land redistribution—individuals that assisted the newcomers in consolidating their military position were rewarded with land. The difference, of course, was that integration was undertaken in the name of Islam (peoples' justice?), which provided the justification for it.

The emerging dominance of the Near Eastern pressure point in the region was not perceived as a political threat to either the European or the Mediterranean pressure points. The religious connotation of the expansion was problematic to religious authorities in the West, but not enough to organize considerable reaction. This became evident in the ill-fated attempt against the emerging Ottomans in Nicopolis in 1396, in the same location where the Romans finally subjugated the remnants of regional fragmentation more than fourteen centuries before. Fleeing for his life, the defeated Catholic king, Sigismund of Hungary, barely escaped to Constantinople. Returning to Europe on a naval vessel through the Dardanelles, he was exposed to the "sound of the piteous cries of the Christian captives, whom the Sultan had ordered to be lined up on both shores of the straits in order to humiliate the defeated king."[9] Sixty-eight years later, Pope Pius II died brokenhearted in 1464 waiting at Ancona for a Christian crusade against the Ottomans that never materialized. European diplomacy had become "too secularized to allow for crusades. The new nation states placed dynastic and commercial considerations before religious ones. The outstanding example of this new attitude was the alliance concluded with the Ottomans in 1536 by the 'most Christian' king of France against 'the apostolic majesty,' Charles V of the Holy Roman Empire."[10]

On the other hand, after the Hungarian defeat at Mohacs in 1526 the Europeans began seeing the Ottomans as a threat. This became evident during two Ottoman attempts to capture Vienna, one in 1529 and the other in 1689. It was during the first attempt that Luther himself declared, "I fight until death against the Turks and the God of the Turks."[11]

Despite Luther's proclamation, no concerted European efforts were made against the Ottomans, who once they stopped being a threat to Europe, significantly contributed to European commercial interests by suppressing fragmentation in the peninsula, as the Romans had before them. Western commercial exploitation in the Balkans continued and actually increased in both scale and scope. Both the French and the British, and to a lesser extent the Dutch, having broken Italian monopolies, were free to exploit resources and sell their commercial goods without trade or tariff obstacles imposed by the Ottomans. In the meantime, the consolidation of Hapsburg rule in Central Europe meant that what used to be exclusively Hungarian interests were now combined by a German interest to lessen Franco-British influence. Subsequently, other than having to deal with the Turks instead of the Byzantines, the European pattern of involvement in the Balkans scarcely changed during the Ottoman period. At the same time, the fusion of the Near Eastern pressure point with one of the most important regional power centers, Istanbul—the polis of Constantine, now simply referred to with the Greek expression *is tin poli* (to the city)—ended the perennial conflict between the regional centers and the Near Eastern point—the Near Eastern pressure point won.

The Ottoman victory and subsequent domination of the region exhibited different mechanics than that of the Romans and the Byzantines. Where the last two homogenized the region ideologically by Romanizing it and Christianizing it, the Ottomans continued to exploit fragmentation in order to maintain their domination. Fragmentation was now reinstated at the extreme local level and along the lines that had existed in the days of the city-state and the early Roman period. Once separated between free citizens and slaves, the people were now divided between Muslim believers and Christian infidels— with the walled-in center of the cities inhabited by the Muslims and the outskirts by Christians. This social bifurcation was accompanied by the regional fragmentation according to interests that articulated themselves in religious terms as well. Thus the power centers on the Adriatic coast, which traditionally had been the stepping-stones for the intrusion of the Mediterranean pressure point, and conceivably of the European pressure point, were Islamized, along with the approaches from the Near East and, as it will be seen later, with the northeast (against the Russians). Inevitably, this bifurcation made it most difficult for the Ottomans to maintain control, despite the absence of major activity from the Near Eastern pressure point.

Since the Europeans appeared least concerned toward the parochial interests of the Balkan Christians vis-à-vis the Muslim Turks, the justification was found to facilitate the emergence and increase of Russian influence along the Eurasian pressure point targeting the straits. It became necessary for the Russians to revoke moral imperatives for justifying their projection of power into the Balkans for two reasons. First, the Western Europeans were vulnerable to the charge of having neglected Christian rights, and second, having vested economic interests in the Ottoman Empire, the Western Europeans were threatened by the projection of Russian power—they could, and they would, lose their trade privileges. To soften the Western European determination to defend the Ottoman Empire against the Russians, the Russians projected themselves as the protectors of the Balkan Christians. With the advent of nationalism, and in order to reinforce their argument, they also projected themselves as the protectors of the Balkan Slavs.

In turn, the French, the British, and, to some extent, the Austrians counteracted the Russian arguments by branding their intentions as simply expansionistic. What gave the Russians the advantage in the competition was the rapid decline of the Ottoman Empire after its failure to capture Vienna. Not being in the position to acquire and distribute more land to the people, the Ottoman system gradually and steadily reverted to feudalism, with the added twist that the landowners were now Muslims, while the serfs were Christians. More important, the inefficient and overcentralized Ottoman administrative system proved counterproductive to controlling fragmentation—it reinforced the forces of fragmentation according to interests that, as pointed out, were increasingly articulated in religious terms. As a result, the Western European efforts to maintain the Ottoman Empire as a means of safeguarding economic advantages became unsustainable. Wherever the control of the Ottoman Empire collapsed, both the central European and the Eurasian pressure points projected themselves as the defenders and promoters of the rights of the subjugated Balkans, insofar as such an approach would not help the competition. Consequently, Slovenia and Croatia came under the influence of the Hapsburgs; Bessarabia, Wallachia, and Moldova came under Russian influence; while Greece came under the influence of the British, the French, and the Italians—with the Ottomans clinging desperately to Istanbul and the landlocked power centers in the interior. All and all, both the Ottomans and the outside pressure points reinforced fragmentation, which, along with its existing religious articulations, found increasing articulation in nationalistic outbursts.

The 1804 revolt against the Janissaries in the landlocked Morava Valley (a Serbian revolt?) was pretty much left to its own fate despite appeals for help. Fearing that they might push the janissaries toward Napoleon, the British stayed clear. Exhausted from its war against Napoleon, Austria stayed away despite its desire to become involved. Russia paid lip service to the Slavic cause but, not wishing to alienate Britain and Turkey in the face of the Napoleonic threat, did nothing to help either. In contrast, when the Greeks revolted a few years later (1821), and following a series of highly publicized massacres, the combined Christian fleet of the European states intervened to defeat the Ottoman fleet at Navarino in August 1827 and "liberate" the Greeks. To be certain, intervention was justified on moral grounds, but the objective was the preservation of economic, political, and strategic advantages in the face of the Ottoman's increasing inability to maintain stability. Certainly, the Ottoman atrocities in Greece exposed the moralistic declaratory policies of the Europeans and threatened to undermine their actual objectives. The maintenance of their objectives made intervention on the basis of morality absolutely necessary.

When declaratory moral policies were incompatible to geopolitical interests, the active pressure points did not hesitate to set aside or overlook human rights. For example, England and the other Western European powers failed to intervene on behalf of the Christian subjects who revolted against Ottoman rule in Bosnia in 1876, despite widespread violence. The revolt received the same official reaction when it spread onto the Serbian autonomous state. As the revolt spread into Bulgaria, however, and as Ottoman irregular forces moved to subdue it with uncharacteristic barbarism (destroying villages and massacring their entire populations), the Russians agitated for intervention. Having first dismissed all atrocity charges made against the Ottomans by the British press, and after having aroused public indignation and an outcry for autonomy for the Christian subjects in the Ottoman Empire, Disraeli still refused to consider intervention for the sake of maintaining the balance of power in Europe.

Another incident illustrative of European involvement in the Balkans was the widespread revolt against the Ottomans in Macedonia in 1903. Both Austria and Russia intervened on behalf of the Christian subjects, but their effort to create administrative districts along ethnic lines failed to take into consideration the interests of the regional power centers. As a result their effort precipitated ethnic strife—the different parties involved (Serbians, Bulgarians, Greeks) began vying for positions in anticipation of impending permanent border demarcations. In this case, it was the pressure points that fell victim to the regional balance of power priorities of the emerging state system in the region. Finally, in October 1944, after Churchill's initiative, Britain and Russia took sole responsibility for the regional balance of power by creating spheres of influence that remained in place until the end of the Cold War—they were able to freeze the geopolitical pattern of interaction I have described.

The most recent illustration is the ongoing Yugoslav conflicts, of which too much has been written already (and probably ineffectively). Suffice it to say that the Yugoslav conflicts manifested themselves along the lines delineated by the geopolitical triangles in the beginning of the chapter—as conflicts in the region have for the last fifteen centuries and certainly before the people there developed a group consciousness as Christians (Catholic and Orthodox), Muslims, communists, Montenegrins, Serbs, Croats, Bosnians, Albanians, or Kosovars. These conflicts resurfaced at the end of the Cold War because Yugoslavism, far from undermining regionalism, reinforced it by relying on force and on political and economic practices that failed to bring about political and economic homogenization. In other words, the Yugoslavs—like the Byzantines and the Ottomans before them, who relied on force and religion—reinforced regionalism by relying on a communist ideology that, no matter how ambitious its plans for achieving homogeneity, simply failed to deliver the political and economic miracle it promised.

Once modern feudalism reemerged as ethnic nationalism, the outside pressure points intervened, always uncoordinated, always too little, always too late, always for reasons camouflaged in moral imperatives and grandiose political aspirations, and always for their own specific interests. For example, NATO's involvement in Kosovo may have, at least partially, been motivated by humanitarian concerns, but NATO intervention was undertaken with a view toward the preservation of the EU and NATO, against Russian objections, with too little force, too late, and without any clear vision of political objectives and pragmatic solutions.

Conclusion

In terms of understanding conflict in the Balkan region, the pattern of geopolitical interaction reveals that geographical realities have produced a geographical fragmentation and corresponding political and economic interests that articulate themselves through whatever ideology is fashionable at a specific time (struggles against slavery, religious struggles, ethnic struggles, national struggles). In essence, the problems in the region stem from the failure to create or maintain a viable domestic and regional political system that can provide opportunities for growth and development of the people in the region. Topography-based fragmentation has encouraged and maintained barely viable political and economic entities that not only are unable to respond to real human needs, but also tend to externalize their problems through futile military adventures and grandiose territorial visions. Thus we witness the vicious circle of local and interregional violent conflicts that has come to be known as Balkanization. The irony is that as much as Balkanization is despised, so have been all attempts at political homogenization. On the other hand, the outside pressure points tend to consider the regional developments either as a great opportunity for promoting their specific interests or as an unfortunate political situation that should be avoided at all costs. This has given rise to such expressions as The Balkans is not worth the bones of a single Pomeranian grenadier and The Balkans is the powder keg of Europe. The second statement is completely wrong. A careful examination of history reveals that Europe has been the powder keg of Europe and that the Balkans are the powder keg of the Balkans. It just so happens that when one of the two kegs blows up, the tendency has been to blame the other and deny all responsibility. The first statement needs rephrasing, especially since no one has ever asked any Pomeranian grenadier if he would like to leave his bones in the Balkans. Better to ask, How can the vicious cycle of violence be stopped?

The idealistic response to this question is to try to promote regional cooperation between the competing power centers, promote international cooperation between the extraregional pressure points, and then coordinate cooperation between the regional and the extraregional actors. This is a huge undertaking that will require vast resources and the kind of diplomatic and military undertaking that simply is not logistically possible. For example, the difficulty of coordinating cooperation between regional power centers and extraregional pressure points can be demonstrated by the EU's attempt to include Turkey. Western Turkey can be easily incorporated—it has been one of the regional power centers—but the rest of Turkey represents the Near Eastern pressure point, with interests that do not coincide with those of western Turkey and the European Union. Just like previous authorities who controlled the regional power centers (Istanbul and Asia Minor) found themselves in constant military struggle with Anatolia and the Middle East, so now the Turkish government (the Turkish military) has engaged in a struggle against Islamic fundamentalism and Kurdish revolts, not to mention outstanding issues between Turkey and Syria. Unfortunately, it is safe to assume that it will be doing the same for years to come. This means that the democratization of Turkey will not take place unless the Near Eastern pressure point is managed effectively. Such a scenario is not possible until Europe and the Middle East develop politically, economically, and socially to the same level. Ad hoc approaches tend to bring about temporary retreats of conflict that gradually produce relapses.

On the other hand, the prospect that Russia and the EU will develop common interests and a concerted long-term diplomatic approach toward the region is not realistic (although that seems more feasible than co-opting the Near Eastern pressure point). The realistic approach of trying to promote regional cooperation by military means (what the Romans, the Ottomans, the Yugoslavs, and perhaps NATO have done or are doing) has not worked and will not work. The amount of force necessary to accomplish the task is no longer considered acceptable. Force also becomes quickly counterproductive, as it tends to reinforce fragmentation.

One solution is to do what the Romans eventually did once they established themselves in the region—penetrate the mountains and flatten the region out by creating a network of communication links to undermine the localism that has been entrenched in isolated valleys and regions over the centuries. Communication networks will bring about balanced political and economic development, which will lead to cooperation across the mountains and river valleys. Fragmentation will become too expensive to practice while the benefits of cooperation will just be too great to resist. In turn, the ensuing state of regional cooperation will insulate the region against the tendency of the extraregional pressure points to take advantage of regional fragmentation to safeguard or promote their specific interests. In fairness to the European Union, highway construction has already begun, but it needs to be sped up and expanded rapidly to include the entire region and to be accompanied by the construction of airports and all other means of modern communication. This kind of investment is not only ethical, but also wise in both political and economic terms.

Notes

1. See Ferdinand Schevill, *The History of the Balkan Peninsula* (New York:

Harcourt, Brace, 1922), 13–25; Leften S. Stavrianos, *The Balkans, 1815–1914* (New York: Holt Rinehart and Winston, 1963), 1-5.

2. Stavrianos, *Balkans, 1815–1914,* 2.

3. Thucydides, *History of the Peloponnesian War* (New York: Penguin, 1972), 35–36.

4. Ibid., 37–39.

5. Rebecca West, *Black Lamb and Grey Falcon* (New York: Penguin, 1968), 126.

6. Ibid., 127.

7. Will Durant, *Caesar and Christ* (New York: Simon and Schuster, 1944), 86–87.

8. George Ostrogorsky, *History of the Byzantine State* (New Brunswick: Rutgers University Press, 1957), 48.

9. Ibid., 490.

10. Leften Stavrianos, *The Balkans since 1453* (New York: Holt, Rinehart and Winston, 1958), 226.

11. Dorothy M. Vaughan, *Europe and the Turk: A Pattern of Alliances, 1350–1700* (Liverpool: University Press, 1954), 135. Quoted in Stavrianos, *Balkans since 1453,* 72.

4

Changes and Opportunities Wrought by Exile and Repatriation
New Identities among Guatemalan Refugee Women

Paula Worby

ALTHOUGH EXILE IS a time of terror and disaster, it can sometimes offer an opportunity for change and organization in the lives of refugees. That was the case for many Guatemalans who fled the brutal counterinsurgency war that targeted the rural civilian population in the early 1980s and settled in refugee camps in southern Mexico. The majority spent at least twelve years in exile under the protection of the office of the United Nations High Commissioner for Refugees (UNHCR) and with the additional support of the Mexican government. The Guatemalan refugees were rural peasant farmers and mostly indigenous, belonging to eight of the twenty-two language groups of the country. In the process of surviving displacement, Guatemalan refugee women embarked on a journey of self-discovery and developing newfound skills.

Women refugees turned forced exile and stark personal loss into a unique opportunity to mobilize in ways that probably would not have been possible in their home communities. They were forced into new roles by emergency conditions, given special support and attention by outsiders, and eventually were supported by male leaders who found their activism useful in mobilizing international support for

67

the overall refugee cause. Many women discovered new ways of relating to the outside world and, perhaps to a lesser extent, to their partners at home. The refugees, in general, stopped seeing themselves only as poor, rural Indian campesinos (peasants), but also as active parties in determining their own destiny. Refugee women, in particular, began to be visible and outspoken in public events. Refugee girls went to school in far greater numbers than before. For these women, the seeds of new and important transformations had been planted, but cultivating them was difficult once away from the temporary reality of refugee camps.

This chapter will demonstrate that while forced displacement can be linked to attempted ethnocide (in the context of permanent disruption of community and cultural life), the Guatemalan survivors who managed to reach refugee camps developed new positive group identities. Joining refugees from other regions and ethnic groups and with the common task of returning home to Guatemala, they forged a unity that cut across linguistic differences. As an extension of the refugee experience and because it epitomizes the women's struggle to gain public recognition and decision-making roles in their communities, this chapter will also analyze the refugee women's campaign to become joint owners of community lands as returnees in Guatemala.

Gaining direct exercise of land rights might have seemed secondary to other needs, among them the urgency that the community as a whole be granted land. However, the demand responded to the women's need to protect themselves and their children in the case of separation from their partner. In turn, women's mobilization to gain direct access to land forced men to see women as more important actors in their communities. The movement was reaffirming even to women who were not activists as it prompted widespread reflection for the first time on their role in community and society. These attitudes were bolstered by outside institutions such as UNHCR to the extent that they insisted on the importance of women's presence and inclusion in everything from informal meetings to land acquisition. Equally true is the reverse, the women's efforts were undermined when outsiders no longer gave them visible support and validation. Ultimately the deficient material conditions of the returnee communities have also curtailed women's efforts; women struggling for daily economic survival for their families no longer see themselves as having the "luxury" to organize around long-term aspirations. An overall lesson for the women involved and their supporters is that the more profound the transformation in social consciousness aspired to and the more meaningful its application, the longer the process necessary to consolidate achieved gains.

Violence and Displacement

Five hundred years after Spanish colonization, the Mayan Indian majority in Guatemala found itself increasingly squeezed onto the most marginal lands.[1] Rural families were forced into a subsistence existence, growing corn and beans on eroded hillsides, and to yearly migrations, under exploitative conditions, to harvest the export crops grown by wealthy plantation owners. The extremely unequal land distribution in Guatemala (among the worst in Latin America) and ensuing inequalities helped spur an insurgency war that lasted over thirty-five years until a UN-brokered peace agreement was signed in December 1996. Widespread poverty and hopes for land reform were factors in generating rural support for revolutionary insurgents in the 1970s. The Guatemala military responded to peaceful organizing for civil and economic rights in the 1970s first by targeting individuals and then increasingly through widespread repression.

While international opinion condemned horrific human rights violations in Guatemala in the early 1980s, it is only recently that the charge of genocide has been argued from a legal standpoint. A by-product of the 1996 Peace Accords, the 1999 Guatemalan Truth Commission report concluded that the Guatemalan state committed acts of genocide against different Guatemalan ethnic groups.[2] The commission based its conclusion on the notion that even when the stated *motive* for state violence was to fight communism or insurgent groups and not Indians per se, the *intent* of state policy was to eradicate specific groups of Mayan people.[3] The commission centered its analysis on examining army actions in specific geographic areas that were home to particular ethnic groups and by relating those actions to the definition given by the 1948 UN Convention on the Prevention and Punishment of the Crime of Genocide, ratified by Guatemala in 1949.[4] One Guatemalan human rights organization also argued that the disruption of the social fabric of different ethnic groups caused by displacement was a calculated attempt to destroy their way of life, their ability to be a community, carry out their livelihood, and practice their traditions.[5] A state policy of forced displacement, therefore, could contribute to an act of genocide insofar as it contributes to the physical destruction of the group's members. Firsthand accounts clearly illustrate this link: "We were hiding in the mountains for three months; there were 150 [in our group]. It was very difficult, we only wanted to cry. People died, they couldn't tolerate the conditions. . . . Hiding under the jungle canopy we were frightened, hungry, thirsty, and cold. So many died there; the poor little babies especially didn't tend to make it."[6] At its height, between 1982 and 1983, the Guatemalan conflict caused the internal displacement, at least temporarily, of an estimated one million people or more (of a total population of seven million at the time). Tens of thousands of rural Guatemalans fled to Mexico, fewer to Honduras and Belize. Of these, many continued on to the United States.

Guatemalan refugees in general, and women refugees in particular, were able to turn some of their suffering into something positive, something which ironically has made many grateful for the opportunities experienced in refugee camps. While in Mexico, most refugees developed a new group identity regardless of their place of origin and specific ethnic group. The refugees discovered that they shared the same narrative as victims of repression.[7] In an environment where free expression was not only permitted but encouraged (as opposed to the situation of those who had stayed in Guatemala), the commonalties were reinforced, especially as they were revealed by wartime narratives to foreign journalists and human rights activists.[8]

The refugees were counted, registered, grouped, and regrouped by UNHCR and the Mexican government's refugee aid agency—but the refugees were often in charge of undertaking the registration and organizing themselves, through designated leaders.[9] This reinforced their group identity as refugees and also permitted them direct access to valuable demographic information gathered in the name of institutional needs assessment.

Forming an organization of cadres known as the Permanent Commissions of Guatemalan Refugees, a group of leaders, many with prior experience as community leaders or political organizers, spent years lobbying and negotiating with the Guatemalan government. With the mediation of UNHCR and other international and national entities, their chief demands were finally accepted. While the leaders were virtually all men, the organization enjoyed wide support among both men and women, as it represented the best chance at negotiating a return to Guatemala with safe conditions. The resulting agreements between the refugees and the Guatemalan government, signed in 1992, reiterate basic guarantees, including the rights to life, physical safety, organization, and free expression. The agreements also offer specific benefits, including the promise to aid refugees in recovering prior land claims or obtaining new lands. Given the ongoing conflict in Guatemala at the time and the concern over continuous human rights abuses, the strategy of the refugees was to capitalize on international support in order to raise the government's cost of violating constitutional rights. The slogan of the movement led by the Permanent Commissions was to carry out a "collective and organized" return as opposed to the repatriation program offered by the government. While the latter was maligned among the refugees as a way for the government to control and divide those who returned, the collective movement was touted as a political concession wrested from the government, which was faced with the refugees' people power.

Refugee Women's New Roles— "We Know How to Think Too"

Visible roles and focused attention for women came only after the refugee camps had been established for several years.[10] Coming from rural villages with either no schools or little tradition in educating girls, and initially unable to communicate with each other due to linguistic differences, refugee women had little opportunity and even less confidence to participate actively in the organization of refugee life. Refugees, especially women, often considered the acquiring of Spanish as equivalent to gaining speech or cognizance, as expressed by one female refugee: "I remember that my father used to tell my mother that women have no place in the [community] meetings because they don't understand anything, because in our village the women didn't even know how to speak Spanish."[11]

Nevertheless, the crisis of flight and the emergency demands of forming the refugee camps forced women into new roles. Later, women were singled out to implement small economic projects. Even when these were unsuccessful economically, it brought refugee women together. A new generation of women's organizations began in 1990 with the creation of the organization known as Mamá Maquín (named for a revered female elder and activist, martyred in a 1978 land protest). This organization and others formed later by refugee women typically put the strategy of the collective and organized return at the center of their agenda, echoing the male-dominated collective return movement: "We women will support the return in every way necessary. . . . [We have] always had a close relationship with the Permanent Commissions. Since the beginning we have set the goal of helping and supporting their demands."[12] This agenda in part responded to a prescribed and encouraged role for the women, a sort of ladies' auxiliary for the Permanent Commissions.[13] But many women leaders took their newfound consciousness beyond the party line. They also wanted "to continue developing our own forms of organization . . . [to] become active subjects, women with awareness of gender, class and ethnicity, so that we can participate in national [level] and social projects, in which women play the active role that belongs to us, alongside men."[14]

Once strong refugee women's organizations were established, from 1990 onward, and had consistent support from non-governmental organizations (NGOs), a joint commission between UNHCR, the women's organizations and the NGOs was formed to coordinate their complementary agendas. UNHCR initiated a gender-based approach to its work promoting, among other activities with Guatemalan refugee women in Mexico, the following:[15]

- A literacy campaign designed with women's organizations and as a tool for raising women's self-esteem and contact with one another;
- Implementation of time- and labor-saving devices such as mechanical corn grinders and fuel-saving stoves;
- Reproductive health services;
- Communication skills training for refugee women who ran their own radio program as a vehicle for spreading information to other refugee women and improving the abilities of women involved; and,
- Protection and rights training covering human rights, women's rights, land rights, and awareness of sexual and domestic violence (including mechanisms to report such violations to and receive follow-up from UNHCR).

These programs were all undertaken with a clear decision by UNHCR to work closely with NGOs and to create an open-door policy whereby both refugee women and men would feel comfortable approaching and working with UNHCR staff.[16] Three field offices in each of the three Mexican states with refugee camps covered a population that never exceeded forty-eight thousand persons, permitting a staff-to-refugee ratio that facilitated one-on-one contact (although in the state of Chiapas more than twenty thousand refugees were dispersed among more than a hundred sites). Increasingly stable economic and security conditions permitted UNHCR and NGOs to focus on longer-term strategies and more complex issues (including gender roles) when compared to many refugee situations.

The above conditions and parallel efforts by other institutions created new possibilities alongside refugee women's growing enthusiasm. Women began to speak out more in community matters, derived pride from having their own organizations, and young women were designated as promoters of health, education, and human rights. Women report that they had more options to earn money in and outside the camps, which exposed them to new venues and gave them increased economic independence.[17] Families increasingly sent their daughters, as well as their sons, to school, in contrast to common practice in their home communities in Guatemala. It is therefore no coincidence that, among returnees, girls have higher education levels compared to other Guatemalan rural girls and some are choosing to marry later or delay childbearing. In this way they are varying the roles played by women and subsequently increasing men's recognition of their different capabilities.

One overall conclusion that UNHCR was able to draw from this experience is that certain assumptions held by the institution about working with refugee women, and especially indigenous women, were false. It *was* possible for women to represent themselves, to make their needs known directly without using intermediaries.[18] Topics considered taboo by outsiders concerned with cultural sensitivity were less so if both women and men were involved in choosing the topics and the way in which they were presented. For example, in some camps women had more access to discussing their sexuality, and not just in terms of their reproductive health. Incest and domestic violence were addressed more openly, as was the financial obligation of men who abandoned their families.

Without minimizing UNHCR's contribution or that of the NGOs involved, the creation and success of the women's organizations was ultimately an effort by and for the women involved. No amount of outside funding, well-meaning foreigners, or opportunities ceded by male leaders would have created the movement that came to exist if it hadn't been for dozens of dynamic, decisive, and forceful refugee women.

The years of training, traveling, economic work, and organizational experience transformed the outlook of countless Guatemalan refugee women. Compared to many Indian women in Guatemala, they have lost, to use their term, their embarrassment or sense of shame (*pena, vergüenza*) and now engage in public speaking. These are the same women who used to characteristically cover their mouths with their hands and look down when they spoke, if they dared to speak at all. Women often recount a personal experience as either before or after the self-discovery and critical consciousness associated with exile. In the words of one returnee woman, "Now I dare speak out. I'm sure that if I'd stayed in my [pre-exile] village I wouldn't know anything."[19] As will be seen, however, the story does not end with the refugees' triumphant return to Guatemala and the women's best intentions to bring back their new ideas.

Why Land and Why Land for Women?

Land was the battle cry of the collective return movement and a foremost concern of every refugee family. The lands the refugees left were either in ancestral regions in the western highlands or in recently colonized northern lowlands. In the first case, lands were mostly of marginal quality and insufficient in size to maintain a family. In the colonized areas, refugees left behind newly acquired lands planted with cash crops at the peak of production. Land tenure in Guatemala before exile was varied and whereas verbal and informal written agreements had worked well for many for generations, most of these would not constitute sufficient proof when land disputes went before the Guatemala legal system. Refugees knew that many of the lands they claimed had been resettled in their absence, sometimes by colonizers with army backing. New families, formed by young couples during the many years in exile, had children of their own, but stood to inherit insufficient or no land from their parents' generation upon returning to Guatemala. So a mass movement to demand land was appealing to both those intent on recovering land and those who intended to obtain new land.

Physical displacement meant the loss not only of livelihood from the land, but also of the spiritual value of the land itself. For some Mayans, the spirit-gods they pray to correspond to the surrounding hillsides and cannot be prayed to elsewhere.[20] Spiritual, family, and economic ties especially motivated the older generation to attempt the return to their village of origin. Others, however, faced with the option of returning to an ancestral village with poor land, versus better or more land in a region of Guatemala completely new to them, did not hesitate to choose the latter. Skills learned in exile, organizational strength, and the promise of external aid reinforced the idea that such settlements would be successful.

Part and parcel of the refugee experience, women felt the loss of family land as keenly as men. Nevertheless, in the context of mobilizing for a collective return, it was not immediately evident that women should struggle for joint ownership of land. For the most part, women assumed that so-called community land would continue to be in a husband or father's name. The issue of women's direct control of land was more meaningful, however, for women abandoned by their partners. Often abandonment meant deprivation of land or family belongings. In the words of one female returnee: "Look at what happened to [my neighbor], she and her husband separated and she was lucky that he left her with the house, but he took all the [farm] land. This is our problem . . . not that we plan on separating from our husbands but these things happen . . . and if the man leaves us and [we are not landowners] then he can do whatever he wants— we can't fight back because he has all the rights."[21]

In some Guatemalan communities where more traditional leadership structures are intact, family problems, such as a man's desertion of his family, may be brought before an elders' council (of men) or other respected community authorities (or both). Sometimes the man is instructed to surrender the family house or land or both to his children and former wife, but a woman has no guarantee that a decision will be in her favor or that her former partner will comply. In such a case and on the basis of national law, women can theoretically take their cases to a justice of the peace. Redress through the legal system, however, is time-consuming, costly, and particularly intimidating for Mayan women, especially if they do not speak Spanish. In short, it is rarely a realistic option. Although most Guatemalan law is gender neutral, and the Guatemalan constitution stresses that men and women are equal regardless of "marital status" *(estado civil),* practical application is otherwise. Furthermore, until 1998 the Guatemalan civil code designated men as household representatives for married couples and its unconstitutional basis went uncontested for many years.

A potential obstacle was women's fear and lack of self-confidence to accept formal responsibility for credit. This was not insurmountable, however, since payments for family credit (often available for fertilizer purchase or animal-raising projects) often fell to the women anyway if her partner was irresponsible with family funds, even if she was not a named beneficiary. Furthermore, there was new awareness for some women that their daily labor is what permits their spouse to earn "his" income:

> We realized that the women were also paying the credit [granted for land purchase]; the women work in the house, in the fields, in the community. Women put aside household money to meet payments and they leave home to work in order to make enough money for food. Without someone doing the housework and guaranteeing food on the table, men wouldn't be free to go work and they wouldn't get enough money to pay the credit by themselves. In our history no one values or pays for the work we do and that's why the men often say that they are the ones who earn the money and that they should make the decisions about how to spend it and that's why the laws and the government authorities only recognize men as landowners.[22]

Therefore, while the decision of the refugee women's organization to mobilize women in demanding joint ownership of land was an outgrowth of their new awareness of women's rights in general, it also responded to the concrete need to protect women's economic rights in cases of separation. For UNHCR, moreover, supporting this demand was an important way to reaffirm and promote women's importance vis-à-vis the community and the male leaders. In other words, for UNHCR staff intent on addressing gender bias and discrimination, the issue crystallized the strategy of promoting both women's improved condition and position. *Condition* includes women's economic and general well-being; *position* signifies recognition of their capabilities and contribution by participation in decision-making spheres as well as the exercise of legal rights in the community.[23]

Theory Meets Praxis—Initial Attempts for Women to Exercise Land Rights

When the first organized group that was to receive new lands through the government was preparing to return, women were anxious to cosign the legal documents listing the beneficiaries. When they crossed the border into Guatemala in January 1994, however, only the men and widowed women were listed on the collective title. When the community formed a cooperative to which the property of the land was transferred, women with partners were newly excluded. UNHCR on both sides of the border was mystified at first as to "what went wrong" in establishing joint ownership as the logical conclusion of several years of intensive work on the topic in the Mexican refugee camps.[24] Afterward, a process of investigating both the institutional-level and community-level obstacles and the ways to overcome them became a priority for the refugee women's organizations involved and UNHCR.

When it was clear that legal limitations were not at issue in this or in ensuing cases, the corresponding state agencies were asked to emit statements to this effect.[25] Following this, UNHCR devised a strategy whereby the (male-dominated) refugee organizations through their legal advisors in conjunction with the UNHCR office in Guatemala signed a document affirming the lack of legal impediments and, furthermore, the desirability of making men and women equal owners of the lands to be negotiated.[26] This document was later analyzed in a workshop with leaders of the refugee women and made public in a conference setting where the relevant state agencies were asked to formally respond to women's request to be included as joint owners of land. A subsequent 1996 credit agreement between the refugee organizations and the government specifies that family lands should be allocated on the basis of both the male and female heads of households becoming joint owners of the family farming plot.[27] This process of clarification of institutional policies and public debate

- revealed the clear bias that effectively discriminated against women due to the interpretation and application of institutional policy by government officials (of whom most, but not all, were and are male) and the need for appropriate models for preparing and implementing the process of land acquisition. Clear evidence of this problem is that the lists circulated for beneficiary families were designed to include only one name per family;

- forced the male-dominated refugee organizations to publicly accept and even promote the inclusion of women in land titles; and
- reinforced the decision of women to continue to struggle for their right to landownership.

Through publicized agreements and women's insistence, women being taken into account as property owners became an increasingly accepted part of the agenda of the refugees—familiar (and less shocking) to at least some of the institutions (governmental and nongovernmental) working with them.

Finally, sheer persistence started to pay off. Between late 1996 and 1998, seven new return groups that managed to negotiate land purchases through the government included all adult men and women on the document soliciting credit and authorizing the purchase on their behalf *(mandato legal)*. The women refugees and the institutions advocating on their behalf began to believe that an important preliminary battle with the government institutions had been won, although minor setbacks continued.[28]

A Bittersweet Transition to an Unfamiliar Home

Most of the refugees fled Guatemala in 1982 and most of the organized returns occurred between 1993 and 1998. Refugees had spent between eleven and sixteen years in the camps and the women would encounter many new situations and unexpected difficulties upon returning to Guatemala.

First, the return communities were formed from groups of people from different refugee camps, united around a need for land and the common denominator of having been refugees, but heterogeneous in other ways. In many cases, any given family would know just a few other families, but now they were expected (by outsiders at least) to act like a coherent unit, making decisions with people they barely knew. Second, even where groups were going home to their previous place of origin, they were reuniting with old neighbors who had had very different wartime experiences, not all of them in Mexico. Ten or fifteen years apart made coming back together a difficult process. Third, women were often separated from their friends and relatives depending on the return site different people chose. Would a young woman go with her own parents, with her in-laws, or with other women with whom she had formed friendships and bonds? Often the return meant choosing one priority over another.[29] Thus, family ties and the structures of the women's organizations and other communal networks were altered or even dismantled during the return. Fourth, economic conditions were and are difficult despite start-up assistance and other aid. Establishing or reestablishing communities as returnees meant beginning all over again. Whether new settlements or recovered lands ravaged by war, returnee lands were rarely under production when returnees arrived. All but a handful of returnee communities (of approximately fifty associated with the collective return process) are in remote and isolated areas of Guatemala, with no or poor-quality roads. Where returnees opted for lands in regions new to them, there are complex integration issues depending on the ethnic groups and social dynamic of each area.

In addition, there was a severe clash of expectations for women as individuals. The romantic ideal of home is rarely a realistic one for returning refugees. Women's personal sense of loss in returning home is partially due to the anticlimactic and unanticipated conditions of resettlement. It is increasingly recognized in refugee literature that the dynamics of returning refugees has been insufficiently explored; often, the simple equation *return equals happiness* was inappropriately taken for granted by the institutions involved.[30] The pace of the Guatemalan return process, however, was driven less by the governments involved and external institutions such as UNHCR (often dragged reluctantly into supporting return movements) than by the refugees themselves. The latter were prone to vote with their feet and return with or without institutional support. Leaving aside for the moment how refugee sentiment was influenced for political purposes by their own leadership and others, nostalgia for home was paramount in individual decision making.[31] The majority of Guatemalan refugees old enough to remember their country of origin more often than not would complain about most aspects of life in exile while expressing longing for *mi tierra* (my land or place). They tried to instill in their Mexican-born children (with mixed success) the idea that Guatemala was where they belonged. Such was the collective ideal of going home that it belied both personal memories of the hardships of Guatemala and the sometimes negative information that arrived in the camps from those who had already repatriated.

I met with a woman leader—known for her militancy and outspokenness—in Guatemala City a few months after her return to her village of origin in the jungle. She commented that home was not as she expected: "It is *so* difficult to live there!" I expected her to relate the privations of living in the one region where the war continued, where land mines had been found and military overflights were common, but her explanation was less dramatic: "Yes, imagine! Two hours of walking in terrible mud to get to a road!"[32] She had left this same village as an adult, when getting to the road took days instead of hours, but the distance of years and selective memory had betrayed her in preparing for her new life as a returnee.

How Women Lost Ground

In January 1998, Mamá Maquín leaders visited several communities where women had signed all the preliminary documents related to obtaining funding for land purchase. To their surprise they found communities where women were losing the land rights they thought they had won. In these cases, community male leadership had created cooperatives for the community to which land rights were being transferred and women (with the exception of some widows and single mothers) were being excluded from the cooperatives and therefore losing land rights. Furthermore, the Mamá Maquín leaders found that many women were demoralized, isolated, and their support structures all but gone. It was evident that the campaign to have women "sign the papers" while still in Mexico was necessary but, in and of itself, insufficient. Other challenges included exploring the difficulties women faced in becoming cooperative members and understanding the reasons why women, apparently so involved in politics and camp life in Mexico, were back at the hearth and feeling helpless about, if not resigned to, playing a quieter role.

In retrospect, it is possible to see where the women's organizations were just not aware of, let alone prepared for, the challenges that awaited them. In seeking an explanation for the organizational crises faced by the women's organizations after returning, in addition to logistical problems created by the isolated conditions of returnee communities there was a lack of consolidation of the organizing in Mexico and common goals were no longer obvious. The fact that strategizing in Mexico both by the women and by the agencies that supported them neglected research or reflection on the possible problems that could occur once back home indicates a first weakness. Also the experiences and abilities were not uniform among all the women and this left only a handful of leaders who were in a good position to withstand the setbacks that began to occur. Another observation, which is only possible in retrospect, is that women were just barely reaching the point of consolidating their gains and they were still very dependent on outside support (moral, organizational, and financial).[33] In fact, concerted efforts by outsiders to help the women did not begin until after 1990 and the collective return movement started the return exodus only two years later.

The women had organized around one primary common goal: the struggle to return home. Around that common goal they had achieved many other changes, but there was no longer a single objective once back in Guatemala. Some women thought that their organizations should bring them economic projects; others thought they should forge links with other women's groups in Guatemala and intervene in national politics. Others just didn't know why they should still exist except that their affiliation to a women's group had made them feel proud and positive about themselves.

Another issue is that of men's opposition to women's participation. The creation and promotion of women's refugee organizations that began in 1990 was not only permitted, but was promoted by male leaders in a moment of political opportunism while in Mexican refugee camps. Women demanding the right to return home with a political platform stipulating specific conditions, rejecting the role and presence of the Guatemalan army in rural communities, and demanding land, made for a powerful image in the media and for international organizations and embassies. Thus, women's visibility had been convenient for the male-dominated refugee organizations. However, when women began to take charge of their own organizations and engaged in consciousness raising to demand visible and formal roles in decision making, men may have perceived it, consciously or unconsciously, as overstepping the acceptable limits they had prescribed for women's roles.

Community men, and some leaders in particular, have discouraged women in different ways, both in regard to their organizations and to their role in the male-dominated structures. In a few cases, hostility has been open: What did you accomplish anyway, men have asked the women publicly, or: You played your part in Mexico, but there is no longer any need now that we are back home. This would follow the rule played out in many a wartime scenario: "women are welcome to assume counter-traditional roles only where there is a perceived need. Once the crisis has ended they are supposed to return to the private sphere of the household."[34] How men regarded women organizing and women's organizations was also complicated by the political landscape and the national role of male-run refugee organizations. As some male returnee leaders sought to renegotiate or reject support for the guerrilla organizations (when these were in the midst of becoming a political party), individual women were also taking sides on this political debate and had to redefine their organizational positions as well. Some women were trapped by conflicting loyalties to their own political beliefs, their husband or partner, and their women's organization. Their organizations also had to decide how autonomous they would be in relation to the men in their communities and the male-dominated organizations, regardless of the political position of the latter.

In one extreme case in 1997, in the midst of an internal political struggle in one community, one group openly backed the emerging political party of the guerrilla organizations and another group opposed them. The opposing group declared publicly that the local women's group was made up of guerrilla supporters and in a violent fit a small mob burned their humble meeting house. Through simple red-baiting and guilt by association, the male leaders in this community had conveniently and symbolically silenced the outspoken women who dared to denounce them for their unfair and authoritarian practices. Was it a coincidence that the political debate was taken as an excuse to quiet the women's organization? In the view of the women affected, one was linked to the other: "The reason for this aggression against our organization and our right to free association is that we do not share some of the political stances held by the [community's cooperative] directorate, [since] these opinions relegate women to second place in social and community participation."[35] It is ironic, but not unexpected, that male refugee leaders continue to demand that the state uphold the universal primacy of human rights for them, but overlook their own role in limiting these same rights for women in their homes and communities.

Finally, there were numerous obstacles put forth by institutions (both governmental and nongovernmental) interacting with returnees and this was another important factor in debilitating the women's quest for landownership and other visible ways of participating. In general, the Mexican NGOs had proved more sensitive to incorporating and calling on women, whereas the Guatemalan NGOs were used to relegating women to secondary roles even when outwardly conforming to donor pressure to work with women or analyze their activities through the lens of gender. One leader recounted in a workshop for returnee women how development workers called a meeting in her community with the male leaders of the cooperative to address funding a community (not cooperative) project. As the aid workers left, the women confronted them: "Why didn't you include us," they asked. At this point the narrator imitated the aid worker's condescending look and pat on the shoulder: "Oh, we knew you were busy and there wasn't time to convene everybody, but next time. . . ." The women in the workshop exploded with laughter. The story was familiar.[36]

For the government institutions involved in working with the refugees to find land and obtain credit from the government, the presence of women during this process seemed useless or sometimes amusing. When queried about women's participation, the standard answer was, Of course we include widows. Even when some government agency directors began to mimic the language of including all women, other employees—agronomists, accountants, and lawyers—had no training or contact with the notion of women's possible role. Excluding them from the process seemed normal and taking them into account, very novel.

For example, in October 1998 a group of refugees was negotiating a combined credit from two government institutions: one that normally worked with refugees and the other, a program that had never had contact with refugees or with the issue of considering that a beneficiary family could be represented by two people. As the extremely drawn-out credit approval process drew to a close, the pressure was on to finalize the purchase before the owner selling the property backed out of the deal and to permit the returnees to arrive in time to harvest the already ripe coffee on the farm. In this context, the government lawyers were surprised to see that both men and women had signed the legal document soliciting credit approval and told the group's representatives (all men) that this would not be permitted. When the government officials were pressured to give explanations, they ranged from explaining, Its never been done, to the affirmation that the real problem was that many couples lived in common-law relationships and the women's rights would be most adequately addressed by them becoming legally married.[37] While no one could point to a specific law prohibiting the notion of two persons representing each family, the government representatives affirmed that the inclusion of women would imply lengthy delays and the possible loss of the coffee harvest or even the finalized purchase. Faced with the implicit ultimatum, the male refugee leaders opted to exclude the women.

Institutional bias has also been manifested via those agencies that work with cooperatives. Both the Guatemalan law regulating co-ops and government extension workers reinforce the concept that every single member must contribute with co-op dues and community labor in the same way. Men therefore put pressure on women to pull their own weight with equal contributions of cash and physical labor in order to be members. While this is especially onerous for widows and single mothers, this approach also misses the heart of the matter articulated by women leaders: women's work (in the fields and with children and domestic responsibilities in the home) subsidize the labor and cash contributions credited to their husbands. Were this work visible and valued, the community would recognize that women are already paying membership dues and have been for some time.[38]

What Is Next?

It would be easy to dismiss the process that women underwent in exile when the disappointing outcomes to date are measured against the women's own expectations. Women are not involved in community decision making, are mostly excluded from the cooperatives that have been formed around approving and administrating economic projects in the community, and have often been denied legal control of community land. Women are often called upon to validate decisions put before a community assembly, but they are not involved in the leadership structures that set priorities and create strategies for community norms and daily life. Women are often called by NGOs and agencies to participate in or control small so-called women's projects, but are routinely ignored for the implementation of so-called community projects, which tend to be those with more funding and broader scope.

But reality of course is more complex and the process the women underwent cannot be reduced to a zero-sum game. The women themselves—who remain open to discussing their opinions with numerous outsiders—remain positive and distinguish between the conditions they live and what they feel. It is the intangible gains of having participated and having contributed that women speak of, even when complaining about the current state of affairs and their personal difficulties as poor rural women. Even while women have difficulty putting into practice some of their new ideas with their own daughters and sons, they are aware that their endless domestic and agricultural labor is indeed work, they are conscious of needing rest, and they feel freer circulating in their community and engaging with other women. Such things can be taken as evidence that women were touched profoundly by their experiences and have begun to apply it in their own lives.[39] Other gains for these women and their daughters, with support and time, can and will come.

As values and cultural practice among Guatemala's rural Indians continually evolve there are increasing gaps in the mechanisms that used to support and protect women and those envisaged for the future. For example, in the tightly knit, less mobile communities of decades ago (at least in today's nostalgic retelling), there were probably more effective safety nets for women who became widows—through extended family networks and the expected show of community solidarity. On the other hand, an ideal version of the modern future that the returnees seek (using cooperatives as a basis for social organization, for example) also might afford protection to all women if laws were fully complied with and—in the case of cooperatives—women were allowed to be members. Mexican psychologist Itziar Lozano, who collaborated with UNHCR in conducting research with refugee women, has argued that it is the present situation in which the women have the worst of both worlds insofar as they are excluded from the new community structures: "[This exclusion] situates women as they were before exile in regard to domestic, productive, communal, and political relations but without the protection, small or large, previously offered by indigenous custom, now broken up by war and displacement."[40]

Notes

All Spanish-to-English translations in this chapter are mine.

1. The term Mayan has been adopted increasingly by different indigenous organizations during the 1990s to describe the vast majority of indigenous and linguistic groups in Guatemala. Previously, other terms such as *natural, indigena,* and *indio* have been used to distinguish those who marked themselves or were marked by dress, language, and often more subjective criteria from those considered non-Indian, ladino, or mestizo. Mayan and Indian are used here interchangeably. Based on primary language spoken, 86 percent of

refugees in Mexico were classified by aid agencies as Indian, although more were undoubtedly of Indian origin. *Memoria de Silencio. Informe de las Violaciones a los Derechos Humanos y los Hechos de Violencia que han Causado Sufrimientos a la Población Guatemalteca,* [Memory of Silence. Report on the violation of human rights and the acts of violence that have caused suffering to the population of Guatemala] Comisión de Esclarecimiento Historico (CEH), 1999, ch. 3.

2. The commission's official title was the Commission for Historical Clarification, and its subtitle, "[of] past human rights violations and acts of violence that have caused the Guatemalan population to suffer." Its mandate was to explain and detail the conflict and its context without assigning individual blame. The commission's structure and information-gathering process constitute an innovative model within the international genre of truth commissions and its final report is made up of fifteen lengthy volumes.

3. Greg Grandin, "Chronicles of a Guatemalan Genocide Foretold: Violence, Trauma, and the Limits of Historical Inquiry" (paper presented at the Latin American Studies Association Congress, Miami, 2000).

4. According to the convention, genocide is defined as "any of the following acts committed with intent to destroy, in whole or in part, a national, ethnic, racial or religious group." One of the five examples of such acts is "deliberately inflicting on the group conditions of life calculated to bring about its physical destruction in whole or in part." Convention on the Prevention and Punishment of the Crime of Genocide, December 9, 1948, 102 stat. 3045, 78 UNTS 277, UN GA res. 260, UN GAOR, 3d session, 179th plenary mtg. at 174, UN doc. A/810 (1948). Cited in Grandin, "Guatemalan Genocide Foretold."

5. Interview with staff of CHRLA (Center for Human Rights Legal Action), January 2000.

6. CEH, *Memoria,* 408–9.

7. Finn Stepputat, "Hacia un Marco de Análisis de los Procesos de Migración Forzada: Identidades y Modernización entre Refugiados y Retornados Guatemaltecos" [Toward an analytical framework for forced migration: identities and modernization among Guatemalan refugees and returnees] *Revista Estudios Interétnicos* 7 (11) (1999): 7–19; Deborah Lynn Billings, "Identities, Consciousness, and Organizing in Exile: Guatemalan Refugee Women in the Camps of Southern Mexico" (Ph.D. dissertation, University of Michigan, 1995).

8. Stepputat, "Migración Forzada."

9. Finn Stepputat, "Repatriation and Everyday Forms of State Formation in Guatemala," in *The End of the Refugee Cycle? Refugee Repatriation and Reconstruction,* ed. Richard Black and Khalid Koser (New York: Berghahn Books, 1998), 210–26.

10. The quote in the heading is from Carolina Cabarrús, Dorotea Gómez, and Ligia González, *Y nos saltamos las trancas: Los cambios en la vida de las mujeres refugiadas retornadas guatemaltecas* [We jumped the pole: Changes in the lives of returned refugee women in Guatemala (Guatemala City: Consejería en Proyectos/Project Counseling Services [PCS], 2000), 58. Additional field notes from this project used by permission.

11. Ibid., 53.

12. Mamá Maquín and CIAM (Centro de Investigación y Acción para la Mujer), *From Refugees to Returnees: A Chronicle of Women Refugees' Organizing Experiences in Chiapas* (Mexico: CIAM, 1994).

13. To the extent that the Centro de Investigación y Acción para la Mujer revolutionary left sought support among and influence over the organizing male refugees, so the refugee women's organizations were anticipated as a way of broadening support for the revolutionary cause. Indeed, some women had arrived at their consciousness about the need to change women's roles based on their experiences (both negative and positive) as guerrilla collaborators. A recent description of women's role in the revolutionary left in Central America details the case of El Salvador, where organizing women was key for both raising funds (since international funding agencies were so supportive of women's work) and for the support roles the women played in the war. See Ilja A. Luciak, "Gender Equality and Democratization in Central America: The Case of the Revolutionary Left" (paper presented at the Latin American Studies Association Congress, Miami, 2000).

In general, refugees had become more sympathetic to the "struggle" after experiencing repression at the hands of the Guatemalan army that caused their exile (CEH, 1999). The overlaps and differences in agenda, however, meant that from the very beginning of their organizing, the leaders of the women refugees had to reflect upon and then negotiate their autonomy from the organizational structures of the revolutionary left.

14. Mamá Maquín/CIAM, *Refugees to Returnees*.

15. Itziar Lozano, *Lessons Learned in Work with Refugee Women: A Case Study of Chiapas* (Mexico City: Consultancy for UNHCR [United Nations High Commissioner for Refugees], 1996).

16. Ibid.

17. Interviews carried out in camps in rural Chiapas in 1993, however, showed women complaining of the lack of mobility and paid employment. See Billings, "Identities, Consciousness, and Organizing." On the other hand, interviews in 1998 showed returnee women who lived in different places in Mexico nostalgically recalling the numerous work opportunities available to them as refugees. See Cabarrús, Gómez, and González, *Y nos saltamos las trancas*. Given

the increased mobility that refugees were permitted through the years, differences from camp to camp, and the tendency to lament the present and romanticize the past, both findings are compatible.

18. Lozano, *Lessons Learned;* Terry Morel, "Mujeres guatemaltecas refugiadas y retornadas: Su participación en las estructuras comunitarias y los procesos de toma de decisiones" [Guatemalan refugee and returnee women: Their participation in community structures and decision making] (paper presented and distributed at UNHCR seminar in Guatemala, 1998).

19. Cabarrús, Gómez, and González, *Y nos saltamos las trancas,* 69.

20. See Richard Wilson, *Maya Resurgence in Guatemala: Q'eqchi' Experiences* (Norman: University of Oklahoma Press, 1995).

21. Cabarrús, Gómez, and González, *Y nos saltamos las trancas,* 105.

22. Mamá Maquín, *Nuestra experiencia ante los retos del futuro: Sistematización del trabajo de las mujeres de Mamá Maquín durante el refugio en México y su retorno a Guatemala* [Our experiences and future challenges: The work of Mamá Maquín during exile in Mexico and the return to Guatemala] (Mexico City: Mamá Maquín, 1999).

23. Efforts by specific, mostly female, UNHCR staff members in Central America to apply in a systematic and genuine manner vague institutional mandates on "refugee women" and "gender focus mainstreaming" were both parallel to and influential over changes taking place at the institutional (Geneva) level, pressuring UNHCR to practice what it preached in regard to women. See Paula Worby, *Lessons Learned from UNHCR's Involvement in the Guatemala Refugee Repatriation and Reintegration Programme: 1987–1999* (Geneva: UNHCR, 2000).

24. Ana Patricia Ispanel, "Diagnóstico de la participación de la mujer en los niveles de organización comunitaria: El caso de Nueva Esperanza" [Assessment of women's participation of different levels of community organization: The case of Nueva Esperanza] (unpublished consultancy for UNHCR, Guatemala office, 1995).

25. Itziar Lozano, "El mandato del ACNUR y la equidad de género: El acceso de las mujeres a la tierra en el refugio, el retorno y la reintegración" [UNHCR's mandate and gender equity: Women's land access in exile upon return, and during reintegration] (consultancy for UNHCR, Mexico, 1997).

26. UNHCR and Comisiones Permanetes de los Refugiados Guatemaltecos, "Dictamen Juridico sobre el Acceso de la Mujer Desarraigada a la Propiedad de la Tierra y a Créditos para la Compra de la Misma" [Legal analysis regarding displaced women's access to property rights and credit for land purchase] (Guatemala, 1995).

27. Simultaneously, partial topic-by-topic peace agreements were being

signed between the government and the insurgent organizations grouped in the National Guatemalan Revolutionary Unity (URNG). Three of these agreements, regarding the resettlement of uprooted populations, the identity and rights of indigenous peoples, and socioeconomic and agrarian issues, contain explicit mention of women and land. In each, the government's obligation is to eliminate any legal or de facto discrimination against women and simultaneously promote their access to land, housing, or credit, though no specific timeline or mechanism is described. All agreements took full effect in December 1996 with the conclusion of the final Peace Accords.

28. In 1996 government officials visiting Mexico about a land purchase transaction canceled the meeting when "only" the women had arrived to the meeting on time and were present. Later, only men signed the land papers in a hastily rescheduled meeting. In another incident, in April 1997, a legal advisor for the Permanent Commissions argued against men and women refugees who had agreed that all would be included on the document soliciting the land purchase. Then he offered to make two legal documents to present to the government, one with and one without the women, if and when he was paid a double honorarium.

29. Sometimes women admit to having submitted to the decision of her partner or pressure from her parents in choosing her destination, but equally often the men ceded these choices to women or used her preference as a pretext to opt for a particular destination without needing to further justify the choice. In short, the available choices—staying in Mexico or choosing where to go in Guatemala—were always fraught with pros and cons. The multiple factors involved in weighing options made for a complex process for all involved. Adolescents (over fourteen) were asked individually by UNHCR Mexican staff about their voluntary choice to repatriate and the more private the interview, the more likely they would differ with their parents. An inevitable part of repatriation was the separation of families already split by displacement and migration; women are vocal about the ongoing sadness this causes them.

30. John R. Rogge, "Repatriation of Refugees: A Not Simple 'Optimum' Solution," in *When Refugees Go Home: African Experiences,* ed. Tim Allen and Hubert Morsink (Geneva: UNRISD, Trenton, N.J.: Africa World Press), 367–78; Daniel Warner, "Voluntary Repatriation and the Meaning of Return to Home: A Critique of Liberal Mathematics," *Journal of Refugee Studies* 7 (2–3) (1994): 160–74; Laura Hammond, "Examining the Discourse of Repatriation: Towards a More Proactive Theory of Return Migration," in *The End of the Refugee Cycle?* ed. Richard Black and Khalid Koser (New York: Berghahn Books, 1998), 227–44.

31. Nostalgia for the homeland and hopes for rebuilding a new and better Guatemala with the skills learned in exile were secondary priorities for the

approximately forty-four hundred families (made up of eleven thousand persons of the original refugee caseload together with eleven thousand born in the refugee camps) who opted to remain in Mexico. While the Mexican government had for years purposely avoided raising the hopes of refugees who wished to stay, it eventually faced up to the fait accompli of thousands of refugees loath to leave and refugee children who had Mexican citizenship, and initiated the road to permit refugee naturalization in December 1995.

32. My notes, 1995.

33. See Cabarrús, Gómez, and González, *Y nos saltamos las trancas.*

34. The dismantling of Rosie the Riveter (U.S. women mobilized for World War II industrial work) is a classic example. Luciak, "Gender Equality"; Cynthia Enloe, *Does Khaki Become You? The Militarisation of Women's Lives* (Boston: South End Press, 1983).

35. Mamá Maquín, communiqué, June 11, 1997.

36. My notes, 2000.

37. The urban cultural bias against the rural and Indian practice of living *unidos,* without state or church sanctioned marriage, is clear and was defined as a problem principally by government officials. While marrying or formalizing common-law relationships (before a notary public) theoretically improves a woman's claim to her husband's property, there is no reason that married or unmarried women should not represent themselves directly in regard to jointly held belongings.

38. Paula Worby, "Security and Dignity: Land Access and Guatemala's Returned Refugees," *REFUGE: Canada's Periodical on Refugees* 19 (1) (2000).

39. Cabarrús, Gómez, and González, *Y nos saltamos las trancas.*

40. Lozano, "Mandato del ACNUR."

5

Religion and National Identity
in Stalin's USSR
Implications for Post-Soviet Politics

Steven Miner

SINCE THE IMPLOSION of Soviet Communism in 1991, the western borderlands of the former USSR have been spared the sort of violent ethnic conflict that has erupted in the Caucasus, Central Asia, and the former Yugoslavia. This does not mean, however, that ethnic tension—much of it rooted, or at least reinforced by, religious differences—is absent. In Estonia and part of Latvia, a numerically small enclave of Protestantism clings to the shores of the Baltic. In Poland and Lithuania, Catholicism is both powerful in numbers and in vigor, having only been revitalized by its adherent sense of repression at the hands of the Russians and Soviets, and by the elevation of a Polish pope in 1978. In western Ukraine, a shard of Catholicism—the Uniate, or Greek Catholic, Church—managed to survive severe repression at the hands of the Soviet authorities, to emerge by 1991 as one of the most important kernels of a new Ukrainian nation. Throughout Estonia, Belarus, Moldova, Ukraine, and Russia itself, Eastern Orthodoxy, battered and compromised by its ambiguous relations with the region's Communist regimes, shows signs of recovering its former centrality, both politically and religiously. Religious tension adds a dangerous element to an already combustible mix of conflicts over political loyalties, regional and national boundaries, and scarce material resources.

The sudden disappearance of established political authority in the former Soviet Union has led to a reemergence of the power and importance of religion as a unifying and defining social and national force. The collapse of Communist power has also brought about a jumbling of political, national, and even religious loyalties. In nationalist, right-wing demonstrations in Moscow, one is treated to the strange spectacle of disgruntled Communists, holding aloft images of Stalin, mingling with Russian Orthodox believers displaying copies of icons (Serbia has witnessed a similar odd mix). This strange blending of seeming irreconcilables is the direct result of the Soviet state's decades-long manipulation of national forces and images; in its desperate attempts to establish the legitimacy of its power, the Soviet regime was forced to accommodate itself to historical and national forces that were inimical to the professed goals of early Bolshevism.

This chapter argues that the Second World War provided a preview of the reemergence of nationalism as a political force in the post-Soviet period. Soviet religious policies during the Second World War both tapped into and aggravated existing religious-national forces. Not only did Soviet religious policy crystallize these forces' opposition to the Soviet regime, but it also entrenched them into a potential collision course with each other due to the political vacuum created by the collapse of the Soviet system. In this regard, the effect of Soviet religious policies, which contributed to the reinforcement or emergence of spontaneous local and regional religious institutions and identities during World War II, is analogous to the effect that Soviet policies of nationalism and ethnicity had on national and ethnic identities for the post-Soviet period.

Religion and the Soviet State

Embedded deep within the DNA of the Bolshevik regime, born in 1917, was hostility to religion in general—Marx's opiate of the people—but especially to Russian Orthodoxy. In the Bolsheviks' view, the Russian Orthodox Church was not only, in effect, the tsarist government at prayer, it was also the repository of peasant values and national identities that the new Communist regime sought to root out. In the reasoning of the Communists, the mysticism, magic, and mystery of the church merely served to cloud peasant minds, preventing them from seeing that the establishment of a workers' state served their own best interests. Bolshevism was, in its very essence, an urban phenomenon; even for many years after the revolution, the countryside—and thus the majority of the Soviet domain—remained a virtual terra incognita, a region inhabited by a largely hostile mass of people whose worldview and loyalties ran more along religious, rather than political, lines.

The Bolshevik regime sought to extirpate religion through various means: outright repression, destruction, and confiscation of church property, the banning of religious education among the young, forced state registration of baptisms, the denial of opportunity and state benefits to clergy and their children, desecration of holy sites and relics, the propagation of materialist, antireligious education, and many other tactics. One particular approach toward undermining religion later came back to haunt the Soviet regime. Russian Orthodoxy had been the official state church of the Russian Empire; accordingly, within the tsarist domain it embraced all Orthodox believers from the various regions and national groups that together constituted the empire. Once in power, the Bolsheviks sought to fracture the church from within by encouraging splinter movements based along national lines; thus, they encouraged Belorussian, Baltic, and especially Ukrainian Orthodox secessionists. While these groups had their own reasons for wishing to remove themselves from Muscovite ecclesiastical authority, the Communist authorities' support of religious national determination was purely tactical. The Kremlin was playing the traditional imperial role: *dividum et imperium*.[1]

Churches, especially in non-Russian areas, served as foci for the peasant masses, and, given the numerical weakness of Communist Party cadres in the countryside, these churches were often numerically more powerful than state organs. The linking of agrarian discontent over Communist rule with religious-nationalist organizations proved to be an especially hard nut for Moscow to crack. This dangerous nexus goes a long way toward explaining why, during the campaign to impose collective agriculture, Soviet power especially targeted Ukrainian Orthodox churches.[2]

During the 1920s, Soviet antireligious campaigners tried another approach to divide the Russian Orthodox Church from within: they encouraged and facilitated the creation of the so-called Renovationist, or Living, Church (*Obnovlencheskaia tserkov'*). Never as successful as the various nationalist schisms, the Renovationist sect claimed to be founded by "progressive" clergy who professed to see in the Communist order elements of Christian brotherhood and equality. Under the dubious, and entirely nominal, leadership of Archpriest Aleksandr Vvedenskii, this attempt to create a form of liberation theology, well before the invention of that specific term, failed to garner a mass following among Soviet Orthodox believers.

In the years before 1939, Communist repression of religion peaked in three great waves: immediately after the civil war, during collectivization, and during the purges of the late 1930s. The first wave begun when Lenin sought to undermine the authority of the Orthodox Church by blaming it for failing to assist the victims of the postwar famine.[3] Lenin arranged for show trials to indict church leaders, and many thousands of priests throughout the country suffered various forms of repression. As already mentioned, the second wave came during the first five-year plan and collectivization of agriculture (1929–1933).[4] The third, and most lethal, wave started in April 1937, when Georgii Malenkov wrote to Stalin, "The time has come to finish once and for all with all clerical organizations and ecclesiastical hierarchies." Accordingly, nineteen thousand of the remaining twenty thousand open churches were shut; and many thousands of priests were arrested, shot, or driven into other, safer occupations.[5]

As a result of the above policies, the position of the Russian Orthodox Church on the eve of World War II and of religion generally within the USSR was highly precarious. Ironically, the outbreak of the war, so ruinous and destructive in every way for the masses of the Soviet population generally, most probably saved the Russian Orthodox Church from destruction; the dynamics of war also planted the seeds of the current religious-national situation in Russia.

In contrast with the general opinion among historians, the Soviet regime's decision partially to restore the Russian Orthodox Church was actually made before the entry of the USSR into the war. As a reward for assuring Hitler of a quiet Eastern front, following the Nazi-Soviet Pact of August 1939, and for actually assisting the German economic war machine, Moscow received compensation in the form of vast swathes of territory along its western border, encompassing more than 20 million new subjects. Between September 1939 and June–July 1940, these new "western borderlands," including the three Baltic states, the eastern half of Poland (along with eastern portions of Belorussia and Ukraine), Bessarabia, and Bukovina, were occupied by the Red Army. It has long been known that the imposition of Soviet authority in these areas entailed great violence and strife, including the arrest, execution, or deportation to the Soviet Far East of hundreds of thousands of inhabitants deemed unreliable by Moscow; historians have also long known about the partisan war that sprang up throughout the region, most strongly in Polish, Baltic, and Ukrainian lands.[6]

Until the opening of the Soviet archives, however, it had not been clear that the various modes of resistance to the imposition of Soviet rule were deeply intertwined with local churches and with religious institutions. The publication of Soviet documents from the occupation period, including many thousands of communications from the Soviet political police, the People's Commissariat of Internal Affairs, and the People's Commissariat of State Security (the NKVD/NKGB), show that local clergy played a leading role in organizing resistance, as well as providing means for clandestine communication, printing presses, and safe houses for resistance commanders.[7] Try as they might during the months before the German invasion on June 22, 1941, Soviet security forces could not eradicate either the anti-Communist resistance forces or the religious personnel and institutions that fostered them.

It was the very intractability of this problem that led the Kremlin to adopt a new policy toward the Russian Orthodox Church: having tried to erase the church entirely as late as the previous year, the

Kremlin decided to employ the few hierarchs that were not sent to the Gulag to assist the process of imposing Stalinist rule in the western borderlands. The obedient remnant of Russian Orthodox clergy provided a religious cover for the assertion of Soviet power: non-Russian local Orthodox parishes were transferred to the control of the Moscow Patriarchate, which assured their political compliance; in the case of the Greek Catholic Church, predominant in western Ukraine, Soviet authorities authorized and enforced the transfer of property away from the Uniates (whose loyalty was with the papacy), and to the Moscow Patriarchate—itself entirely obedient to the Kremlin's will and thoroughly penetrated by the NKGB.

Had it been given sufficient time to take effect, this almost entirely unknown operation might well have yielded substantial results, assisting Moscow's overall occupation design. The program was, however, cut short by the German attack; nonetheless, the Kremlin remembered the services rendered by the Moscow Patriarchate, and, when Red Army forces recovered the region from the Nazi invaders in 1943–44, it would employ the church in the same manner, although on an altogether grander scale.

The War and Russian Orthodoxy

The role of the Russian Orthodox Church during the Nazi-Soviet War has been much misunderstood by historians. The general view has been that, finding itself hard pressed by the German attack, and lacking legitimacy of its own, the Stalinist regime was forced to ease up on religion in a desperate attempt to rally Russian nationalism. In fact, this widely held view is an oversimplification, even a distortion, of the actual sequence of events. During the first two years following the German invasion, the Russian Orthodox Church played only a marginally heightened role. To be sure, on the first day of the war, the acting patriarch, Archbishop Sergii, issued a declaration calling on believers to support the Soviet cause as a Russian national crusade; further declarations followed, summoning believers behind German lines to support Soviet partisans, calling on the laity to donate money to the Soviet armed forces, and pronouncing anathema on those Orthodox who were lured away from Stalin by Hitler's false promises of liberation.[8] Too much should not be made of Sergii's appeals, however; they were printed in very small numbers and posted in the few remaining open churches, or they were broadcast via shortwave to German-occupied regions. The vast majority of Soviet citizens heard little or nothing of the Russian Orthodox Church during the first two years of the war, though specific antireligious propaganda was suspended from the first days of the fighting and would not be resumed until near its end. Furthermore, recruits in the Soviet armed forces continued to be denied the spiritual services of chaplains; religious gatherings and celebrations remained banned, other than a distinctly limited public celebration of Easter 1942; and the vast majority of churches remained closed. In fact, the British embassy noted that as late as autumn 1941 the Soviets continued to close functioning churches, even in Moscow.[9]

This situation began to change in early 1943. The position of the church did not improve because of the desperation of the Soviet military situation in the early days of the German invasion, as historians have been inclined to believe, but rather because of the sharp improvement in Soviet fortunes following the Red Army's victories in the battles of Stalingrad in February and of Kursk in July. These victories, and the retreat of the German army from territories it had occupied since 1941, presented dilemmas as well as opportunities for the Kremlin. As Soviet forces advanced and reasserted Moscow's control over the reconquered regions, Communist political authorities faced a deeply fractured civilian populace. Certainly, the inhabitants were pleased to be rid of the German occupiers, and consequently they were grateful to the Red Army, but this by no means meant that they were eager to see the return of Stalinism.

The Central Committee of the Communist party sent agents to the newly reacquired regions to discern the mood of the civil population, and the results must have been disquieting: people were concerned about the return of Stalinism—the collective farms, police repression, and terror—and they also feared that the partial wartime liberalization of Soviet life, including the reappearance of the Russian

Orthodox Church, had come about owing to pressure from the Western Allies, rather than from any change in spirit in the Kremlin. They feared—rightly, as it turned out—that these things would disappear once the war ended.[10] In the non-Russian regions further to the west, especially in the western borderlands annexed to the USSR following the Nazi-Soviet Pact, hostility to the return of Stalinism took sharper, more violent forms: nationalist guerrillas, many armed with weapons left behind by the retreating Germans or captured from Soviet forces, forcibly resisted the reinstitution of Soviet power. As in the period from 1939 to 1941, much of this resistance was centered on local churches, relying on nationalist clergy and clandestine church networks for essential sustenance.

For Moscow the situation was enormously complicated by the fact that, as the Germans faced defeat in the war, in a desperate and doomed attempt to appeal to the population of the occupied lands, they eased up on religious practice.[11] As a result, as Soviet power advanced westward, it encountered open churches, many of them hotbeds of non-Russian nationalism. Much of this was non-Russian Orthodox; but the single largest anti-Russian religious community was that of adherents to the West Ukrainian Greek Catholic Church, a community numbering between four and five million. Furthermore, a widespread religious revival, triggered no doubt by the mass killing and limitless human suffering of the war, presented Soviet rulers with the prospect of a many-headed religious hydra, even among the ethnic Russian populace. Religious groupings sprang up spontaneously in the chaotic conditions of the war and in regions where Soviet power had not yet been securely reestablished. Priests who had survived terms of exile or imprisonment played an important part in this phenomenon. One worried NKGB official wrote: "Itinerant priests exert a special influence on the religiously minded, appearing in recent times in [the writer's Ukrainian] *oblast'* after serving a term of punishment, from exile cities."[12]

By 1943, the Kremlin thus faced a host of religious-national dilemmas: along the western borderlands of the USSR, untamed churches acted as nuclei for anti-Soviet sentiment, and even armed resistance; even in the ethnically Russian regions that had undergone German occupation, newly reopened churches, unregistered and therefore uncontrolled by Soviet authorities, acted as a barrier to the reimposition of "normal" Stalinism; and throughout the Soviet Union, the war had given birth to a revitalization of religion, in the face of the atheist state. In seeking a solution to these problems, former seminarian Stalin adopted a policy that would have been familiar to his tsarist predecessors, such as Nikolai I or Aleksandr III: he used the Russian Orthodox Church as a tool of Russification.

In September 1943, Stalin met personally for several hours with the patriarch locum tenens, Sergii. During this meeting, the dictator authorized the church to convene a church Sobor, which could elect a new, genuine patriarch, resume publication of a regular journal, open seminaries for the training of new priests, and establish a procedure for the opening of churches and the restoration of church property.[13] On the surface, this appeared to be a momentous change in church-state relations, an impressive liberalization of Soviet religious repression. That was the stated intent, but the effect was rather different.

Each element of this new plan was designed to restore state control over religion, rather than to guarantee its free practice. At first glance, the opening of seminaries, and the shortened training of priests that allowed these newly minted clerics to occupy parishes in record time, seemed to be a great concession to popular religious sentiment. In fact, many of the new priests were either themselves NKGB agents or had been compromised by the security organs in some way. They were destined to occupy newly opened parishes, to be sure, but they were sent out from Moscow to replace unauthorized or anti-Soviet clergy in the regions formerly occupied by Nazis. Thus, while maintaining the façade of religious tolerance, Soviet authorities worked to monitor and tame open religious practice. The publication of a journal, the *Zhurnal Moskovskoi patriarkhii,* also seemed to betoken greater freedom of religion in the realm of ideas. In practice, however, the journal became a forum for exposing and denouncing clerics and laity who resisted Moscow's latest line; it also attacked the Kremlin's foreign religious foes, especially the Vatican.

Even the opening of churches was stage-managed by Soviet security organs. The newly created Soviet for the Affairs of the Russian

Orthodox Church, which was granted the power to refuse or approve requests to maintain open churches, or to open closed ones, was placed under the leadership of Georgii Karpov, a major-general in the NKVD. Karpov's new soviet sought to convey the impression that it was merely a facilitator, opening churches where public opinion demanded. In reality, almost all such requests were denied, and those approved were invariably in areas that had undergone German occupation. The result of these authorized church openings was a massive westward shift of Russian Orthodoxy's center of gravity. By August 1945, of the 10,243 registered active churches in the USSR as a whole, 6,072 (almost 60 percent) were in Ukraine alone, a republic with only 15 percent of the total Soviet population; 633 were in Belorussia; and a further 615 were in Moldavia (now Moldova). In the Baltic states, where the Russian Orthodox population was a small minority, 343 churches were authorized by the state. In Russia itself, by far the largest republic both in area and population, only 2,297 churches (less than 25 percent) were operating at war's end, and most of these were in regions that had either experienced German occupation or had been near the front lines. In short, more than 75 percent of open churches were in non-Russian, western border regions.[14] There, the legal reestablishment of the Moscow Patriarchate gave it a virtual monopoly on Christian worship. As part of its concordat with the Soviet state, the patriarchate received an unwritten charter to subdue and subsume all the rival schismatic branches of Orthodoxy.

As a result of these policies, Moscow was indeed able temporarily to declaw spontaneous Orthodox practice in ethnically non-Russian regions, but only at the price of storing up problems for the future. By dint of its property and interests, the Russian Orthodox Church became a church of empire even more completely than it had ever been under the tsars; its fate became bound with a desire to keep the western borderlands under Moscow's control, since national independence for the USSR's non–Russian Orthodox population threatened the loss of the vast majority of the church's working parishes and existing property.

The Russian Orthodox Church performed another, even more valuable, service for the Stalinist state at war's end. It provided cover for the extinction of the Greek Catholic Church.[15] This church had been a bone in the throat of many tsars, and it was now an obstacle to Stalin's designs in the west. Uniting within its ranks as it did the strongest forces of Ukrainian nationalism, the Uniate Church also provided aid and comfort for the strong western Ukrainian partisan resistance. By a process of internal subversion and external pressure from the security organs, in 1946 the Uniate Church was "reunited" with the Russian Orthodox Church, under the aegis of the Moscow Patriarchate. Thus, Moscow took a giant step toward the decapitation of the Ukrainian resistance, while at the same time tying Russian Orthodoxy's fate even more closely with Soviet imperial interests.

Legacy of the War

As described above, as the centerpiece of its wartime religious policies the Soviet government used the Russian Orthodox Church as a tool to assist the reestablishment of Communist power in the western borderlands. It did this, however, by placing Moscow's wager on specifically Russian nationalism as a means of subduing the centrifugal powers of non-Russian and anti-Soviet national forces. Like so many of Stalin's repressive policies, however, his religious program solved a number of short-term problems even while storing up, and increasing, enormous pressures for the future.

In the first place, the readmission of religion into Soviet life—even as attenuated in form and content as it was under the leadership of the Moscow Patriarchate—was in the long run incompatible with the materialist, internationalist, and "scientific" pretensions of Soviet Communism. As long as he lived, Stalin would not launch another wave of anti-Orthodox repression, not because he valued Orthodoxy as such, but rather because for many years after the war the church was still performing useful services for the Soviet government, by channeling religious sentiment and practice into open, controlled conduits. Furthermore, the church also aided Soviet foreign policy in significant ways, denouncing foreign claims about religious repression in the USSR, establishing useful ties with religious communities in the Balkans and throughout the Soviet imperium, and sanctioning Soviet international policies. So useful did this particular role become over time that, during the closing years of the USSR, the personnel of the church's Department of External Church Affairs actually outnumbered that of all its other departments combined.[16]

Stalin's immediate successor, Nikita Khrushchev, perhaps because his power base had been in Ukraine, saw the negative consequences—from the Soviet point of view—of allowing the church to continue to operate openly. So long as it existed and drew adherents, the Russian Orthodox Church, for all its obedience to state power, gave the lie to the pretense that Soviet Communism was spiritually satisfying to the citizens of the USSR. It also contained within itself the seeds for a renascent civil society, undermining the Kremlin's desired monopoly over civil life. Even while he liberalized much of Soviet society during his campaigns of de-Stalinization, Khrushchev once again ordered a crackdown on religion in the USSR. Many of the churches that had been reopened during the war were closed once again, and religious life was once again cast into the shadows. At the same time, however, Khrushchev too clearly saw the benefits of maintaining a tame, though much reduced, Moscow Patriarchate to dispense with its services entirely. Far from being the defender of religious freedom within the USSR, the patriarchate continued to act as monitor and check on unauthorized religious practice: far better, from the Kremlin's view, for the rump church to remain above ground and under careful supervision, than to allow religious practice to slip underground, where it might take on threatening forms.

Although this latest wave of antireligious repression ended with Khrushchev's ouster, so long as the Soviet state lasted, Russian Orthodoxy never regained the prominence of the war years. Rather, like a battered child that cannot leave its abusive parent, it served as a pliant prop for the very Communist order that was its oppressor.

There are several implications of this legacy for post-Soviet Russia. In the first place, given its very dubious role under the Communist regime, the Russian Orthodox Church was neither inclined nor able to play the crucial role in the reestablishment of civil society that Catholicism played in Poland, or that Protestantism briefly played during the collapse of East Germany. Instead, as the Soviet Union imploded, the Russian Orthodox Church hierarchy actually pleaded with the Soviet officials to halt the disintegration of the Union.[17] Bishops and metropolitans of the church denounced Gorbachev for imperiling the USSR, and allowing the reemergence of religious splinter groups in the western borderlands—the groups that Stalin had ordered subordinated to the Moscow Patriarchate.

The leaders of the Russian Orthodox Church had entered into a bargain with the Stalinist devil. Of course, they had not had much choice in the matter. But, in exchange for being allowed to extinguish their own ecclesiastical rivals, and also for being permitted to carry on a half-life in the quasi-legal shadows, the patriarchate had served the atheist state loyally, informing the security forces about all manner of religious activity not specifically authorized and, in fact, acting as the agent of religious repression. Following the demise of the Soviet state, the church was left demoralized, weak in numbers, short of funds, and massively discredited in the eyes of many citizens who could remember the church's dubious collaboration with the Communists. In this regard, the church hierarchy experienced the same fate as those ethnic political elites who, having been co-opted by the Soviet bureaucracy, found themselves alienated from their surfacing ethnic lot in the post-Soviet period. As the next chapter illustrates in reference to the Caucasus, they either became nationalistic or were politically marginalized and or replaced by more assertive and nationally minded local elites. Similarly, as the constituent republics of the USSR seceded one by one, the Russian Orthodox Church lost the bulk of its remaining churches to the very nationalist religious rivals that it had seemingly defeated in 1945.

Notes

1. On encouragement of atheism and the Bolsheviks' multifarious attempts to extinguish religion during the early years of the regime, see Daniel Peris, *Storming the Heavens: The Soviet League of the Militant Godless* (Ithaca, N.Y.: Cornell University Press, 1998). On splinter movements, see Arto Luukkanen,

The Party of Unbelief: The Religious Policy of the Bolshevik Party, 1917–1929 (Helsinki: SHS, 1994), esp. 181–98.

2. Robert Conquest, *The Harvest of Sorrow: Soviet Collectivization and the Terror-Famine* (New York: Oxford University Press, 1986), 199–214.

3. See Lenin's particularly chilling letter to V. M. Molotov in *The Unknown Lenin: From the Secret Archive,* ed. Richard Pipes (New Haven: Yale University Press, 1996), 152–54. In fact, Lenin's charges against the church were entirely fabricated.

4. See Nicholas Werth, "A State against Its People: Violence, Repression, and Terror in the Soviet Union," in Stéphane Courtois et al., *The Black Book of Communism: Crimes, Terror, Repression,* translated by Jonathan Murphy and Mark Kramer (Cambridge, Mass.: Harvard University Press, 1999), 172–74.

5. Ibid., 200–201.

6. See, for example, Jan Gross, *Revolution from Abroad: The Soviet Conquest of Poland's Western Ukraine and Western Belorussia* (Princeton, N.J.: Princeton University Press, 1988).

7. The most useful such collection is Federal'naia sluzhba kontrrazvedki rossiskoi federatsii (Federal service for Russian counterespionage), *Organy gosudarstvennoi bezopasnosti SSSR v velikoi otechestvennoi voine* (Soviet Russian organs for state security in the Great Patriotic War), *Sbornik dokumentov* (Collected documents) (Moscow, 1995). There are also several helpful collections of documents related to specific regions, for example, V. I. Pasat, ed., *Trudnye stranitsii istorii Moldovy, 1940–1950* (Difficult pages of Moldovan history, 1940–1950) (Moscow: 1994).

8. These appeals were later published by the Moscow Patriarchate in *Russkaia pravoslavnaia tserkov' i velikaia otechestvennaia voina* (The Russian Orthodox Church and the Great Patriotic War) (Moscow: 1943).

9. Moscow Chancery to Foreign Office, September 30, 1941, Great Britain Public Records Office, FO 371/119663.

10. The results of these surveys are contained in the former Party Archive in Moscow, RtsKhIDNI, f. 17, op. 125, r. 1392.

11. The Nazi policy on religion was contradictory and ineffective. In the early days following the invasion, certain elements within the Nazi and Wehrmacht hierarchies favored freeing religious practice among the occupied peoples of the East. Hitler himself squelched these policies, fearing that open churches would present long-term problems for German occupation. Being antireligious himself, he did not wish to see the revivification of religion in the East, which might then spread back to the Reich itself via returning Wehrmacht soldiers. Only when faced by the prospect of defeat in 1943–44 did the Nazis relent on the religious question. By then, the murderous Nazi plans for

the East were clear for all to see, and the new religious policy did little to win hearts and minds. Still, it did present the Soviets with the fait accompli of open churches. See Alexander Dallin, *German Rule in Russia, 1941–1945: A Study of Occupation Policies* (New York: St. Martin's, 1957), 472–93.

12. E. Novosel'tsev to Khodov, relay of *sovershenno sekretno* (top secret) report from Colonel Nikolaev of U[krainian]NKGB in Penza, June 28, 1943, RtsKhIDNI, f. 17, op. 125, r. 1378.

13. The record of Stalin's meeting with Sergii has been translated into English and published in Felix Corley, ed., *Religion in the Soviet Union: An Archival Reader* (London: Macmillan, 1996), 139–47.

14. Karpov to Aleksandrov, *sovershenno sekretno* (top secret), August 30, 1945, RtsKhIDNI, f. 17, op. 125, r. 1408.

15. See Bohdan Bociurkiw, *The Ukrainian Greek Catholic Church and the Soviet State, 1939–1950* (Edmonton: Canadian Institute of Ukrainian Studies Press, 1996).

16. Pedro Ramet, *Cross and Commissar: The Politics of Religion in Eastern Europe and the USSR* (Bloomington: Indiana University Press, 1987), 4.

17. A. Lukianov memorandum for TsK KPSS, February 7/9, 1990, TsKhSD, f. 89, op. 8., d 41.

6

Ethnic Conflict in Georgia

Neil MacFarlane, with George Khutsishvili

THE CAUCASUS REGION (north and south) was one of the most active zones of ethnic conflict[1] in the 1990s. Two of the three states of the southern Caucasus have experienced civil war along ethnic lines, and the northern Caucasian jurisdictions of the Russian Federation (e.g., Ingushetia, North Ossetia, Chechnya, and Daghestan) have all been seriously disrupted by violence. As late as November 2001, Georgia continued to experience political upheaval, and conflict in Abkhazia threatened to break out again. In this paper, we examine the roots and significance of ethnic conflict in the region through a close analysis of the conflicts in Georgia. We provide first a summary account of the two major ethnic conflicts affecting the republic in the 1990s. In attempting to explain these conflicts, we then examine the ethnodemographic situation in the country and the historical roots of Georgian and minority nationalism, and conclude with an analysis of the effect of perestroika on the ethnic politics of Georgia.

Ethnic Conflict in Georgia

Georgia has been significantly affected by two ethnic conflicts since independence. The first was the conflict in the South Ossetian autonomous oblast of the republic (Shida Kartli). Open conflict began in 1990, after Georgia's effective declaration of independence.[2] In the fall of 1990, the South Ossetian regional soviet threatened by this development responded by adopting a declaration transforming the oblast into the South Ossetian Soviet Democratic Republic. A day later, the supreme soviet of Georgia annulled this decision. The declaration was renewed in October 1990 and was followed by elections to the new republic's supreme soviet in December. The meeting of the newly elected supreme soviet on December 11, 1990 provoked the Georgian supreme soviet (then dominated by partisans of Zviad Gamsakhurdia, after Georgia-wide elections in October) to abrogate South Ossetia's status of autonomy.

Violence broke out in the region in December 1990 and military operations continued until mid-1992. By all accounts, the conflict between local militias at the village level was particularly brutal. Local forces were strengthened on one side by the Georgian national guard and the paramilitary organization Mkhedrioni, and on the other by volunteers from North Ossetia.[3] Tskhinvali, the capital of the region, was shelled over a considerable period, with massive damage to buildings and infrastructure. Estimates of casualties from the Osset conflict vary. Most believe that by mid-1992, when the cease-fire went into effect, there were over one thousand dead and wounded. Georgian authorities maintain that upward of forty thousand Georgian refugees fled South Ossetia to the Gori region and to Tbilisi. Osset authorities claimed a flow of refugees of around one hundred thousand from Georgia to North Ossetia.[4]

By the time of the Sochi Accord (June 1992), which established a monitored cease-fire and a process for political resolution, the economy of the region had been destroyed. Beyond Tskhinvali itself, law and order collapsed and the countryside degenerated into heavily armed banditry. The lack of central control over the region, the loose authority of the regional government in Tskhinvali, and the region's contiguity to the Russian Federation have created, according to many reports, a haven for organized criminal activity, notably smuggling, in which Russian, Osset, and Georgian peacekeepers have been implicated. The lack of progress toward a final resolution of the conflict is probably related to the fact that various groups in South Ossetia benefiting from smuggling and other illegal activities are resistant to any final settlement that would permit Georgia to impose effective law enforcement and customs control in the region.[5]

Since the Sochi Accord, a reasonably effective cease-fire has operated in South Ossetia. A peacekeeping force of Russians, Georgian government forces, and a North Ossetian military unit has done a reasonably good job of minimizing the continuation of violence. Nonetheless, there has been little progress on the political track,[6] owing to Georgian reluctance to restore significant autonomy to the oblast and to serious political divisions within Georgia's elite on this and other issues, to the radicalization of and lack of unity within the Osset political elite, and also presumably because those forces in Ossetia benefiting from the continuation of this abnormal situation have no desire to see it normalized. At a deeper level, normalization has been impeded by the deep bitterness of the resident population and refugees.[7]

Once the situation in South Ossetia had stabilized, attention turned to the Autonomous Republic of Abkhazia. The roots of the conflict between the autonomous republic and the central government predate Georgia's reestablishment of independence and the collapse of Soviet rule. In the summer of 1989 the government announced its intention to make the Georgian section of Abkhaz State University a branch of the University of Tbilisi. Civil violence ensued and twenty-two people died.

In 1990 "sectional parties" were excluded from the Georgian supreme soviet elections, a move clearly aimed at the Abkhaz, Ossets, and other minorities—as discussed further below their political formations were ethnically and regionally based. Abkhaz delegates to the autonomous republic's supreme soviet responded by declaring Abkhaz independence from Georgia. The supreme soviet of the Republic of Georgia then annulled this action.

When Gamsakhurdia's Round Table/Free Georgia coalition took power in October 1990, Abkhaz authorities refused to accept the centrally appointed prefect. In March 1991 they defied his authority again by participating in the USSR referendum on the future of the union. Of the 52.4 percent of the Abkhaz republic's population that voted, 98.4 percent opted for the preservation of the union.[8] Nonetheless, relations between the Gamsakhurdia government and Abkhaz authorities were reasonably quiet in 1991, largely as a result of the preoccupation of the Georgians with the Osset question. That said, a conflict was eventually likely, since the ethnic Abkhaz authorities had not abandoned their movement toward secession.

Matters changed rapidly in 1992. Zviad Gamsakhurdia, the first president of independent Georgia, was overthrown and forced to flee Tbilisi at the end of 1991. Forces loyal to him mounted an insurrection against the new central authorities in the spring of 1992 in Mingrelia, a region of western Georgia contiguous to Abkhazia. As hostilities in Ossetia wound down in the summer of 1992, the Georgian government and Mkhedrioni were able to transfer substantial forces to the west to engage the supporters of Gamsakhurdia. This conflict, too, was notable for the disorganization and brutality of forces supporting the government.[9] The insurgents used sanctuaries in the Gali district of southern Abkhazia in their struggle against the central government. In the summer, they kidnapped a number of Georgian officials, including then Deputy Prime Minister Sandro Kavsadze, and took them to hiding places in Abkhazia.

This drew the attention of central authorities back to Abkhazia. In a general sense, a solution to the security problem in Mingrelia required the denial of Abkhaz sanctuary to Gamsakhurdia's supporters. More specifically, the Georgian government sought to move into southern Abkhazia in order to free the kidnapped officials. Reports at the time suggested that the Georgian government had received tacit if not explicit agreement from the Abkhaz authorities for a limited operation in the Gali region.[10] When Tengiz Kitovani, then defense minister and head of the national guard, encountered little resistance in his advance on Gali, he decided, reportedly on his own initiative (and arguably on the pretext created by the reversion of the Abkhaz government to the 1925 constitution of Abkhazia, which defined a far looser relationship between Abkhazia and the rest of Georgia), to continue to Sukhumi in order to bring the autonomous republic's government under central control.[11] The chair of the Abkhaz supreme soviet fled along with his government to Gudauta, and the Georgian government, impressed by Kitovani's apparent success, dissolved the Abkhaz supreme soviet, installing a Georgian-dominated military council in the region.

The result was a civil war in Abkhazia. The Abkhaz side, benefiting from the arrival of volunteers from the northern Caucasus, and from the support of Russian forces stationed in the region, reasonably rapidly consolidated its control over northwestern Abkhazia. In the spring of 1993, this was followed by an offensive on Sukhumi. Its failure in March and again in July to take the city, coupled with shifts in the Georgian government in May that rendered negotiation easier, led to a cease-fire agreement on July 27, 1993, that was both mediated and guaranteed by the Russian government.

The cease-fire agreement provided for the separation of combatants, the withdrawal of Georgian forces from Abkhazia, and the encampment of Abkhaz forces and equipment, all under Russian supervision. The Georgian side largely (although slowly) complied with the withdrawal stipulation, leaving southern Abkhazia defenseless. In mid-September, 1993, the Abkhaz returned to the offensive and after eleven days took Sukhumi and then the rest of Abkhazia up to the border with Mingrelia.[12]

The fall of Abkhazia initiated a further major flow of displaced persons, as the Georgian majority of the republic fled the Abkhaz advance, crossing into Georgia through the mountain passes of Svanetia or south into Mingrelia. According to the UN, this brought the total number of internally displaced persons in Georgia to some two hundred forty thousand.[13] The success of the ethnic cleansing of Abkhazia is indicated by the comment of a UN official who visited Georgian-populated zones of the republic in the spring of 1994. It resembled, in his words, an empty desert.[14] Initial informal efforts at repatriation to the Gali region of Abkhazia in 1994 resulted in violence against returning civilians.

The denouement of this phase of the Abkhaz conflict coincided with the renewal of rebellion in Mingrelia, as Gamsakhurdia took advantage of Shevardnadze's vulnerability to return. Mingrel insurgents took control of all the major towns in Mingrelia, and then took the port of Poti, critical to the supply not only of the interior of Georgia, but also of Armenia and Azerbaijan. Sources in Tbilisi suggest that the insurgents were assisted by the Abkhaz, the latter presumably seeking to establish a buffer between their own region and central Georgia, and by ex-Defense Minister Kitovani, who by this time had joined the opposition to Shevardnadze's government.[15]

By mid-October, Mingrel insurgents were threatening the city of Kutaisi, at the gates to central Georgia, and preparing for an offensive on Tbilisi itself. Government forces, demoralized and disorganized by their ordeal in Abkhazia, and operating in a region (Mingrelia) the population of which was sympathetic to the rebels, showed little capacity for effective resistance. It was at this stage that Shevardnadze capitulated to Russian pressure to join the Commonwealth of Independent States (CIS). After his October meeting with Boris Yeltsin in Moscow, the Russians finally weighed in on the side of the government. With Russian military assistance, the Georgians succeeded in eliminating the insurgency in Mingrelia in short order.

In Abkhazia, the Russians again brokered a cease-fire between the belligerents in April 1994. This involved the interposition of a Russian-dominated peacekeeping force along the Inguri River and in the Kodori Valley. The cease-fire turned out to be reasonably durable, despite occasional violations in areas where the Georgian withdrawal was incomplete, as in the Kodori Gorge in the spring and summer of 1994.[16]

As in South Ossetia, there seems to have been little progress toward a political resolution, despite the renewal of direct contacts between the two leaderships in mid-1997. Talks have stalled on several related questions. The Abkhaz side maintained that the future of their region should be decided by referendum. This was a referendum they could never win if full repatriation of Georgian displaced persons occurred. The Georgian side, of course, maintained that a referendum without repatriation would be invalid. The Georgian side also sought more effective guarantees for the security of returnees, either through a police role for UN forces in the region, or through an extension of the geographical and functional mandate of the CIS (Russian) peacekeeping force deployed in the security zone between Georgian and Abkhaz forces. The two sides also remained far apart on the question of the eventual constitutional status of Abkhazia. Although the Georgians moderated their initial rejection of any substantial devolution of power from the center, embracing the principle of federalism and even contemplating an asymmetrical federal arrangement for Abkhazia, while the Abkhaz have formally abandoned their quest for a complete separation, Georgian compromise proposals remain far short of the Abkhaz preference for a confederal union of two essentially sovereign entities. As in South Ossetia, movement is complicated by the lingering bitterness of the two populations.

Despite the success of peacekeeping operations in forestalling any renewal of hostilities, Georgian impatience with the situation grew. In the mid-1990s, increasing numbers of Georgians were returning spontaneously to the Gali region of Abkhazia. Estimates of spontaneous returnees ran as high as fifty thousand in the summer of 1997. With them came trained and increasingly effective partisan forces who were committing acts of sabotage against Abkhaz militia and officials. The result was that the Abkhaz lost control over the area between Gali and the Inguri cease-fire line, and were under increasing pressure as the return expanded northward into the area between Gali and Ochamchira.

In the face of Georgian pressure and despite Russian resistance, the CIS approved an extension of the mandate of CIS peacekeepers in early 1997. Russia—citing the unwillingness of the Abkhaz party to consent to a broadened mandate—failed to implement it. Georgian officials and parliamentarians in turn threatened to withdraw their consent to the presence of the force when the mandate expired on July 31, 1997. In the meantime, attacks on CIS Peacekeeping Forces (CISPKF)—including mining and hostage-taking—increased. By 1998, CISPKF was largely confined to its barracks and checkpoints, unwilling to accept the risks of extensive patrolling.

This phase culminated in massive Abkhaz retaliation against

Georgian returnees in May 1998, in which some thirty thousand were once again expelled from Abkhazia, their homes burned to the ground. Subsequent efforts (both multilateral and bilateral) to rekindle the peace process have again largely failed.

Ethnodemographic Profile of Georgia

The 1989 Soviet census indicated that Georgia had a population of some 5.4 million people. Their ethnic distribution is indicated in table 6.1.

Table 6.1. The Ethnic Makeup of Georgia, 1989

Ethnos	Percent of Population
Georgians	70.1*
Armenians	8.1
Russians	6.3
Azeris	5.7
Ossets	3.0
Greeks	1.9
Abkhaz	1.8
Ukrainians	1.0

*The Ajar (Georgian Muslim) population is included in the total for Georgians.
Source: Census of the USSR, 1989.

Several factors are worth noting with regard to table 6.1. First is the clear primacy of the Georgian ethnos in the republic's demographic makeup. Georgian national identity has never been threatened by outside migration. Soviet census data show the Soviet period as a whole to have been one of the gradual ethnic homogenization of Georgia in favor of the Georgians. In 1939, Georgians made up 61.4 percent of the population, Armenians 11.7 percent, and Russians 8.7 percent. In 1970, the analogous figures were 68.8 percent, 9 percent, and 7.4 percent; in 1979, 68.8 percent, 9 percent, and 7.4 percent; and in 1989, 70.1 percent, 8.1 percent, and 6.3 percent. Since the last census, although reliable data are hard to come by, it is reasonable to assume that, as a result of Russian, Greek, Armenian, and Osset emigration, the Georgian position has been further consolidated although this effect is probably mitigated by the outflow of young Georgians seeking employment in the Russian federation and elsewhere.

With regard to assimilation, neither miscegenation nor language acquisition appears to pose a significant threat. As of 1970, 93.5 percent of Georgian marriages were endogamous. In the same year, 63 percent of urban Georgians and 91.4 percent of rural Georgians were not fluent in Russian. Demographic and cultural pressure, consequently, did not play a major role in the kindling of Georgian nationalism.

Second, the diminutive share of the two minority groups involved in ethnic conflict is striking. The war in Abkhazia pits a group comprising less than 2 percent of the country's population against the majority; that in Ossetia involves a group comprising only 3 percent. Larger minorities (e.g., the Russians, Armenians, and Azeris) have, on the whole, remained apolitical and thus far have enjoyed reasonably quiet relations with the majority. The quiescence of these larger groups is a result of a number of factors. In the case of the Azeris and Armenians, both home countries are dependent on Georgian transport links, and therefore their governments are careful to discourage ethnopolitical activity by their coethnics inside Georgia. The Russian minority is weakly organized and, not being indigenous, has no territorial claim against Georgia.[17]

With regard to those ethnic groups actively in conflict with the Georgian government, the Abkhaz are concentrated in the Republic of Abkhazia, with insubstantial numbers resident in Mingrelia and elsewhere. The Ossets, by contrast, were more widely spread throughout the country. Only a minority of Ossets lived within the autonomous oblast of South Ossetia prior to the conflict, the rest having lived in urban areas and in concentrations of villages in the Gori and Kareli districts and in the area of Borjomi, among others.[18] Osset preponderance in the former autonomous oblast was not and is not threatened by the Georgian population. In Abkhazia, by contrast, the Abkhaz were a minority in their own jurisdiction.

Table 6.2. Ethnic Distribution in Zones of Conflict, 1989 (percent)

	Abkhazia	South Ossetia
Georgians	45.7	30
Ossets	—	66
Abkhaz	17.8	—
Russians	14.3	3
Armenians	14.6	—

In short, the ethnodemographic profile of Georgia has contributed in a number of ways to the initiation and perpetuation of conflict. Although Georgian majority status in the republic as a whole is strong and growing stronger, the existence of compact minorities along Georgia's peripheries constitutes a significant potential challenge to the integrity of the Georgian state.[19]

The Historical Roots of Ethnic Conflict in Georgia

THE PRE-SOVIET ERA

There is a striking discrepancy between the prevalent Georgian self-image of ethnic and religious tolerance on the one hand,[20] and the explosive and bitter quality of the two ethnic conflicts that have beset the country since 1990. The myth is not too far from historical reality. Relations among ethnic groups have been peaceful for long periods in Georgia, not least during the Soviet period. Moreover, the society had developed sophisticated mechanisms for the prevention of intercommunal tensions.[21] There was statistically significant miscegenation between ethnic groups now involved in deep conflict. For example, nearly half of Osset marriages involved Georgian partners. It is noteworthy that the Georgians and neighboring ethnoi did not, on the whole, form cohesive ethnically based political communities until the modern era. For much of its history, Georgia was divided into two or more political units, often under the influence of contiguous states. Although communities of Georgians shared certain

basic traits, the topography of the country discouraged a national co-
alescence of identity. Identities had strong regional roots. Two groups
generally identified as Georgian (the Mingrels and the Svan) speak
languages that, in linguistic terms, are distinct members of the southern division of the Caucasic language family. They are not easily comprehensible to mainstream Georgians (Kartvelians). That these
regional and subnational identities can place significant limits on
ethnonational identification is evident in the outbreak of serious
conflict in 1992 and 1993 between the central government and the
mainly Mingrel supporters of ousted president Gamsakhurdia. The
key question, then, is why interethnic relations were so profoundly
exacerbated from 1990 to 1994.

Many, including Ronald Suny, date the effective politicization of
Georgian ethnicity to the nineteenth-century Russian occupation of
Georgia: "The Georgians, who were incorporated into the Russian
Empire in the first decades of the nineteenth Century, were still a divided, defeated, inchoate people, sharing an ethnicity with recogniz-
able cultural features. Despite periods of unity and glory in the past,
they had faced virtual extinction by the end of the eighteenth Century and, except for a few nobles and clerics, possessed little sense of
their own nationhood."[22] The emergence of Georgia as a conscious
political nation during the nineteenth century was a product of numerous conditions, among them the political and economic stability
produced by Russian rule, increasing ease of communication within
the country and the consequent integration of regionally diverse
communities, and the spread of modern education to the Georgian
political elite. Georgia's emergence followed a course quite typical for
smaller nations in the nineteenth century, from renewed attention to
history and language, through the dissemination of this new consciousness in the educational system and the press, to the emergence
of open political nationalism.[23]

The Georgian nobility—attempting to cope with economic
change and its own loss of political power—was the principal pro-
genitor of the movement, both in culture and in politics. The union
with Russia and the gradual imposition of Russian modes of governance deprived them of the considerable power that the class had

enjoyed before union. The commercialization of the economy and the beginnings of industrialization destroyed their economic primacy, displacing them with a predominantly Armenian bourgeoisie. The emancipation of the serfs in 1861 deprived noble landowners of the low-cost rural labor force on which they had depended. Their general failure to adapt to the structural change through adopting modern agricultural techniques caused many to accumulate growing debts (held largely by Armenians) and ultimately to lose their land.[24] As the century passed, the growing economic pressure faced by the Georgian elite was increasingly joined by the more and more openly chauvinistic cultural approach of the central government to national minorities in the Russian empire.

Given the narrow social base of both conservative, aristocratic nationalists and of the liberal political alternative that appealed mainly to the Armenian bourgeoisie, and the emergence—as a result of industrialization—of an ethnic Georgian working class, Georgian political thought in the early twentieth century developed a clear social democratic bent, with a view to the mobilization of this new force. Marxism provided a "non-nationalist ideology that was a weapon against both their ethnic enemies: Russian officials and the Armenian bourgeoisie." It was social revolution that would return Georgia to the Georgians by eliminating both.[25] By 1905 the social democratic movement was the most influential political organization in Georgia.

Largely owing to the belief that Georgian self-determination could be achieved only through a revolution in Russia, as well as to the still strong internationalism of the Russian socialist movement, the Georgian struggle for national liberation was folded into the larger struggle against tsarism. Noe Zhordania and Irakli Tsereteli, leaders of the Georgian social democratic movement, played leading roles in the Menshevik wing of the Russian Social Democratic Labor Party (RSDLP) between the first (1905) and second (1917) Russian revolutions.

With the collapse of tsarism in February 1917, the social democrats inherited power in Georgia. After a brief experiment with Transcaucasian federalism, and as the Bolsheviks consolidated power in

Russia, Georgia declared its independence on May 26, 1918. Georgian authorities chose this route as a result not so much of nationalist aspiration, but of differences with the Bolsheviks in Moscow, the collapse of central authority in the Caucasian region, and the growing military threat from Turkey. In this sense, their exercise of national self-determination through secession was a product of circumstances beyond their control.

The principal significance of the period of Georgian statehood for this analysis is twofold. First, it afforded the Georgians a moment of independence that provided a potent symbol for future nationalist discourse. The extinction of a viable, orderly, and more or less democratically legitimate Georgian state as a result of an invasion by the Red Army—and this after Soviet Russia had recognized in treaty instruments the independence of Georgia—gave this symbol a clear anti-Soviet and anti-Russian content.[26] Second, the period of independence complicated Georgian relations between the Georgian majority and the Osset minority in particular. The Osset peasantry reacted to the Georgian government's land reform policy in 1920 by mounting a rebellion against the central government. This was expeditiously suppressed by the Georgian military, leaving a bitter taste in Osset mouths. One result was that many Ossets cooperated with the Red Army when it entered Georgia in 1921. This in turn created the impression that the Ossets were a Russian fifth column within Georgia.[27]

THE SOVIET ERA

Several important further preconditions for conflict in the Republic of Georgia originated in the Soviet era. First, it is probably the case that, in the Caucasus as elsewhere, modernization itself encouraged the crystallization of national identities. Second, as elsewhere in the former Soviet Union, the federalization of the Soviet state provided a locus for the development of nationally oriented political consciousness. The state not only tolerated but promoted national cultural symbols, such as language and folk custom. It fostered, albeit in truncated form, the growth of national educational institutions such as Tbilisi State University. In its later stages, it provided Georgian political elites with a degree of autonomy that allowed them to consolidate ethnic control over the Party and institutions of state power. In all these respects, the Soviet state laid important political cultural foundations for the renaissance of Georgian statehood and for the flowering of Georgian nationalism, once the political constraints of Soviet power evaporated. In these respects, Georgia is a good example of the general proposition that "rather than being a melting pot, the Soviet Union became the incubator of nations."[28]

Third, also as elsewhere in the former Soviet Union, Soviet nationality policy encouraged the national consciousness not only of the titular nationality, but also of minority groups within Georgia. South Ossetia received its institutional form as an autonomous jurisdiction for the first time in April 1922. Abkhazia enjoyed several years as a union republic before being reintegrated into Georgia as an autonomous republic. Minority political elites evolved around the new political institutions. Central government support underwrote the blossoming of minority cultures and languages. Protection by the center also provided insurance against any recrudescence of nationalism on the part of the Georgian majority. The net result was the development of political nationalism not only among the Georgian majority, but also among those minorities that enjoyed a degree of political autonomy. The impact of this political institutionalization of ethnicity is evident in the fact that, whereas the Georgian government has had few problems with the much larger and territorially compact Azeri and Armenian minorities that did not possess autonomous political structures, two of the three autonomous territories in Georgia have been implicated in civil wars since independence.[29]

Fourth is the question of economic development and its effects on Georgian identity. The Bolshevik seizure of power was followed reasonably rapidly by the more or less complete integration of Georgia's economy into that of the USSR proper. Soviet planners replaced the reasonably diverse agricultural sector in Georgia with a number of cash crop monocultures, notably tea, wine, and citrus fruit. Although from the Soviet perspective this made sense, given the limited capacity to produce semitropical products elsewhere, it rendered Georgia much more dependent on Russia for staple foods than it had been historically. Georgian industrial development displayed similar dependency links. The mining sector produced for factories elsewhere in the USSR. The Rustavi metallurgical complex relied on raw material and energy imports from the rest of the USSR. The aviation industry that grew up around Tbilisi during and after World War II was dependent on factories in other union republics for essential spare parts, and dependent on the Soviet military as a monopsonistic consumer. In short, the modalities of integration of Georgia into the Soviet planning structure greatly deepened Georgian economic dependence, and provided ample fodder for nationalists who argued that the relationship between Georgia and the union was essentially exploitative.

More basically—although in many indices (e.g., housing, medical care, education) Georgia did as well as or better than the rest of the union—the gap between Georgia and Russia widened during the Soviet era, as it did for many other republics on the southern fringe of the USSR.[30] In the Caucasus as a whole, the standard of living, while increasing in the post-Stalin era, rose less rapidly than that of the union as a whole, as a result of disproportionately high rates of population growth. The growth of total fixed capital formation in Georgia was the second lowest for any republic in the USSR from 1961 through 1975. Georgian per capita GNP was conspicuously lower than the national average.[31] Georgian indices of real income were slightly below the union average. Average annual wages in Georgia also grew more slowly than they did in the union as a whole or in Russia.[32] These results, in other words, provided further economic grist for the nationalist mill.[33]

Fifth was the impact of de-Stalinization. Georgian attitudes on Stalin and Stalinism were ambivalent. On the one hand, they too suffered at the hands of Stalin. On the other, for many Georgians, he was one of theirs. Stalin was frequently credited with the protection or restoration of Georgian national symbols, as in 1943, when he restored the autocephaly of the Georgian Orthodox Church, extinguished by the tsars in 1828. The Stalin museum at his birthplace in Gori has operated continuously since the dictator's death, in stark contrast to the closure of other institutions honoring Stalin during the Khrushchev era. In the vicinity of Gori, toasts are still drunk to Stalin at festive occasions. In the era of de-Stalinization, Soviet denigration of Stalin was symbolically conflated with Russian oppression of the Georgian nation.[34] The first public manifestation of Soviet-era nationalism occurred in Georgia in mid-1956 in student demonstrations in response to Khrushchev's speech at the Twentieth Party Congress. The rapid and violent suppression of these demonstrations in turn hardened nationalist opinion against the center.[35]

The post-Stalin decentralization of power led to increasing control over local affairs by republican party elites in Georgia as elsewhere in the union. This control was used to consolidate Georgian ethnic primacy in the economic and cultural affairs of the republic, often at the expense of minority nationalities.[36] By the early 1970s, the emergence of Georgian nationalism was of sufficient concern to the central Party apparatus that, along with corruption, it became one of the principal issues in a purge of the Georgian Party apparatus. In 1972, upon assuming the post of first secretary of the Georgian Communist Party, Eduard Shevardnadze repeatedly attacked manifestations of national chauvinism among both the Georgian majority and minority populations. Among his victims was Zviad Gamsakhurdia, subsequently elected as the first president of independent Georgia.

The 1970s also witnessed the emergence of organized dissident groups in Georgia. Their origins lay in concern over the treatment of Georgian architectural monuments and over the theft of religious artifacts by individuals linked to the Mzhavanadze patronage network[37] for sale abroad. In 1974, Zviad Gamsakhurdia, Merab Kostava, and others established the Human Rights Defense Group in Tbilisi, and following the Helsinki Accords, this evolved into the Helsinki Watch Committee in Georgia. However, dissidence in the Georgian case evinced a substantial nationalist inclination with a corresponding de-emphasis on principles of liberal democracy. Ultimately, the group was suppressed with the arrest of Gamsakhurdia and Kostava in 1977. Its suppression was perceived as a Soviet effort to deny the national aspirations of the Georgian people. The importance of this movement lay in its establishment of a political elite that could, in time, serve as an alternative to the Party during the later period of reform, about which more will be said below.

One final element of the process of de-Stalinization and political development in the post-Stalin era deserves mention. As already noted, Georgia was one of the few republics outside Central Asia in which the proportion of Russians in the population as a whole declined significantly during the Brezhnev years. This was in part a manifestation of the consolidation of authority by Georgian ethnic elites during this period and the growing national exclusiveness of Georgian society mentioned above. Beyond this, it reflected the rise of what Russians have come to call *bytovoi natsionalizm* (everyday nationalism) among Georgians. This enhanced the general sense of unwelcomeness, if not insecurity, on the part of non-Georgian populations, and particularly those (like the Russians) not living in compact communities. In turn, the gradual homogenization, of which everyday nationalism was a part, strengthened the appeal of nationalism for society as a whole.

In sum, the Soviet era strengthened the ethnic preconditions for the emergence of Georgian nationalism in the perestroika era. It also increased popular and elite distrust of the cultural intent of the Soviet center. Finally, it provided a set of concrete grievances to animate nationalist discourse and witnessed the beginning of organized nationalist political activity. Yet at the time of Gorbachev's accession to power, there was no broadly based national movement in Georgia. The Gorbachev era created one.

Perestroika and Georgian Nationalism

Three questions need to be addressed in discussing the proximate causes for the rise of majority and minority ethnic nationalism in Georgia. Why did Georgian political elites seize upon ethnic nationalism as an ideological device? Why did minority elites embrace a parallel nationalist agenda to challenge that of the Georgian majority? Why were majority and minority populations receptive to these appeals?

At least four factors relevant to the Gorbachev period are useful in answering these questions. With regard to mass receptivity, however advantageous or disadvantageous the traditional Georgian economic relationship with the center may have been, it is clear that the contradictory and fitful effort at economic reform in the USSR produced considerable hardship in Georgia, as elsewhere in the USSR. Increasing economic privation appears to increase mass receptivity to revisionist or revolutionary ideologies and to the advocacy of collective violence.[38] There were important perceptual components to this decline in standards of living. In the first place, as elsewhere in the former USSR, Georgians had come to expect a low, but guaranteed standard of living. They were unaccustomed to economic uncertainties common and accepted in free market societies. As a result, they were psychologically unprepared for the ambiguities of the reform economy in the USSR. Moreover, in Georgia as elsewhere, people were promised rapid improvement in the context of economic reform. The economic reform was botched. This disappointed expectations and raised the issue of whether the center was capable of serious economic change. Given the centrally directed character of the Soviet economy, the locus of blame was clear when things went awry. Unaccustomed insecurity and disappointed expectations—both attributed to failures in Moscow—favored the politicization of ethnicity.

Economic insecurity was only one component of a broader sociopolitical context of uncertainty, confusion, instability, and frustration. This was particularly uncomfortable for people who were accustomed to order and stability in their political lives. In such uncomfortable conditions, people may be drawn to individuals and groups who provide simple and coherent answers. To put it another way, they were susceptible to populist demagoguery.[39] Such susceptibility was encouraged also by both elite and mass political acculturation under Soviet rule. Georgians—and other former Soviet nationalities—were conditioned to expect single definitive answers to political questions and had no experience of the pluralism and ambiguity characteristic of democratic politics.

One should also note the dynamic dimension of evolving political process and its effect on the Georgian perception of their dilemma.

The last years of perestroika left many with the impression that the union was collapsing. The logical response to this perception was to develop one's own exit option. In this context, nationalist assertion at the expense of the center built on its own momentum. The farther it went in the union as a whole, the less credible was the option of re-formation within the union, and hence the more intense the momentum toward disintegration.

The nationalist agenda of independence was an attractive option in these circumstances. It was credible in terms of the Georgian perception of the problem they faced—the ineffectiveness of the center in the implementation of serious reform. And it provided a simple and comprehensible solution, far more so than the complex, tentative, and often contradictory programs of the center.

The attractiveness of the nationalist agenda is related to a further factor: the credibility of the coercive power of the center. Just as the complex and halfhearted central approach to economic reform drew into question the capacity of the union to sustain the economic well-being of the various communities in the USSR, the ambiguous and ineffectual Soviet response to national self-assertion drew into question the will or the capacity of the center to sustain the union. The farther the various republics of the USSR went in successfully asserting themselves in the face of opposition from the center, the deeper this problem of credibility became. This in turn invited still stronger challenges. Elites and publics both sensed that the emperor had no clothes.

Finally, the center was, in the past, quite careful to co-opt indigenous national elites through the party and the *nomenklatura.* All other things being equal, such elites, being closely associated with a Soviet system, were likely to be discredited by its demise. In some instances (as in Central Asia and Ukraine),[40] local elites moved sufficiently quickly to limit their vulnerability by seizing components of the nationalist agenda. The Georgian party elite, like that in the Baltics, failed to do so until rather late in the game. In the context of the transition away from monolithic party rule and the incomplete formation of the political spectrum (a development which had been precluded by the previous emphasis on one-party rule and democratic centralism), the population, when allowed to choose, chose those least tainted, those who had most consistently opposed the Communist system. In Georgia, these were nationalist dissidents, such as Zviad Gamsakhurdia and Merab Kostava, who had suffered imprisonment and persecution under the Communist authorities.[41]

Perestroika had significant effects on minority elites and populations as well. As has already been suggested, the autonomous republics of Abkhazia and Ajara and the autonomous oblast of South Ossetia were creations of Soviet nationality policy, and particularly of Stalin's propensity for diluting the cohesion of the union republics by creating within them subsidiary jurisdictions along ethnic lines. As these jurisdictions were of questionable legitimacy from the perspective of titular national elites, they depended for their existence on the support of the center. Any weakening of the center and of its resolve to control political processes on the periphery was threatening to these minority jurisdictions and the elites controlling them. The resurgence of titular nationalism was viewed likewise. In these circumstances, it was natural that the reemergence of Georgian nationalism in the context of the decaying credibility of the center would enhance the sense of insecurity among elites in the autonomous zones of Georgia and would encourage efforts to depart from the republic.

Thus far we have accounted for the development of majority nationalism directed primarily against Russia and for the quickening of minority concerns regarding the intentions of the majority. This, however, is a long way from an account of the intensity that the Georgian independence movement assumed in 1989–90 and the rejection of a tradition of national tolerance which was a prominent part of Georgia's own national mythology. What is needed is an additional catalytic dimension to the analysis that would account for the deep radicalization of Georgian politics during this period. The events of April 1989 in Tbilisi provide one answer. This disturbance in Tbilisi—and its suppression by the Soviet army, with some thirty deaths and numerous injuries owing to the use of chemical agents—joined the pantheon of episodes of Georgian victimization. There is substantial evidence that the demonstration was constructed in such a way as to induce a violent response on the part of the authorities in the hope that this would galvanize popular support behind the nationalist movement's striving for independence. This is, in fact, exactly what happened. The events were quickly mythologized in Georgian nationalist discourse.[42]

The event was particularly strongly felt because of the political context in which it occurred. It was a period of unambiguous political liberalization in Soviet society. This liberalization appeared to enjoy the support of the central hierarchy itself. The suppression in Tbilisi was not what people expected from such a leadership at such a time. There was a dissonance between the articulated commitment to reform and pluralism and the reality of blood in the streets. This further confused and embittered the populace.

The response of the center to the event was also deeply frustrating and offending. Responsibility was denied by Gorbachev, who disclaimed knowledge and said that the commander exceeded his instructions. The commander claimed that he had acted within his instructions. When complaints about his conduct surfaced in the Supreme Soviet, he was vocally supported by large numbers of Russian deputies. The impression from the television footage of the debate on the subject was that a large portion of the Russian deputies felt that the Georgians deserved what they got. No significant disciplinary action was taken against General Rodionov or his subordinates. Indeed, Rodionov subsequently became Russian defense minister. No apology was forthcoming.

The effect on Georgian perceptions of the center is clear. The political process in Moscow was thoroughly delegitimized. The lack of meaningful response caused the Georgians to internalize the experience and the sense of humiliation and powerlessness associated with it. Although the principal villain in the piece was Moscow, and the principal impetus to Georgian nationalism from the event was anti-Russian, it had spillover effects with consequences for civil peace in Georgia. One saw in the subsequent year an acceleration of efforts at "purification" of Georgia, a growing intolerance of non-Georgian minorities, and an increasing sense of Georgia for the Georgians.

To summarize, the politicization of both minority and majority ethnicity in Georgia was a result of social, political, and cultural changes rooted in the Soviet era. More proximately, it reflects the impact of perestroika on both elite and mass politics during the Gorbachev era. Finally, the dysfunctional Soviet response to mass political activity in Georgia in April 1989—and the manipulation of these events by the Georgian nationalist movement—deeply radicalized the political agenda among the titular population, with grave consequences not only for Georgian attitudes toward reform of Georgia's relations with the center, but also for majority-minority relations within the republic itself.

Independence and Ethnic Conflict

The chronological development of ethnic conflict in South Ossetia and in Abkhazia has been addressed above. It suffices to note here two points. First is the essential role that the Gamsakhurdia government played in the initiation of open conflict in South Ossetia and, indirectly, in Abkhazia.[43] Gamsakhurdia came to power committed to a policy of ethnic Georgian primacy in the republic. The isolation of his government from the international community, a product of the latter's concern about minority rights, contributed to the atmosphere of extremism. This was intrinsically threatening to minority elites. However, specific policies of the government also played a role in the exacerbation of tension. The appointment of prefects for the regions of Georgia was perceived as an explicit challenge to the authority of minority jurisdictions. The situation was not improved by efforts to reconsecrate mosques as orthodox churches in western Georgia.

The policy adopted by the government toward the activities of the South Ossetian autonomous oblast at the end of 1990 was foolishly confrontational. The attacks on Osset populations outside the South Ossetian oblast caused massive flight and, although these attacks may not have been inspired by the government, they were certainly not prevented. The renewal of Georgian assaults on Tskhinvali after the return of Shevardnadze in the spring of 1992 spoiled what might otherwise have been a promising opportunity for a negotiated resolution of the conflict.

The latter point invites a related observation. Georgians account for the renewal of attacks on Tskhinvali in the spring of 1992 in terms of the weakness of the chain of command after the coup and return of Shevardnadze. It was the latter's incomplete control over the levers of power that allowed local commanders to steal the initiative.[44] This problem recurred elsewhere. The initiation of hostilities in Abkhazia was reportedly the result of a deliberate violation of state policy by one of Shevardnadze's principal subordinates, Tengiz Kitovani. In none of these instances were the perpetrators of these actions effectively disciplined. In short, the weakness of central authority under Shevardnadze and the autonomy enjoyed by other actors—both in government and at the operational level in affected theaters—were major factors in explaining both the initiation of hostilities (in Abkhazia) and their continuation (in South Ossetia).

Loose control and lax discipline also played a role at lower levels. The excesses of the Georgian campaign in Mingrelia in the summer of 1992, for example, resulted from incomplete government control of paramilitaries and the manifest inhumanity and corruption of their personnel in the field. The campaign of looting, rape, torture, and murder mounted by Mkhedrioni in the region did much to poison relations between Mingrelia and the rest of Georgia. Georgian forces behaved similarly upon their entry into Abkhazia in the summer of 1992.[45] One sympathizes in this context with Aslan Abashidze's view that the only way he managed to keep the lid on in Ajara was to keep government forces out.[46]

The mention of incomplete government control over forces in the field brings us to the second point—the role of Russia in provoking and sustaining ethnic conflict in the republic. It is facile to accept the position frequently articulated in Georgia that the civil conflicts in the republic are the result of foreign (i.e., Russian) meddling rather than internal conditions. However, just as it is not possible to explain the development of nationalism in post-Soviet Georgia without reference to the politically and socially distorting effects of Soviet rule, so it is hard to account fully for the course of ethnic conflict in the country without reference to Russia's role.

This issue has both permissive and proactive aspects. In the former category, one should note the obvious inability or unwillingness of Russian authorities to control their own borders and the behavior of their own citizens. Insurrection in South Ossetia was possible because of the uncontrolled border between this region and its northern neighbor—a situation that allowed reasonably free movement of both matériel and volunteers into the conflict zone. Likewise, in Abkhazia, resistance to central authorities was mounted with ample assistance of Cossack and Chechen volunteers, who crossed freely from the North Caucasus. Arguably, these permissive factors were the result of the collapse of Russian authority in the region, rather than any deliberate design.

It is reasonably clear in the case of Abkhazia that insurgents benefited from substantial supplies of Russian heavy weaponry. It is difficult to account otherwise for the appearance of an Abkhaz air force in the skies over Sukhumi in the spring of 1993, or for the plenitude of heavy weapons deployed by the Abkhaz in the last weeks of their push against Sukhumi. Here too this may have been the result not of Russian government policy, but of the actions of specific groups in Russia with access to or control over military resources, and willing either to sell them to the Abkhaz or to use them as an instrument in an effort to punish Georgia for its early rejection of Soviet rule or to reclaim this desirable piece of real estate, or both.[47] Alternatively, much of it may have been the result of illegal arms sales or transfers by local Russian commanders seeking either to line their pockets or to feed their troops at a time when the logistical chain back to Russia was not operating.

Certain components of the Abkhaz story, however, cause one to push the interpretation farther. After the cease-fire accord of July 1993, Russian military observers were introduced into the zone of conflict to monitor both sides' implementation of the accord. To judge from the outcome of the renewed offensive in September 1993, they did a much better job of monitoring Georgian compliance than they did of Abkhaz. Moreover, they signed on as a guarantor of the cease-fire, and yet did nothing as the Abkhaz took the offensive and then cleansed the area of its Georgian population. In so doing, they created a situation in which Georgia had no choice but to capitulate to Russian pressure that they join the CIS and legitimize the stationing of Russian forces on Georgian soil, not only as peacekeepers, but in permanent bases.[48] The evidence is admittedly circumstantial, but it points strongly to a deliberate Russian policy of destabilization aimed at a restoration of Georgian dependence and Russian influence. Independent observers, including Russian ones,[49] generally accept that it was a matter of Russian state policy to manipulate Georgia's ethnic conflicts in order to restore Georgia to the fold, and as part of a broader effort to reestablish primacy in the former Soviet region.

Conclusion

The case of ethnic conflict in Georgia highlights the hazards of monocausal explanation of conflicts of this type (e.g., those based on external meddling or those appealing to "ancient hatreds"). Civil war was a product of deep historical and demographic factors conducing to tension between ethnic groups and between Georgia and Russia. It also reflected the constitutional design, nationality policies, and economic dispensation of the Soviet era. More proximately, it was a product of the opportunities, uncertainties, and disappointments of the Gorbachev period. The emergence of the more virulent strain of Georgian nationalism was catalyzed by profound errors on the part of central authorities in dealing with nationalist demonstrations in the capital in 1989.

Once hypernationalists had taken power in Georgia in 1990, some degree of conflict with minorities was quite probable. However, the weakness of the Georgian state also played its role, as did conflict within the Georgian majority between supporters and opponents of Zviad Gamsakhurdia. The course of the conflicts themselves, and the course of the effort to resolve them were strongly influenced by external agency (the Russian Federation). In all these respects, and despite the attractions of simple explanation and grand theory, the Georgian case highlights the importance of awareness of context and changing historical circumstance in coming to grips with the phenomenon of ethnic conflict.

Notes

1. By ethnic conflict, we mean conflict that occurs along ethnic lines. We are not suggesting a direct causal relationship between ethnicity and conflict, for reasons elaborated in the chapter.

2. In March 1990 the supreme soviet of the Republic of Georgia abrogated the 1921 agreements by which Georgia joined the Russian Federated Soviet Socialist Republic.

3. Georgian sources maintain that Russian forces, stationed in Tskhinvali until early 1992, also provided assistance to local Osset militias.

4. These figures are somewhat higher than those mentioned by the United Nations in its assessment of humanitarian needs in Georgia in 1993. See UN, 1993, 2–3. At the time the report was written, the UN cites numbers of displaced Georgians at fifteen thousand, and of Ossets at twelve thousand six hundred. These UN figures do not, however, include Ossets who crossed the frontier into North Ossetia. The North Ossetians claim that around fifty thousand such people took refuge in the North Ossetian autonomous oblast of the Russian Federation.

5. In this respect, South Ossetia may be an example of the problem of war economies and their inhibiting effect on transitions from war to peace. For discussions of this problem, see David Keen, *The Economic Functions of Violence in Civil Wars,* Adelphi Papers, no. 320 (Oxford: Oxford University Press for the International Institute for Strategic Studies, 1998); Mats Berdal and David Malone, eds., *Economic Agendas in Civil Wars* (Boulder, Colo.: Lynne Rienner, 2000).

6. The signature of a memorandum on security and confidence building measures in 1996 occasioned renewed optimism regarding a settlement, but, despite repeated contacts between the two leaderships since that time, little further movement has been evident. It appears that the Osset leadership is awaiting settlement of the Abkhaz conflict, since it will seek a similar deal to the one that the Abkhaz receive.

7. In interviews in Tbilisi in 1993, monitors from the Commission on Security and Cooperation in Europe reported that the most striking aspect of their work in the field was the depth of the hatred dividing Georgian and Osset populations in the region. These feelings are perhaps strengthened by the cultural milieu, which is one of close kinship ties and a tradition of vendetta.

8. Catherine Dale, "Turmoil in Abkhazia: Russian Responses," *RFE/RL Research Report* 2 (August 27, 1993).

9. For example, as Elizabeth Fuller recounts, in July 1993, Mkhedrioni forces reacted to an attack in Tskhalendzhika with massive reprisals against the civilian population. See "Transcaucasia: Ethnic Strife Threatens Democratization" RFE/RL Research Report 2 (1) (January 1, 1993): 23.

10. See Svetlana Chervonnaya, *Abkhazia - 1992: Postkommunisticheskaya Vandeya* (Abkhazia 1992: Post-communist Vendée) (Moscow: Mosgorpechat', 1993), 188. The author maintains that on August 11, 1992, Eduard Shevardnadze called Vladislav Ardzinba (the chairman of the Abkhaz supreme soviet) and secured his agreement on cooperation to free those detained by the insurgents.

11. Dale, "Turmoil in Abkhazia," 48. The author notes the significance of the Abkhaz supreme soviet's declaration of sovereignty in July 1992 in explaining Kitovani's decision. Interviews in Tbilisi in 1992 and 1993 suggested, however, that his motivation was essentially political. He felt that a rapid victory by forces under his leadership in Abkhazia would make him a national hero.

12. For useful accounts of the evolution of the conflict in Abkhazia, see Fuller, "Transcaucasia"; Elizabeth Fuller, "The Transcaucasus: War, Turmoil, Economic Collapse," *RFE/RL Research Report* 3 (January 1, 1994).

13. United Nations, "Consolidated Interagency Appeal for the Caucasus, April 1, 1994–March 31, 1995" (Geneva: UN, 1994), 8. Georgian sources put the total number of refugees from the outflow at approximately two hundred thousand. Interviews in Tbilisi, August 1994.

14. Interviews in Tbilisi, August 1994.

15. Interviews with officials and independent analysts in August 1994.

16. Small-scale violence also occurred as a result of infiltration by armed groups of Abkhaz Georgians across the Inguri River. Interviews in Tbilisi, Zugdidi, and Gali in March 1995.

17. This is not to say that these relations are stable. There is substantial concern within the Georgian population about Armenian irredentism and the possibility that after the conclusion of the Nagorno-Karabakh episode, Georgia may be next. Relations between Georgians have also been exacerbated by the fact that many Armenians joined the Abkhaz in their offensive of September 1993. An Armenian battalion served in the Abkhaz armed forces. In the late 1990s, the Armenian population of the Samtse-Javakheti region of Georgia became increasingly active, and in 1998, Georgian forces were prevented from holding military exercises in the area by local Armenian militias. There is also concern about the rapid natural growth of the Azeri population in southeastern Georgia and in agricultural lands in the vicinity of Tbilisi, and the possibility that this might lead to pressure for frontier rectification. In the 1980s, there

was violence between Azeris and Georgians resettled from the mountains of Svanetia to this area over land. Interviews in Tbilisi, 1992–96.

18. The 1989 Soviet census reported that of the one hundred sixty-four thousand Ossets in Georgia, seventy thousand lived in the oblast and the rest elsewhere in the country. In addition, thirty thousand Georgians lived in South Ossetia.

19. Compact settlement of minorities is a result of the poor fit between state borders and ethnic frontiers in the Caucasus, the settlement policies of the Soviet era, and, more basically, the country's fragmented geography.

20. All visitors to the old city of Tbilisi are greeted with the information that within a few city blocks there have existed for centuries an Armenian Apostolic Church, a Georgian Orthodox Church, a Russian Orthodox Church, a mosque, and a synagogue without any apparent difficulties between their congregations.

21. In the mountain villages of South Ossetia, for example, there were long-standing exchanges of children between Ossets and Georgians, where children from one ethnic group would live for long periods with families of the other. Interview with Peter Mamradze, then with the State Committee for Human Rights and Ethnic Relations, August 1992.

22. Ronald Suny, *The Making of the Georgian Nation* (Bloomington: Indiana University Press, 1988), 114.

23. This process in the Georgian case is well presented in Suny, ibid., 113–43.

24. In many respects, as a response to the nobility's declining economic and political position, the emergence of Georgian nationalism resembles Liah Greenfeld's account of the emergence of French nationalism out of the aristocracy under Bourbon absolutism in the seventeenth and eighteenth centuries. Greenfeld, *Nationalism: Five Roads to Modernity* (Cambridge, Mass.: Harvard University Press, 1992).

25. Suny, *Georgian Nation,* 145.

26. See the relevant clauses of the May 1920 treaty between Russia and Georgia as cited by Richard Pipes, *The Formation of the Soviet Union* (Cambridge, Mass.: Harvard University Press, 1964), 228. Pipes gives a historical account of Georgian relations with Russia during the period of independence and reannexation on pages 210–14, 227–28, 234–41.

27. Georgian sources attribute unrest among the Ossets during the period of Georgian independence to Bolshevik manipulation. See Georgii Zhorzholiani, Solomon Lekishvili, Levan Mataradze, Levan Toidze, and Edisher Khoshtaria-Brosset, *The Historical, Political, and Legal Aspects of the Georgian-Ossetian Conflict* (Tbilisi: Samshoblo, 1992), 6.

28. Ronald Suny, *The Revenge of the Past* (Stanford, Calif.: Stanford University Press, 1993), 87.

29. The third—Ajara—has been the most stable zone of Western Georgia since independence. This reflects in part a belief among Georgians that the Ajars are a distinct part of their own community, rather than an alien apparition. Even here, however, there were significant problems when the Gamsakhurdia government sought to impose central control on the area in 1991. This again threatened the position of institutionalized Ajar elites. Interviews in Batumi, August 1992.

30. See Roland Dannreuther, *Creating New States in Central Asia,* Adelphi Papers, no. 288 (London: International Institute for Strategic Studies, 1994).

31. In 1970, taking the USSR as a whole at 100, Georgia came in at 66.5.

32. Wages in the union as a whole in 1978 averaged 199 percent of those in 1960, in Russia 202 percent, and in Georgia 179 percent.

33. The above figures on the relative standing of Georgia were taken from I. S. Koropeckyj, "Growth and Productivity"; Gertrude Schroeder, "Regional Living Standards"; James Gillula, "The Growth and Structure of Fixed Capital in Union Republics"; and Oleg Zinam, "Transcaucasus"—all in *Economics of Soviet Regions,* ed. I. S. Koropeckyj and Gertrude Schroeder (New York: Praeger, 1981), esp. 95, 122, 124–25, 138, 143, 412. Whatever the "objective" truth, it is nonetheless clear from interviews with Georgian political figures, civil servants, and intellectuals from 1991 to 1994 that the prevailing view was that Georgia had been continually exploited as a member of the union and that its economy was substantially distorted by Soviet economic planning.

34. Suny, *Georgian Nation,* 303–4.

35. Shevardnadze comments on these events and on the government response in Eduard Shevardnadze, *Moi vybor: V zashchitu demokratii i svobody* (My choice: In defense of democracy and freedom) (Moscow: Novosti, 1991), 54–55.

36. Suny illustrates this point by reference to enrollment trends in higher education. Suny, *Georgian Nation,* 304–5. By 1969–70, Georgians (67 percent of the population) comprised 82.6 percent of students in higher education. At the other end of the spectrum, Armenians (9.7 percent of the population) made up 3.6 percent of advanced students.

37. Mzhavanadze was Shevardnadze's predecessor as secretary of the Communist Party of Georgia.

38. For a discussion of relative deprivation, see Ted R. Gurr, *Why Men Rebel* (Princeton, N.J.: Princeton University Press, 1971), 24–122. Gurr argues that the potential for collective violence varies strongly with people's subjective sense of deprivation "with reference to their expectations," noting in this context that a person's point of reference "may be his own past condition" (24–25).

39. For a discussion of the relevance of populism to the emergence of Georgian nationalism, see Stephen Jones, "Populism in Georgia: The Gamsax-

urdia Phenomenon," in *Nationalism and History: The Politics of Nation Building in Post-Soviet Armenia, Azerbaijan and Georgia,* ed. Donald Schwartz and Razmik Panossian (Toronto: University of Toronto Centre for Russian and East European Studies, 1994), 127–49.

40. On this point see Dannreuther, *Creating New States,* 16.

41. In this respect, Georgia differs from the predictions of much recent theory on the origins of ethnic conflict, which focuses on the instrumental use of ethnic nationalist rhetoric by established elites during periods of political transition to defend their positions that are threatened by broadened political participation. See Jack Snyder, "Democratization, War, and Nationalism in the Post-Communist States," in *The Sources of Russian Foreign Policy after the Cold War,* ed. Celeste Wallander (Boulder, Colo.: Westview, 1995), 21–40; Edward Mansfield and Jack Snyder, "Democratization and the Danger of War," *International Security* 19 (4) (Spring 1995); reprinted in *Debating the Democratic Peace,* ed. Michael E. Brown, Sean Lynn-Jones, and Steven Miller (Cambridge, Mass.: MIT Press, 1996), 301–36; Neil MacFarlane, "On the Front Lines in the Near Abroad: The CIS and the OSCE in Georgia's Civil Wars," *Third World Quarterly* 18 (3) (Spring 1997): 509–25.

42. See, for example, Givi Pantsuria, Ludmilla Esvandzhia, Eka Eliava, and Roland Dzhalagania, *Deviat Aprelya: Dokumental'nye svidetel'stva o tragicheskikh sobytiakh v Tbilisi* (April 9: Documentary evidence of tragic events in Tbilisi) (Tbilisi: Izdatel'stvo Merani, 1990).

43. Stephen Jones, "Georgia: The Trauma of Statehood," in *New States, New Politics: Building the Post-Soviet Nations,* ed. Ian Bremmer and Ray Taras (Cambridge: Cambridge University Press, 1997), 513.

44. This explanation is rejected by officials in South Ossetia. Interviews with Southern Osset Information Ministry officials and supreme soviet deputies in August 1992 and summer 1996.

45. For a concise description of the behavior of Georgian military, paramilitary, and civilian personnel toward non-Georgians in Abkhazia after their entry, see Chervonnaya, *Abkhazia,* 149–50.

46. Interviews in Batumi, 1992. When I asked a Georgian taxi driver in 1993 whether he felt that conflict would spread to Ajara, he responded that of course it would. After all, it was the only place in the country where there was anything left to steal.

47. In the post-Soviet context, control over Abkhazia would have roughly doubled the Russian coastline on the Black Sea at a time when the status of the major former Soviet naval bases in the region (those in Ukraine) was in doubt. There were identifiable factions in both the Russian parliament and in the defense ministry who were publicly sympathetic to Abkhaz aspirations.

Chervonnaya concludes an extensive analysis of the causes of the Abkhaz conflict with the more ambitious assertion that its most important proximate cause was interference and manipulation by operatives of the KGB seeking to neutralize Georgia's drive toward independence by stimulating internal conflict. According to Chervonnaya, their behavior changed little subsequent to the collapse of the union, the adjusted intention being to "punish disobedient colonies and to return them to the imperial system." Chervonnaya, *Abkhazia 1992*, 150–51.

48. A Russian-Georgian agreement on military cooperation, including provision for twenty-five-year leases on four Russian bases in Georgia, was initialed in March 1995. The agreement was finalized in 1994–95. It still awaits ratification by the Georgian parliament, the delay resulting from what Georgians see as a Russian failure to deliver on their promise to assist in the reestablishment of jurisdiction over its territory. More recently, the fate of the agreement has become entangled in the dispute between Georgia over extension of the CISPKF mandate mentioned above. It is noteworthy that some six years later at the Istanbul summit of the Organization for Cooperation and Security in Europe, the two countries signed an agreement on the withdrawal of Russian troops from several of Georgia's bases.

49. See Chervonnaya, *Abkhazia 1992*.

7

Democratic Governance and the Roots of Conflict in Africa

Muna Ndulo

FOR THE MOST part of its postcolonial era, Africa has been torn by strife. Africa has the largest share of conflicts in the world today. Since 1970, more than thirty wars have been fought in Africa, the vast majority of them within individual states. In 1996 alone, fourteen of the fifty-three countries of Africa were afflicted by armed conflicts accounting for more than half of all war-related deaths worldwide and resulting in more than 8 million refugees, returnees, and displaced persons.[1] Africa remains host to the largest population of refugees and displaced persons on any continent. Too many Africans are trapped in conditions of grinding poverty, face violence and abuse daily, suffer under corrupt and oppressive regimes, and are condemned to live their lives in squatter settlements or rural slums with inadequate sanitation, schooling, and health facilities. About 240 million Africans live on less than one dollar a day, have no access to safe drinking water, and are illiterate.[2]

Africa has the dubious distinction of being both the least developed and, in terms of natural resources, the most endowed continent in the world.[3] With a land area three times the size of the United States, and a population of some six hundred million people, Africa enjoys the resources required to attain sustainable development, defined in terms of increasingly productive employment opportunities and a steadily improving quality of life for all its people.[4] The continent has vast mineral, oil, water, land, and human resources.[5] The ambiguity in Africa's position is revealed with particular clarity in relation to the production of food, a sector in which during precolonial times the continent was self-sufficient. Nowadays, it is increasingly dependent on external supplies. On the face of it, the apparent inability of the African continent to feed itself is paradoxical, since one of the region's chief assets is its huge agricultural potential. It has all the conditions for becoming one of the world's major food producers.[6]

Ironically, the above factors contribute to conflict, instability, and misery.[7] In turn, conflicts have seriously undermined Africa's efforts to ensure long-term stability, prosperity, and peace for its peoples.

This chapter examines the constitutional roots of conflict in Africa in the context of the crisis of governance and sustainable development. It seeks to identify some of the key issues that must be considered in the process of developing durable constitutions that are acceptable to the people of the country they are intended to govern. It sees the design and implementation of governance as a means of handling political conflicts and a way to ensure that peace endures.

Sources of Conflict

The source of African conflict is a complex interlocking web of factors that are steeped in history and contemporary realities, including social, economic, and political conditions. Since the advent of colonialism, African societies have experienced protracted changes.[8] At the 1885 Berlin Conference, the colonial powers developed an international code regulating the territorial partition of Africa. Kingdoms, states, and communities were arbitrarily divided or created. Prior to the colonial period, traditional African societies had their own system of social and political organization.[9] Max Gluckman, for instance, observes that the Lozi of Zambia had a complex economy that required many people to cooperate in various productive activities. The basic unit of organization in the structure of their economic, political, and domestic system was the village. It was the center from which they exploited gardens and other parcels of land. The village was headed by a headman, who was responsible to the King's Council, headed by the chief. The chief governed with the assistance of councillors.[10] The era of colonialism initiated (and independence consummated it) a dynamic process of disruption in traditional social structures and life. The foremost act of disruption was the unification of ethnic communities under the umbrella of sovereign states with overriding powers of political control within their whole area of jurisdiction. The result was that the political, military, and financial security of African societies no longer depended on traditional organizations and custom. The new philosophy of governance was expressed in laws, which gave almost unlimited discretion to colonial officials, and the absence of formal controls over their exercise.[11]

Colonial rule was philosophically and organizationally elitist, centralist, and absolute. There were no representative institutions. The colonial administration not only implemented policy, they made it as well. As colonial rulers sought expedient interlocutors, they distorted or destroyed precolonial governance systems by creating or encouraging arrangements such as indirect rule, which made existing local chiefs more despotic and created new ones (warrant chiefs) where none existed before.[12] There was a departure from agrarian self-subsistence communities to a money economy dependent on the capitalist economic system. The character of commercial relations instituted by colonialism created long-term distortions in the political economy of Africa. Transportation networks and related physical infrastructure were designed to satisfy the needs of trade with the metropolitan country, not to support the balanced growth of an indigenous economy. In addition to frequently imposing unfavorable terms of trade, economic activities were strongly skewed toward extractive industries, while primary conditions for export stimulated little demand for steady and widespread improvements in the skills and educational levels of the workforce. African societies became divided into two—the rural and the urban. Traditional culture continued in the rural areas, where the great majority of the people lived and which was largely outside the framework of colonial elitism and the "modern" culture of urban areas. The urban economy and culture was the link between the metropolitan country and the colony in the export of raw materials.[13] Since colonial economic policies kept African economies small, excessively open, dependent, and poorly integrated,[14] the colonial state was characterized by a huge gap in standard of living between the rural and urban areas. Dislocation of African peoples from their lands and communities continued throughout the colonial period as the needs of the colonial economy expanded, further undermining traditional economic and social organization that might have been left in place after the initial establishment of colonial rule.[15]

This colonial legacy endured long after independence,[16] and so did the rural-urban divide. The rural areas are still neglected, marginalized, and impoverished. The state is extremely weak and is almost completely irrelevant as a provider of services in rural areas.[17] This is further reinforced by the lack of popular participation in governance and exacerbated by the lack of effective devolution of power to local communities. Subsequently, colonial rule bequeathed to independent African states undemocratic governments and bureaucracies that emphasized hierarchy, compliance, and discipline, without addressing other equally important concerns, such as public accountability, responsiveness, and participation.[18] Many governments that emerged after independence soon became undemocratic, overcentralized, and authoritarian. Predictably, political monopolies led to corruption, nepotism, abuse of power, and conflict.

African presidents replaced their colonial governors both in title and in deeds. Like the colonial governors, they became the sole embodiment of the social will and purposes of the countries they ruled. Their rule saw the emergence of repressive one- or no-party systems of government.[19] With one-party systems, power came to be concentrated in one man. Dissent, for which there had always been a secure and honored place in traditional African society, came to be viewed with ill-concealed hostility, almost as if it were treason. Multiple parties, even if originally formed around national agendas, generally tended to lead to ethnically based parties—a system that made African states ungovernable.[20] Single-party or military rule was often regarded as a viable and sometimes desirable solution to the ethnically based parties in Africa's new modern states.[21] Ultimately, the party supplanted the machinery of the state, and the differences between the two became blurred.[22]

The nature of political power in Africa, together with the real and perceived consequences of capturing and maintaining power, is a key source of conflicts across the continent. Frequently in politics the winner takes all: wealth and resources, patronage, and the prestige and prerogatives of office. A communal sense of advantage or disadvantage is often closely linked to this phenomenon, which is heightened in many cases by reliance on centralized and highly personalized forms of governance. Where there is insufficient accountability of leaders, lack of transparency of regimes, inadequate checks and balances, nonadherence to the rule of law, absence of peaceful means to change or replace leadership, or lack of respect for human rights, political control becomes extremely important and the stakes become dangerously high. This situation is exacerbated when, as is often the case in Africa, the state is the major source of wealth accumulation and political parties are largely either regionally or ethnically based. In such circumstances, the multiethnic character of most African states makes it even more likely that conflict will lead to an often violent politicization of ethnicity. In extreme cases of competition between rival communities, a community's survival can often be ensured only through acquiring state power. Conflict in such cases becomes virtually inevitable. And because a viable middle class is seldom present due to the lack of industrialization, there is usually no countervailing force to blunt the excesses of warlords or the state itself. This situation leads easily to the intensification of conflict.

During the Cold War, external efforts to bolster or undermine African governments were a familiar feature of superpower competition. With the end of the Cold War, external intervention has diminished but has not disappeared. In the competition for oil and other precious resources in Africa, interests external to Africa continue to play a large and sometimes decisive role, both in suppressing conflict and in sustaining it. Foreign interventions are not limited, however, to sources beyond Africa. Neighboring states inevitably affected by conflicts taking place within other states may also have other significant interests, not all of them necessarily benign. Despite the devastation that armed conflicts bring, there are many who profit from chaos and lack of accountability, and who may have little or no interest in stopping a conflict and much interest in prolonging it. Very high on the list of those who profit from conflict in Africa are international arms merchants. Indeed, a key component in the surge of violence in Africa is the ready availability of cheap arms—imported mainly from Eastern Europe. This is one reason African wars have lacked positive technological side effects. Coupled with the ready availability of cheap arms is the presence of mercenaries who can be contracted to wage interminable war.

Yet, high on the list usually are the protagonists themselves. In Liberia the control and exploitation of diamonds, timber, and other raw materials was one of the principal objectives of the warring factions. Control over those resources financed the various factions and gave them the means to sustain the conflict. The same can be said of Angola, where protracted difficulties in the peace process owed much to the importance of control over the exploitation of the country's lucrative diamond fields. In Sierra Leone the chance to plunder national resources was a key motivation of those who seized power from the elected government in May 1997. As Nelson Mandela observed, in reference to the Great Lakes conflicts, wars of Africa are not inevitable, they are caused by leaders who yield to the narrowest of definition of self-interest and sacrifice their own citizens to their greed, their ambition, and their weakness.

At the root of the problem for Africa is the worldwide perception of it as an unstable, poorly governed, and conflict-ridden continent that cannot guarantee the safety of foreign investments.[23] Africa receives only 5 percent of all direct foreign investment flowing to developing countries.[24] This in spite of the fact that investments made in Africa consistently generate high rates of return. For example, from 1990 through 1994, the average annual return on the book value of U.S. direct investment in Africa was nearly 28 percent, compared with

8.5 percent for U.S. direct investment worldwide.[25] Not only do authoritarian governments keep potential investors away, they simply do not have the institutions by which conflicts can be peacefully expressed and resolved. They generally try to deal with such conflicts by ignoring or denying them, by suppressing them or by attempting to eliminate them. Authoritarian systems can present an illusion of short-term stability but are unlikely to be sustainable over the long term. In its 1989 report on sub-Saharan Africa the World Bank concluded that "underlying the litany of Africa's development problems is a crisis of governance. . . . By governance is meant the exercise of political power to manage a nation's affairs. Because countervailing power has been lacking, state officials in many countries have served their own interests without fear of being called to account. The leadership assumes broad discretionary authority and loses its legitimacy. Information is controlled, and voluntary associations are co-opted or disbanded. This environment cannot readily support a dynamic economy."[26]

Thus, some thirty years into independence, Africa was left in crisis, a litter of failed states whose characteristics included: highly centralized systems of governance; excessive state control coupled with limited capacity to govern; arbitrary policymaking and abuse of executive power; erosion of the boundaries between the state and civil society; weak institutions of both state and civil society with few countervailing forces to the executive branch of authority; unaccountable bureaucracies; widespread corruption; unenforceable or unjust legal systems; limited participation in governance by the general citizenry; and preferential access to power and resources, often determined by religious, ethnic, or geographical considerations.

The Relationship between Governance and Conflict

When the rules of the game are not universally accepted and respected, the political process becomes controversial and a source of conflict rather than a mechanism for resolving strife.[27] Another unfortunate legacy of the colonial model has been the extremely detailed approach in African constitutions. The postindependence constitutions in Africa were the result of agreements reached at independence conferences, which followed nationalist campaigns for independence.[28] The texts of the constitutions bequeathed to the new states followed colonial models developed by the various colonial powers for newly independent states. For example, a typical African constitution contains hundreds of detailed provisions, which might in effect undermine its dynamic development and its ability to meet the needs of a rapidly changing society.[29] Another practice in many African countries has been to adopt new constitutions through the use of commissions.[30] The commission typically tours the country, solicits views relating to possible constitutional arrangements from the public, and ends its work by recommending a draft constitution for adoption by the national legislature. This approach fails to produce durable and lasting constitutions for many of the countries that have used it. Zambia is a case in point; there the opposition parties continue to dispute the constitution adopted in May 1996 on the grounds that it does not reflect the views of the Zambian people and that the ruling party manipulated the process.[31] This experience suggests that the use of commissions to recommend a constitution is susceptible to manipulation by the government in power and often results in the imposition of its preferred constitutional model. Matters are made worse by the perception held by most people that such commissions are populated by people sympathetic to the ruling party. Moreover, on practical grounds too, the use of a commission with a broad and unregimented agenda, to collect constitutional proposals, is inappropriate for the elaboration of a complex document such as a constitution.

A major drawback of the commission method as practiced in Africa is that people come to the commission hearings and, without any guidance whatsoever, voice their opinions about what they individually consider to be constitutional issues.[32] Typically, the issues they address are not appropriate for inclusion in a national constitution. A large number of petitioners take advantage of the process to air grievances relating to unemployment, land allocation, lack of schools, lack of health care, inadequate transport facilities, and development rather than those relating to the constitution. Questions of relevance and weight to be attached to the individual submissions are glossed over for political or expediency reasons or decorum. It is this scenario that provides a perfect opportunity for the government in power to manipulate the constitution-making process. Besides, with thousands of submissions, an average lawyer could easily write any number of versions of a constitution and find justification in submitting each to the commission.

Some African scholars have criticized the move toward written constitutions and the current constitutional arrangements on the grounds that they are based on, or follow too closely, Western models of governance, rather than on African ideals of governance, and have questioned the relevance of Western models to the African condition.[33] Be that as it may, the impact of history seems clear: one may interpret history, or reinterpret it, but no one can repeal it. Besides, while transplanting European models into Africa might be problematic, the motives of some of those who advocate African solutions to Africa problems are often suspect. Many postindependence dictatorships—and indeed the African one-party system of governance in Zambia, Kenya, Tanzania, and elsewhere in Africa—were justified on the grounds that they were the variant of democracy best suited to the peculiar African circumstances, and, at the same time, they were a natural facilitator for economic growth and promoter of national unity.[34] Today it is quite evident that these justifications had little to do with African concepts of governance and more with the consolidation of political power through the elimination of all political opposition.[35]

Without constitutional and institutional effectiveness, urgent social issues are left unresolved. In central Africa, for example, such issues include competition for scarce land and water resources in densely populated areas. In Rwanda, multiple waves of displacements have resulted in situations where several families often claim rights to the same piece of land. In other words, the lack of resolution of earlier conflicts fuel new ones. In African communities where oil is extracted, conflict has often arisen over local complaints that the community does not adequately reap the benefit of such resources, or suffers excessively from the degradation of their natural environment. In addition, a large percentage of the people remain outside the formal structures of the state and rely on themselves for law enforcement and for their survival. As pointed out earlier, postindependence African governments, like their colonial predecessors, tend to be overly centralized. In the institutional sense, centralization of power refers to the constitutional concentration of power in the hands of a few executive offices (and, therefore, a few people) and greatly undermines the constitutional importance of courts, legislatures, and subregional governments. This is usually reinforced by the tendency of most governments to concentrate the most critical human and financial resources at the headquarters, while leaving rural administration with a lean administrative structure that lacks adequate resources or discretionary authority. The above practices are typical of centralized states, whose preoccupation remains with bureaucracy and planning and, therefore, tend to produce concentrated structures, rather than diversified and decentralized institutions that emphasize the grassroots empowerment of the people.

Centralized bureaucracies go hand in hand with financial centralization. The central state collects all the most important and buoyant tax resources and makes scarce funds available to subnational organs. Compounding this problem is that financial transfers to subregional organs are done via grants, which are given on a sporadic, rather than on a regular and systematic basis. It can alleviate the workload of overstretched central government, something that is especially important in Africa in view of the numerous tasks of development and transformation that face a typical African government.[36] Interestingly enough here, there is mounting evidence that the International Monetary Fund (IMF)–World Bank stabilization and structural adjustment programs that are in place in almost all African countries have worsened the situation.[37] For instance, the withdrawal of state marketing agencies has exposed poor farmers to exploitation by large city traders.[38]

As much as intuitional change is necessary, it is not easily possible because, instead of providing the impetus for change, many elections in Africa have been disputed and have sometimes led to conflict rather than the advancement of democracy. As Andrew Reynolds has observed, "although appropriate electoral laws are insufficient to ensure stability and good governance in divided societies, poorly designed laws can entrench societal divisions and exacerbate pre-existing conflict."[39] In the Republic of the Congo, formerly Congo/Brazzaville, for instance, the 1992 election precipitated an incipient civil war between supporters of rival presidential contenders. Similarly, the May 1998 elections in Lesotho led to a total breakdown of law and order and the intervention of the Southern African Development Community's military forces to restore law and order in the country. The 1996 Zambian elections led to unprecedented tensions in the country and to an attempted coup.[40] This is largely because national elections are often manipulated by the party in power and often result in substantial minorities being unrepresented in Parliament or feeling cheated by the process. In addition, many elections have been riddled with irregularities not always calculated to defraud, but which are sometimes a result of the sheer inability of the state to effectively conduct such a formidable managerial and logistical undertaking.[41]

Naomi Chazon notes that "in Africa, elections provide ritual occasions for sanctioning the existing power constellation but allow for precious few opportunities for affecting the composition of the ruling circles or policy outcomes."[42] Clearly, the electoral process is not accompanied by the building of institutions that foster accountability and greater transparency in the governance of the country.[43] In many African countries election results show the main political party as having overwhelming support in a core region. According to B. O. Nwabueze, this is because

> for most African politicians the tribe is the base for political activity and tribal sentiment the focus of appeal, which inevitably disables them from rising above tribal interests and pressures in the administration of government. The result is that the government comes to be regarded as one huge cake, already baked, and it is the duty of a political leader to secure for his tribe as large a share as possible. Every question, whether it be the award of scholarships or contracts, appointments in the public service, economic development, or the siting of industrial projects is viewed from the standpoint of tribal advantage, and support or opposition to it is dependent upon whether or not it advances the interests of one's tribe.[44]

The system of winner take all, which is applied in most African countries, tends to reinforce this kind of approach to politics as it creates permanent losers and permanent winners. The winner-take-all system is based on the principle of territorial representation, emphasizing the relationship between the voter and the representative.[45] The size of a party's representation is thus determined not only by the number of votes received but also by their geographical concentration. Should a party's votes be too widely scattered or too highly concentrated it could be underrepresented in parliament. In such a situation, groups that are numerically small can never win an election. They therefore remain permanently aggrieved. Such a system will be unable to implement democratic principles in deeply divided societies.[46]

Democratic Governance and the Process of Elaborating a Constitution

The future of democracy in Africa is predicated on the development of constitutional arrangements that set up viable institutions within which to conduct the business of governance and that foster an environment where peace and development can flourish. Such arrangements will ensure that the exercise of governmental authority is conducted in a predictable, responsible, and legally regulated way to the satisfaction of civil society.[47] Democratic governance permits grievances to be expressed openly and to be responded to. In short, democracy operates as a conflict management system without recourse to violence. It is this ability to handle conflicts without having to suppress them or be engulfed by them that distinguishes democratic governance from its major alternatives.

The United Nations Development Program (UNDP) has defined good governance as "the exercise of political, economic and administrative authority in the management of a country's affairs at all levels."[48] Good governance is, among many things, participatory, transparent, and accountable. It is also effective, equitable, and promotes the rule of law.[49] Good governance ensures that political, social, and economic priorities are based on broad consensus in society and that the voices of the poorest and the most vulnerable are heard in decision making over the allocation of development resources. It creates a capable state. In this context, a capable state is defined as one that espouses good governance and is characterized by transparency, accountability in the conduct of national affairs, the ability to enforce law and order throughout the country, respect for human rights, effective provision of infrastructure, a limited role in the market economy, creation of a favorable policy environment, and seeking to work in partnership with the private sector and civil society.[50]

Other important characteristics of a capable state are: acceptance of opposition and competitive politics; predictable, open, and enlightened policymaking; a bureaucracy imbued with a professional ethos acting in furtherance of the public good; maintenance of fair terms of trade between the rural and urban sectors; and recognition and respect of the boundaries between the state and the private sector and civil society.[51] These characteristics enable a state to effectively perform its role of developing the country and bringing about a better life for its entire people. Democracy means the freedom of the people in their daily lives to determine their destinies (e.g., their right to build their own organizations, residences, schools, cultural institutions). To a large extent, democracy is less a formalistic system than an attitude. It is a way of approaching the business of government, of setting up rules for government, of creating enough checks and balances that the government depends less on individuals and their personal whims and more on systems and processes.[52]

Where citizens of a country have no sense of democracy and are unwilling or unable to insist that their leaders deliver democracy, a written constitution, however eloquently it proclaims democracy, will be insufficient to guarantee it.[53] Additionally, democracy depends on values such as tolerance and trust, which cannot be secured in a constitution. Rather, these values, to gain a foothold in a given country, depend on the political will of a nation. Effective devolution of power to local authorities entails the existence of local communities endowed with democratically constituted decision-making bodies and possessed of a wide degree of autonomy with regard to their responsibilities, the ways and means by which those responsibilities are exercised, and the financial resources required for their fulfillment. Devolution of power to local communities has been recognized in many parts of the world as one of the cornerstones of democracy.[54]

The right of citizens to participate in the conduct of public affairs is more directly exercised at the local levels. The existence of local authorities that are given real responsibilities can provide an administrative set-up that is both effective and close to the citizen. Unlike more centralized systems, local government provides for more flexible responses attuned to local needs. It opens opportunities for innovation and experimentation in policy formulation and delivery. Any examination of the modalities of affecting the devolution of power in Africa must, among other things, address the issue of the future of traditional institutions of governance in modern African political systems.[55] There is a consensus among most Africans that traditional leaders, such as chiefs, should have a role in the governance of the state. But the exact role they should play is a source of disagreement and, as a result, their role remains largely undefined. There is a need to accommodate traditional leaders in constitutional arrangements or at least to face up to their existence. For instance, they could be incorporated into the local government system and form the nucleus of that system. This could, quite conceivably, enhance the legitimacy of local government structures in the rural areas. In these areas, traditional leaders provide the link between the people and the external world (the government). Reaching these communities effectively requires one to confront this reality. If colonial powers were shrewd enough to use traditional institutions in administering the colonial state,[56] why should modern African political systems not make use of them in efforts to reach out to small communities and build national consensus and cohesion?[57]

In advocating the accommodation of traditional structures in modern political systems, one should not ignore the fact that these institutions can at times be oppressive, exploitative, discriminatory, and intolerant, especially to women and children.[58] The argument, however, is not that traditional institutions are perfect, but that it is more effective to build democracy and effective governance through the familiar than the unfamiliar. Since the goal is to establish a demo-cratic order, the need to incorporate traditional institutions into the modern political system cannot take precedence over the needs of a democratic society.[59] With regard to objections that these institutions are discriminatory as to gender, governments must address the areas that need reform, discard the discriminatory aspects of traditional institutions, and confront the traditional values that underpin gender discrimination and authoritarianism.[60]

The most important legal instrument in the scheme of good governance is the national constitution. Thus a major part of the answer to Africa's present predicament lies in the development of constitutions that can stand the test of time and that can deliberately structure national institutions engaged in the management of the country in such a way as to ensure that a capable state is created.

Constitutional democracy in Africa will inevitably involve multiple or concurrent constitutional orders rather than a single center of authority and power, especially as African countries are characterized by large territorial, multiethnic groupings, high rates of illiteracy, and poor communications infrastructure. In general terms, constitutional democracy centers on the following principles:

- using the constitution, as a supreme and fundamental law, to regulate and limit the powers of government and to secure the efficacy of such limitations in actual practice;
- ensuring that the legitimacy of the government is regularly established by requiring that governmental powers are not assumed or exercised except with the mandate of the people given at periodic intervals through free and fair elections or referenda that are executed and administered according to the constitution and well-defined electoral laws and in the context of a system-wide pluralism;
- protecting the fundamental rights of the people;
- resolving disputes, including disputes relating to the constitutional propriety of legislation and other government acts, impartially and in accordance with the constitution and by regular, ordinary courts that are independent of the disputants;
- applying ordinary laws regarding the execution of governance and

adjudication of disputes in conformity with the limitations imposed by the constitution and in accordance with the procedure for law making prescribed therein and ensuring that such procedures conform to internationally accepted norms;

- holding political leaders and government officials accountable for their actions to the people through clearly formulated and transparent processes;

- assuring the security of citizens and the rule of law such that contracts can be fairly enforced both between public and private operators and between private operators and the state;

- requiring public agencies to be responsive to the needs of the public and to promote social and economic development for the benefit of all citizens, not for a particular ethnic group;

- providing information that permits accountability to be achieved, laws to be carefully applied, markets to function, and people to be creative and innovative;

- promoting freedom of expression and association and the protection of human rights.[61]

Freedom of speech is vital to the success of a democratic enterprise. Unless a people tell one another the truth about what they know and think and see, they cheat themselves of their courage and destroy the opportunities that freedom provides. This is because democratic institutions do not renew themselves as effortlessly as flowering trees. They require cultivation by people brave enough and honest enough to admit their mistakes and to accept responsibility for even their most inglorious acts.

Against this background the issue of ethnicity could potentially be destabilizing to the democratic process. Democracy may magnify rather than reduce the adverse effects of ethnicity. Thus, African states need to accommodate the significant minorities that exist in their countries. Constitutions must deal with this fact sensitively, not only consciously acknowledging the fears and apprehensions of racial minority groups, but also meeting their legitimate demands and involving them, in a meaningful and satisfying way, in the political systems that evolve and also in nation building. Ignoring it will not solve the issue of ethnicity. It has to be addressed in a proactive manner.

The same approach must be applied to the problem of the inequality of the sexes perpetuated by traditional cultural values and roles assigned to women.[62] As John Stuart Mill observed, only complete equality between men and women in all legal, political, and social arrangements can create the proper conditions for human freedom and a democratic way of life.[63] The 1995 Beijing Conference on Women declared that the goal should be to remove all obstacles to women's active participation in all spheres of public and private life through an equal share in economic, social, cultural, and political decision making.[64] The quest for a viable constitution must also anticipate the general unfamiliarity that most of the peoples in an African state have with the philosophy and machinery of modern democratic governance. A viable constitution must accommodate the general economic and social backwardness that exists in these countries and the consequent need for simultaneous development on all fronts. African constitutions cannot ignore the enormous economic and social value/significance of public office to individuals in the midst of widespread poverty and ignorance. A search for a viable constitution must make provisions for the temptations of arrogance, discrimination, abuse of power, and corruption assailing persons in office.[65] It must face the influence of money in the electoral process, especially in economies where a large percentage of voters are unemployed.[66] This is worsened by the fact that most opposition parties in Africa lack the resources to operate effectively, thus the funding of political parties should be addressed. The principle of government funding of political parties is well established across the democratic world. In the absence of state funding arrangements, the party in power has an undue advantage as it has access to state resources and institutions to push its political agenda.

On the electoral front, good constitutional design for divided societies dictates against directly elected presidents. Matthew Shugart and John Carey have identified three key traits of presidentialism that often have negative consequences: temporal rigidity, majoritarianism, and dual democratic legitimacy.[67] In a divided society without a history of stable democracy, there is no assurance that the loser or losers of a presidential race will accept defeat in what amounts to a zero-sum game. Ann Reid of the U.S. State Department lays the blame for the collapse of peace plans in Angola in 1994 and the bloody conflict that ensued largely on the country's presidential system. She observes that since José Eduardo dos Santos and Jonas Savimbi were vying for the only prize worth having, it was inevitable that Savimbi would resume his violent struggle after losing Angola's 1993 presidential election.

The all-or-nothing structure of the 1993 presidential election in Nigeria made it easier than it would otherwise have been for the military to succeed in annulling the election before the final results had been officially announced. Unsuccessful candidates had no immediate stake in the political outcome, and many readily acquiesced in the election's annulment in the hope of being able to run again.[68] In the Republic of the Congo in 1992, Denis Sassou-Nguesso succumbed to popular pressure and permitted multiparty elections; Sassou-Nguesso himself was a candidate for president and lost. After losing the election, he became obsessed with ousting his successor, Pascal Lissouba. He mounted a military campaign against Lissouba and regained power in June 1998.[69]

Directly elected presidents interpret their mandate as distinct from that of members of parliament and as entitling them to supervise parliament in its work. Another danger is that a directly elected president tends to be pressured into ethnic or regional exclusivity. Such presidents have a great incentive to offer special privileges to their own ethnic or regional groups as a means of ensuring reelection through a simple majority or plurality of popular votes. The arrangement in which a president is elected by parliament is more conducive to formal and informal power sharing. In such a system, even without grand coalition requirements, minority parties can influence the choice of president and the composition of the cabinet, particularly where there is no clear parliamentary majority.[70]

Given the factors discussed above, it would seem that a president elected by members of parliament would foster the feeling of greater participation in the election of all stakeholders in the country as represented in parliament. South Africa and Eritrea are examples of African countries that presently follow this arrangement. The adoption of the parliamentary system for the election of a president would be an extension of the proportional representation system to the elections for the office of president.

South Africa and Namibia are unique in the process they adopted in elaborating their national constitutions.[72] In both countries, constitutions were adopted by democratically elected constituent assemblies specially elected to elaborate a national constitution. This process ensured that in each of the countries, before the constitution was adopted, there were extensive consultations with the people and all the principal stakeholders.[73] It is imperative that a broad spectrum of people discuss and voice their opinions as to what the proper constitutional arrangements for the country should be. In Africa, the difficult question is how to do this effectively so as to prevent the manipulation of the system by the party in power. The South African experience teaches us that, to meet the need for the widest possible segment of the population and to make the widest possible consultations meaningful, the method of consultation must be properly structured so that there are meaningful and open discussions. An appropriate strategy would be to select a group of experts representative of the stakeholders in the country to create a draft constitution. The drafting should be informed by theme committees set up as part of the structure to facilitate public participation in the exercise.[74] For example, the South African constitutional exercise was organized along the following six themes: the character of the democratic state, the structure of the government, the relationship between the different levels of government, fundamental human rights, the judiciary and legal systems, and the specialized structures of government.[75]

The main task of the committees would typically be to gather, collate, and refine the views of the political parties and the public on specific issues and submit them to the constitution-making body. The draft constitution, as established by that body, should be based on a list of constitutional principles established and agreed to by all the stakeholders before the drafting exercise commences. The draft constitution should also be accompanied by commentaries analyzing each of its various aspects, highlighting options, and identifying problems that might be encountered in the application of the various suggested provisions. Such a document should then be subjected to public scrutiny in a forum such as a constitutional assembly that has been elected specifically to elaborate a constitution. The existence of a draft would limit the discussion to constitutional issues and would discourage petitioners from addressing the commission on every aspect of human endeavor.

After a constitution is elaborated, the next question that arises is how to involve the people in the adoption of the draft so as to give it maximum legitimacy. The supreme law of the land should not be adopted using the same procedures as those that are available for ordinary legislation.[76] Two methods have been used in the adoption of constitutions in Africa in the postcolonial period: adoption through a two-thirds majority in parliament and adoption through a constituent assembly or national referendum. It could be argued that the adoption of a constitution through a constituent assembly or referendum is unnecessary, as the enactment of a constitution is the legislative preserve of the legislature.[77]

Whether a legislature has the power to enact a constitution is not the issue. The real question is, How do you ensure that the sovereign will of the people, on which the edifice of democracy rests, occupies center stage in the process of producing a legitimate, credible, and enduring constitution? If anything, the process of consulting the people strengthens parliament, as it implies an unequivocal acceptance of the fact that the people delegate parliament's powers. The relationship between parliament and the people can only endure when it is realized and accepted that the people are supreme. Therefore, in matters of great national importance, such as the adoption of a national constitution, parliament must consult the people and defer to their wishes; the people, after all, are the source of popular sovereignty.[78] A successful constitution is one that obtains legitimization by popular will.[79] Popular democracy demands the institutionalization of a culture of consultation and reciprocal control with regard to law making and the use of power and privileges. The adoption of a constitution through referendum is one of the most transparent ways of furthering the culture of consultation in a democracy.

Besides, requiring a two-thirds vote in parliament to approve a constitution is not an effective safeguard against the adoption of an unpopular or unfair constitution or amendments to it. The two-thirds majority requirement is often within the reach of the largest party in parliament, especially in a winner-take-all electoral system.[80] In practice the requirement is therefore not much more than the simple majority required for ordinary law making. In order to safeguard democracy, much more should be required to effect a constitutional amendment than the will of the majority party in parliament. Popular consultation in the form of a referendum should in fact be entrenched in African constitutional practice as a mechanism for obtaining the mandate of the people on constitutional matters and as a deterrent to amendments. In addition, the involvement of the people in the adoption of a national constitution is an educational experience for them and enables them to focus on the contents of the constitution in a manner they would not have done otherwise. Once adopted, the constitution should not be subject to willful amendments. To emphasize this point, the Namibia constitution has adopted a novel approach. It provides that the provisions of the bill of rights within the constitution may not be diminished through amendments and that any such purported repeal or amendment shall be invalid.[81] Recent events in Namibia to amend the constitution and remove the two-term limitation on the presidency in order to facilitate the incumbent president serving a third term are regrettable and can only serve to undermine the sanctity of the Namibian constitution and the development of democracy in that country.[82] If the continent is to respond successfully to the needs of its people and realize its dreams of rapid economic development and political stability, it will have to apply careful thought and inquiry to the proper organization of political, economic, and administrative institutions to ensure the proper governance of the nation-state.[83]

Conclusion

Most of today's conflicts in Africa are not wars between the contending states of former years nor wars of secession, but take place within existing states. Many stem from the competition for resources, recognition, and power and are inextricably bound up with concepts of identity and nationalism. While these conflicts may appear very different from place to place, they often have at their base similar issues of unmet needs and of the necessity to accommodate the interests of majorities and minorities alike. If a continent is to respond successfully to these issues and the needs of its people and realize its dreams of rapid economic development and political stability, it will have to apply careful thought and inquiry to the proper organizations of political, economic, and administrative institutions to ensure the proper governance of the state. In addition, African states have to take measures to cultivate a democratic culture in their countries. Clear ways and means of nation building and promoting the culture and habit of democratic governance must be developed, as well as an ethos of human rights and obligations, cooperative governance, and multicultural tolerance. Whether or not democratic governance is established in Africa will depend on the development of political systems that give people a sense of ownership of the political process. The transition from authoritarianism to greater participation in political decision making requires sustained effort. The enormity of the challenge should not be underestimated. But concerted efforts to overcome the obstacles could ensure that democratic procedures and institutions are developed and that they play an important role in addressing conflicts and thereby ensure that stability is attainable.

Notes

1. United Nations Report of the Secretary-General, *The Causes of Conflict and the Promotion of Durable Peace and Sustainable Development in Africa,* (S/-) SG Report on Africa, 1998.

2. For a discussion of Africa's economic situation, see Adebayo Adedeji, "The Leadership Challenge for Improving the Economic and Social Situation of Africa" (paper presented at the Africa Leadership Forum, Ota, Nigeria, October 24–November 1, 1988); Aguibou Y. Yansané, ed., *Prospects for Recovery and Sustainable Development in Africa* (Westport, Conn.: Greenwood Press,

1996); World Bank, *Sub-Saharan Africa: From Crisis to Sustainable Growth* (Washington, D.C.: World Bank, 1989).

3. World Bank, *Accelerated Development in Sub-Saharan Africa: An Agenda for Action* (Washington, D.C.: World Bank, 1981); Organization of African Unity, *The Lagos Plan of Action for the Implementation of the Monrovia Strategy for the Economic Development of Africa* adopted by the Second Extra Ordinary Assembly of the OAU Heads of State and Government Devoted to Economic Matters, Lagos, Nigeria, April 28–29, 1980 (Addis Ababa: Organization of African Unity, 1980).

4. World Bank, *Sub-Saharan Africa;* Julius Nyerere, "Africa Exists in the Economic South," *Development and Social Economic Progress* 41 (3) (1988): 7–8; United Nations Economic Commission for Africa (UNECA), "Africa Alternative Framework to Structural Adjustment Programs for Socio-Economic Recovery and Transformation," E/ECA/CM.15/6/Rev.3.

5. UNECA, "Africa Alternative Framework," 45.

6. Karl Lavrencic, "Food for Africa," *New Africa* 137 (90) (February 1979).

7. In fact, as Douglas G. Anglin has observed, it can be argued that Africa has slipped into one of the most violent phases of its post-independence history, with political struggles spilling across borders as states interfere militarily in their neighbors' affairs in ways once uncommon. He mentions a number of instances where neighboring states have intervened in internal conflicts. Douglas G . Anglin, "Conflict in Sub-Saharan Africa," *Rapport annuel sur les conflits internationaux 1995–1996,* Institut québécois des hautes études internationales, Université Laval, Québec, Canada, 1996.

8. For example, in 1890, Lord Salisbury, the British prime minister, remarked at a dinner that followed the conclusion of the Anglo-French convention that established spheres of influence in West Africa that "we have been engaged in drawing lines upon maps where no white man's foot ever trod; we have been giving away mountains and rivers and lakes to each other, only hindered by the small impediment that we never really knew exactly where the mountains and rivers and lakes were." M. Mukuwa Wa Mukua, "Why Redraw the Map of Africa ? A Moral and Legal Inquiry," 16 *Michigan J of Int'l L* 1135 (1995), quoting Joseph C. Anene, *The International Boundaries of Nigeria, 1865–1960* (New York: Humanities Press, 1970), 3.

9. Elizabeth Colson, *Seven Tribes of British Central Africa* (Manchester, UK: Manchester University Press, 1959); Max Gluckman, *Politics, Law, and Ritual in Tribal Society* (Oxford: Basil Blackwell, 1965); Isaak Dore, "Constitutionalism and the Post-Colonial State in Africa: A Rawlsian Approach," 41 *St. Louis U L J* 1302 (1997).

10. Max Gluckman, *The Judicial Process among the Barotse of Northern*

Rhodesia (Manchester, UK: Manchester University Press, on behalf of Institute for Social Research, University of Zambia, 1967), 7. See also, Mutumba Mainga, *Bulozi under the Luyana Kings* (London: Longmans, 1973).

11. See Robert Rotberg, *The Rise of Nationalism in Central Africa: The Making of Malawi and Zambia, 1873–1964* (Cambridge, Mass.: Harvard University Press, 1965), 303; Richard Seymour Hall, *Zambia* (Lusaka: Longmans of Zambia, 1964).

12. See generally, A. J. Wills, *An Introduction to the History of Central Africa* (London: Oxford University Press, 1973); L. F. G. Anthony, *North of the Zambezi: The Story of Northern Rhodesia* (Lusaka: Northern Rhodesia Information Dept., in association with the Publications Bureau of Northern Rhodesia and Nyasaland, 1953); Lewis H. Gann, *The Birth of a Plural Society, The Development of Northern Rhodesia under the British South Africa Company, 1894–1914* (Manchester, UK: Manchester University Press on behalf of the Rhodes-Livingstone Institute, 1958); Lewis H. Gann, *History of Northern Rhodesia, Early Days to 1953* (London: Chatto and Windus, 1964).

13. Robert B. Seidman, "Drafting for the Rule of Law: Maintaining Legality in Developing Countries," 12 *Yale J of Int'l L* 85 (1987).

14. Robert B. Seidman, "Perspectives on Constitution-Making: Independence Constitution for Namibia and South Africa," 3 *Lesotho Law Journal* 45 (1987).

15. Okoth Ogendo, "Property Systems and Social Organization in Africa: An Essay on the Relative Position of Women under Indigenous and Received Law," in *The Individual Under African Law: Proceedings of the First All-Africa Law Conference*, ed. Peter Nanyenya-Takirambudde (Private Bag, Kwaluseni, Swaziland: University of Swaziland Department of Law, 1982), 47; Kwamena Bentsi-Enchil, "Do African Systems of Land Tenure Require a Special Terminology?" Northwestern University Program of African Studies, reprint series, no. 7 (1966). In this paper Bentsi-Enchil discuses the colonial heritage in land issues.

16. See Cherry Gertzel, Carolyn Baylies, and Morris Szeftel, *The Dynamics of the One-Party State in Zambia* (Manchester, UK: Manchester University Press, 1984). In their analysis of factors that led to the introduction of the one-party system in Zambia the authors note that the influences of the colonial legacy of bureaucratic authoritarianism continues in many parts of Africa. Isaak Dore observes that the imperfections of postcolonial constitutions were in part a reflection of the fact that those who prepared the colonies for independence were themselves not democratic nor ignorant or insensitive to the prevailing social and cultural dynamics of the societies they had colonized. Isaak Dore, "Constitutionalism and the Post-Colonial State in Africa: A Rawlsian Approach," 41 *St. Louis U L J* 1301 (1997).

17. Isaak Dore, "Constitutionalism."

18. Gertzel, Baylies, and Szeftel, *Dynamics of the One-Party State;* A. Yusuf, "Reflections on the Fragility of State Institutions in Africa," 2 *African Yearbook of Int'l L* 2–8 (1994). See also L. S. Zimba, "The Origins and Spread of One-Party States in Commonwealth Africa: Their Impact on Personal Liberties. A Case Study of the Zambian Model," in *Law in Zambia,* ed. Muna Ndulo (Nairobi: East African Pub. House, 1984), 113; *Nkumbula v. Attorney General* (1972) Z.R., 3.

19. B. O. Nwabueze, "Our March to Constitutional Democracy," Guardian Lecture, July 24, 1989; also published in *Law and Practice,* Journal of Nigerian Bar Association (August 1989), 19–38. Robert B. Seidman, "Perspectives on Constitution-Making: Independence Constitutions for Namibia and South Africa," 3 *Lesotho Law Journal* 45 (1987).

20. Museveni's main justification for his movement system in Uganda is that political parties form on the basis of ethnicity. See Yoweri K. Museveni, *What Is Africa's Problem?* (Minneapolis: University of Minnesota Press, 2000), 42. He observes that one of the biggest factors weakening Africa is tribalism and other forms of sectarianism and that in African politics tribalism is always emphasized. The secretary-general of the United Nations has observed that this is compounded by the fact that the framework of colonial laws and institutions which most states inherited had been designed to exploit local divisions, not to overcome them. See *Causes of Conflict and the Promotion of Durable Peace and Sustainable Development in Africa,* Report of the UN Secretary-General to the Security Council, 1998.

21. Simbi V. Mubako, "Single Party Constitution: A Search for Unity and Development," 5 *Zambia Law Journal* 67 (1973); Republic of Zambia, *Report of the National Commission on the Establishment of a One-Party-Participatory Democracy in Zambia* (Lusaka: National Commission on the Establishment of a One-Party-Participatory Democracy in Zambia, 1972).

22. Gertzel, Baylies, and Szeftel, *Dynamics of the One-Party State;* J. M. Mwanakatwe, *End of Kaunda Era* (Lusaka: Multimedia Zambia, 1994), 101.

23. See UN Secretary-General's Report to the United Nations Security Council, September 1998. See also Ted R. Gurr and Barbara Harff, *Ethnic Conflict in World Politics* (Boulder, Colo.: Westview Press, 1994).

24. United Nations Conference on Trade and Development (UNCTAD), *Foreign Investment in Africa,* UNCTAD/DTCI/19, Current Studies, series A, no. 28, 1995, p. 3.

25. *Foreign Direct Investment in Africa* (New York: United Nations [UNCTAD/DTCI/19], 1995).

26. World Bank, *Sub-Saharan Africa.*

27. Anglin, "Conflict."

28. See Republic of Zambia, *Report of the Constitutional Review Commission*

(Lusaka: Government Printer, 1995). Chapter 2 of the report reviews the constitutional history of Zambia. The 1964 Zambian constitution was provided for in Schedule 2 to the Zambian Independence Order, 1964, promulgated by Her Majesty in Council under the provisions of the Foreign Jurisdiction Act, 1890.

29. The 1973 constitution of Zambia is 291 pages long and contains well over 130 articles, each with several subsections. John Hatchard and Peter Slinn, "Towards an African Zimbabwean Constitution?" in *Building Constitutional Orders in Sub-Saharan Africa* (Valparaiso, Ind.: International Third World Legal Studies Association and Valparaiso University School of Law, 1988), 119.

30. Republic of Zambia, *Report of the Constitutional Review Commission;* Government of Tanzania, *Report of the Presidential Commission on the Establishment of a Democratic One-Party State* (Dar-es-Salaam: Government Printer, 1964); Republic of Zambia, *One-Party-Participatory Democracy.*

31. See *Report of Citizen's Convention on the Draft Constitution,* Lusaka, Zambia, Mulungushi International Conference Centre, March 1–10, 1996. See also Alex Vines and Peter Nanyenya-Takirambudde, *Zambia and Human Rights in the Third Republic* (New York: Human Rights Watch/Africa, 1996), 13.

32. Republic of Zambia, *Report of the Constitutional Review Commission,* 3.

33. Rhoda Howard, in commenting on the issue of cultural relativism, social change, and human rights concludes that during five centuries of contact between Africa and the Western world, social changes have been introduced that increasingly undermine any social structure or cultural uniqueness Africa might once have possessed. Howard, *Human Rights in Commonwealth Africa* (Totowa, N.J.: Rowman and Littlefield, 1986), 16. Yansané observes that colonialism destroyed many indigenous institutions by transforming non-European societies into European replicas. Aguibou Y. Yansané, ed., *Prospects for Recovery and Sustainable Development in Africa* (Westport, Conn.: Greenwood Press, 1996), 7. See also Adrien Wing, "Towards Democracy in a New South Africa," 16 *Michigan J Int'l L* 690 (1995).

34. Zimba, "Origins," 119. For example, in Kenya the postcolonial government justified the one-party state on the basis that "Here we seek out the modern constitutional form most suited to our traditional needs. Our people have always governed their affairs by looking to an elected council of elders, headed by their own chosen leader, giving them strong and wise leadership. That tradition which is an Africanism will be preserved in this new constitution." J. B. Ojwang, *Constitutional Development in Kenya: Institutional Adaptation and Social Change* (Nairobi: Acts Press, 1990), 79.

35. Simbi V. Mubako, "Zambia's Single-Party Constitution—A Search for Unity and Development," 5 *Zambia Law Journal* 67 (1973).

36. Richard Simeon, "The Structures of Intergovernmental Relations"

(paper presented at the International Round Table on Democratic Constitutional Development, Pretoria, South Africa, July 17–20, 1995).

37. Ann Seidman, "Toward an Alternative Development Strategy," in Yansané, ed., *Prospects*, 263.

38. S. M. Shafaeddin, "The Impact of Trade Liberalization on Export and GDP Growth in Least Developed Countries," UNCTAD Discussion Papers no. 85 (Geneva: UNCTAD, 1994).

39. Andrew Reynolds, "Constitutional Engineering in Southern Africa," *Journal of African Democracy* 6 (1) (1995): 86–100.

40. *Post* (Lusaka, Zambia), October 29, 1997.

41. *Report of the Commonwealth Observer Group to the South African Elections, End of Apartheid, 26–29 April 1994,* United Nations Observer Mission in South Africa (UNOMSA), 1994; *Final Report of the United Nations Observer Mission in South Africa to the United Nations Secretary-General, 26 May 1994,* UNOMSA, 1994. Both reports cite difficulties encountered in organizing the South African elections that were due to the enormity of the task of organizing the first-ever democratic elections.

42. Naomi Chazan, *Politics and Society in Contemporary Africa* (Boulder, Colo.: L. Rienner Publishers, 1988), 138.

43. See Human Rights Watch, "Zambia: Elections and Human Rights in the Third Republic," *Human Rights Watch Publications* 8 no. 4(A) (December 1996) or http:www.hrw.org/summaries/s.zambia96n.html. This is a report on the 1996 Zambian elections. The May 1998 elections in Lesotho, which had been pronounced free and fair by international observers and in which the opposition won only one seat, were later found by the Langa Commission of Inquiry to have been riddled with irregularities. See *Daily Mail and Guardian* (Johannesburg) October 12, 1998. The elections led to a crisis, which led to a complete collapse of law and order in Lesotho and to military intervention by the Southern African Development Community.

44. Nwabueze, "March to Constitutional Democracy," 17.

45. B. des Villiers, "An Electoral System for the New South Africa," in *Constitution-Making in the New South Africa,* ed. Alexander Johnston, Sipho Shezi, and Gavin Bradshaw (London: Leicester University Press, 1993), 29.

46. According to Vernon Bogdanor, it seems that a national culture unified both ideologically and ethnically may be a precondition for the successful working of the plurality and majority methods. Vernon Bogdanor, *The Blackwell Encyclopaedia of Political Institutions* (Oxford: Blackwell Reference, 1987).

47. R. P. Meyer, Republic of South Africa, Debates of the Constitutional Assembly, January 24 to February 20, 1995, no. 1, p. 14.

48. Aide Memoire, International Conference on Governance for Sustainable

Growth and Equity, United Nations Development Program, New York, July 28–30, 1997.

49. Apolo Nsibambi, "The Interface among the Capable State, the Private Sector, and Civil Society in Acquiring Food Security" (keynote paper, Conference on Building for the Capable State in Africa, Institute for African Development, Cornell University, October 24–28, 1977).

50. Patricia Armstrong, "Human Rights and Multilateral Development Banks: Governance Concerns in Decision Making," 88 *Am. Soc'y Int'l L Proc* 271.

51. See Nsibambi, "Capable State."

52. Justice Learned Hand, *The Spirit of Liberty* (New York: Knopf, 1960), 189–90.

53. Muna Ndulo, "The 1996 Zambian Constitution and the Search for a Durable Democratic Constitutional Order in Africa," 5 *African Yearbook of Int'l L* 174 (1997).

54. See preamble, *European Charter of Local Self-Government,* Europe Treaty Series (ETS) no. 122 or http://www.xs4all.nl/~tonstam/handvest.html.

55. Nana Wereko Ampem II, "The Role of Chiefs and Chieftaincy in the Development of a Democratic Constitutional Ghana" (paper presented at the International Round Table on Democratic Constitutional Development, Pretoria, South Africa, July 17–20, 1995). At various points some African countries have abolished chieftaincy only to reinstate it. Tanzania and Uganda are cases in point. In the South African constitutional negotiations the question of what to do with traditional institutions was a major point of discussion. In the end the South African constitution provides for the recognition of traditional institutions but leaves it to national legislation to provide for the role of traditional leadership as an institution. This does not really integrate them into the mainstream South African postapartheid political system. See South African Constitution, 1996, ch. 12, "Traditional Leaders," Article 211 (1), (2), (3); Article 212 (1), (2). The South Africa government recently announced the appointment of a commission to look into the role of traditional leaders. *Daily Mail and Guardian* (Johannesburg), October 23, 1998. The Ugandan constitution takes the same approach. It states, "As subject to the provisions of this constitution, the institution of traditional leader or cultural leader may exist in any area of Uganda in accordance with the culture, customs and traditions or wishes and aspirations of the people to whom it applies." Constitution of Uganda, 1996, Article 246 (1).

56. F. D. Lugard, *The Dual Mandate in British Tropical Africa* (Hamden, Conn.: Archon Books, 1965), 149–50.

57. T. Nhlapo, "Accommodating Traditional Forms of Governance in a Con-

stitutional Democracy: A Motivation" (paper presented at the International Round Table on Democratic Constitutional Development, Pretoria, South Africa, July 17–20, 1995).

58. Muna Ndulo, "Liability of a Paramour in Damages for Adultery in Customary Law," 28 *African Social Research* 28 (1981): 179; T. Nhlapo, "The African Family and Women's Rights: Friends or Foes?" *Acta Juridica* 135 (1991); Penelope Andrews, "The Stepchild of National Liberation: Women and Rights in the New South Africa," in *The Post-Apartheid Constitutions: Perspectives on South Africa's Basic Law,* ed. Penelope Andrews and Stephen Ellmann (Athens: Ohio University Press, 2001).

59. Thabo Mbeki, Republic of South Africa, Debates of the Constitutional Assembly, Capetown, South Africa, January 24 to February 20, 1995, no. 1, p. 11.

60. Much of the source of this discrimination is customary law. South Africa and Namibia have provisions in their constitutions that render invalid customary law that is in conflict with the constitution. This practice should be emulated. It gives the courts the ability to declare gender-insensitive customs and practices illegal and unenforceable. See Constitution of South Africa, Article 211 (3); Constitution of Namibia, 1989, Article 66 (1).

61. For an elaboration of some of these issues, see James C. H. Daul, "Developing Constitutional Orders in Sub-Saharan Africa: An Unofficial Report," *Third World Legal Studies* (1988): 1–34. As L. M. Singhvi put it during the elaboration of the South African constitution, "A consistent framework of liberty and restraint is what the constitution assembly is called upon to create for South Africa so that the constitution may at once prove to be the anchor, the compass and the steering wheel for the ship of state" ("Democracy and the Constitution" [paper presented at the International Round Table on Democratic Constitutional Development, Pretoria, South Africa, July 17–20, 1995]).

62. See H. J. Simons, *African Women: Their Legal Status in South Africa* (Evanston: Northwestern University Press, 1968).

63. John Stuart Mill, *The Subjection of Women* (Philadelphia: Lippincott, 1869). For a discussion of Mill's views on this issue see David Held, *Models of Democracy* (Stanford, Calif.: Stanford University Press, 1996), 111. The inequality of the sexes has deprived Africa of a vast pool of talent. See also Penelope Andrews, "Affirmative Action in South Africa: Some Theoretical and Practical Issues," in *The Constitution of South Africa from a Gender Perspective,* ed. Sandra Liebenberg (Cape Town: Community Law Centre at the University of the Western Cape, in association with David Philip, 1995), 49.

64. Platform for Action and the Beijing Declaration, Fourth Conference on Women, Beijing, September 4–15, 1995, p. 17.

65. Thabo Mbeki, Deputy President of South Africa, Republic of South

Africa, Debates of the Constitutional Assembly, January 24 to February 20, 1995, no. 1, p. 10.

66. For a more detailed discussion of some of these issues, see Kwamena Bentsi-Enchil, "Civitas de Africana: Realizing the African Political Dream," 2 (1) *Zambia Law Journal* 65–86 (1969).

67. Matthew Shugart and John Carey, *Presidents and Assemblies: Constitutional Design and Electoral Dynamics* (Cambridge: Cambridge University Press, 1992), 28–43.

68. Ann Reid, "Conflict Resolution in Africa: Lessons from Angola," *INR Foreign Affairs Brief* (1993); Ian Campbell, "Nigeria's Failed Transition: 1993 Presidential Election," *Journal of Contemporary African Studies* 12 (1994): 182.

69. Anglin, "Conflict."

70. Siri Gloppen, *South Africa: The Battle over the Constitution* (Aldershot, UK; Brookfield, Vt.: Ashgate/Dartmouth, 1997), 217–18.

71. Constitution of South Africa, 1996, Article 86. Article 41 of the Eritrean constitution provides that the president shall be elected from among the members of the National Assembly by a vote of the majority of its members. A candidate for the office of the president must be nominated by at least 20 percent of all the members of the National Assembly. Constitution of Eritrea, 1996.

72. See J. Cottrell, "Constitution of Namibia: An Overview," 35 *Journal of African Law* 1–2 (1991); Johnston, Shezi, and Bradshaw, *Constitution-Making;* Commonwealth Observer Group, *The End of Apartheid, Report of the Commonwealth Observer Group to the South Africa Elections, 26–29 April, 1994* (London: Commonwealth Secretariat, 1994); UNOMSA, *Final Report;* Eric Bjornlund, *Nation Building: The UN and Namibia* (Washington, D.C.: National Democratic Institute for International Affairs, 1990).

73. In a study carried out in the mid-1990s, 60 percent of the adult population of South Africa had heard about the Constituent Assembly. When asked whether they believed the Constituent Assembly would treat their submission seriously, 41 percent said yes. An amazing 57 percent of the respondents believed that the constitution would guarantee freedom and equality for all South Africans. Gloppen, *South Africa,* 264–65.

74. South Africa adopted this method. See Republic of South Africa, Debates of the Constitutional Assembly, January 24–February 20, Capetown, South Africa, 1995, p. 3.

75. H. Ebrahim, "The Process of Drafting South Africa's New Constitution" (paper presented at the International Round Table on Democratic Constitutional Development, Pretoria, South Africa, July 17–20, 1995).

76. Republic of Zambia, *Report of the Constitutional Review Commission,* 64.

77. Most African constitutions allow for the amendment of the constitution

with a two-thirds majority. This is not a significant constraint; the required majority is easily obtained in systems where the opposition is often token. See Constitution of Zambia, 1991, Article 72. The government of Zambia argued that way with respect to the 1996 constitution. See Republic of Zambia, *The Mwanakatwe Constitutional Review Commission Supplement,* Government Paper no. 1, 1995.

78. B. O. Nwabueze, *Constitutionalism in the Emergent States* (Rutherford, N.J.: Fairleigh Dickinson University Press, 1973), 135.

79. Ibid., 25.

80. Muna Ndulo and R. B. Kent, "Constitutionalism in Zambia: Past, Present and Future," 40 (2) *Journal of African Law* 257 (1996).

81. Constitution of Namibia, 1989, Article 131.

82. *Daily Mail and Guardian* (Johannesburg), October 31, 1998.

83. But, as Siri Gloppen has observed, "neither ethnic conflict, nor (and even less so) problems of poverty, inequality, and violence are solved by enacting a constitution, not even if the ideal constitution could be found. Some constitutional structures provide more adequate frameworks, however, within which these problems may be addressed." This is what is critical in this whole matter of constitution making. Gloppen, *South Africa*, 264–65.

8

Political Centralization and Social Conflict in Indonesia

Michael Malley

SINCE PRESIDENT SOEHARTO resigned in 1998, after more than three decades in power, violent conflicts have displaced hundreds of thousands of people and resulted in the deaths of thousands more throughout Indonesia. Although all of these conflicts reflect deep-seated ethnic and religious differences, they can be grouped into two broad categories according to the principal dimension along which violence is oriented. In some cases, violence is directed upward at the state, generally to seek independence. In other cases, violence occurs between two or more coexisting communities, usually in response to intensified competition for access to economic resources. During the past two years, it has become conventional to describe the former as vertical and the latter as horizontal conflicts. The major vertical conflicts include predominantly Catholic East Timor's successful separatist struggle, as well as ongoing independence movements in staunchly Muslim Aceh and largely Protestant and animist Irian Jaya. Among the horizontal conflicts, the most notable cases pit Muslims against Christians in Maluku and indigenous Dayaks against immigrant Madurese in West Kalimantan.

Ethnic and religious differences are hardly limited to the regions that have experienced violent conflicts during the past few years. As Hildred Geertz famously noted, "There are over three hundred different ethnic groups in Indonesia, each with its own cultural identity, and more than two hundred and fifty distinct languages are spoken . . . nearly all the important world religions are represented, in addition to a wide range of indigenous ones."[1] No effort has been made to record people's ethnicity since the last Dutch colonial census was conducted in 1930. Since then, the closest measures of ethnic group identity are surveys of language use at home. These tend to indicate that no more than 45 percent of the population is Javanese, about 15 percent is Sundanese, and 7 or 8 percent is Madurese. No other linguistic group comprises more than 5 percent of the country's population, and nearly all ethnic groups have identifiable homelands. The major exceptions are the communities of Chinese immigrants and their descendants, who live mainly in urban areas where they dominate commerce.

The three largest ethnic groups are concentrated on Java and the nearby island of Madura. Together these islands constitute just 7 percent of the country's land area, but account for nearly 60 percent of the country's 215 million people. With a territory about the size of Greece, the islands are among the most densely populated areas anywhere in the world. The rest of the population inhabits nearly half of the thirteen thousand islands that stretch five thousand kilometers along the equator and comprise the world's largest archipelagic state and fourth most populous country. To cope with population pressure on Java, colonial Dutch and independent Indonesian governments have promoted interisland migration. However, even at this policy's peak in the 1970s and 1980s, only about three million people moved out of Java, while about one and a half million, drawn by rapid industrialization, moved in the opposite direction.[2] About one-fifth of the country's people live in Sumatra and speak fifteen major languages and many minor ones. The national language, *bahasa Indonesia*, derives from the Malay language spoken in coastal Sumatra rather than the language of any major group. In Kalimantan and the eastern islands of Sulawesi, the Malukus, the Lesser Sundas, and Papua linguistic groups tend to be smaller.

Indonesia is not an Islamic state, even though 87 percent of its citizens are Muslim. Instead, it requires citizens to profess a belief in God and recognizes several religions. These include Protestantism (6 percent), Catholicism (3 percent), Hinduism (2 percent), and Buddhism (1 percent). Hinduism is nearly synonymous with Balinese identity, Protestantism with the Minahasans of North Sulawesi, and Catholicism with the people of Flores. In other parts of the country, ethnic groups are divided along religious lines. For instance, certain Batak clans in North Sumatra are Protestant, while others are Muslim. The Ambonese are similarly divided. On Java, Christianity is more common among Javanese than Sundanese or Madurese. The main adherents of Buddhism are Chinese, but many Chinese are Christian.

Despite this tremendous cultural diversity, few observers of Indonesian politics considered regional or ethnic differences to be important influences on politics during the Soeharto era (1966–98). For the most part, such conflicts were considered part of the past. Although such issues had dominated politics in the 1950s and early 1960s, it seemed that political and economic changes had eliminated their influence by the 1970s and 1980s. By the early 1990s, prominent scholars noted that "signs of national integration are everywhere," and suggested that rapid industrialization had made rural-urban and class differences much more important aspects of national politics than ethnicity.[3]

Since ethnic and religious identities change relatively slowly, they cannot account for sudden changes in the level of violent conflict. This chapter examines the conflicts that have occurred during the past few years and proposes an explanation for their sudden outbreak. It begins with a pair of observations: the intensification of social conflict occurred as Soeharto's grip on power weakened, and all the major conflicts occurred outside the island of Java. This fact strongly suggests that the centralization of political power under Soeharto is an important source of current conflicts. This chapter finds that much of the recent violence stems from Soeharto-era policies that conferred material benefits in ways that sustained and sharpened generally accepted group identities, and that changes in these policies, due in part to a change in regime but also to an economic crisis, have been the main spurs to recent conflicts.

The Legacy of Political Centralization

One of the most distinctive characteristics of the Indonesian state under Soeharto was its high level of political centralization.[4] The president controlled the appointment of all twenty-seven governors and more than three hundred district heads. During the 1980s and 1990s, nearly half of these officials were active or retired military officers. Through the Department of Home Affairs, the national government managed politics and administration at the provincial, district, subdistrict, and village levels. It vetted candidates for local legislatures and then told them which laws to pass. The central government provided more than three-quarters of the typical provincial government budget and more than four-fifths of the average district government budget, as well as instructions for spending those subsidies. Alongside the provincial- and district-level bureaucracies, the national government constructed a parallel structure. Each department of the national government, such as agriculture or public works, established branch offices that enabled Jakarta to supervise as well as bypass regional governments' own bureaucracies. To ensure that the national government's orders were followed, the army refined a territorial command structure that mirrored the structure of civilian government right down to the village level. Through these structures, the central government offered abundant carrots and wielded powerful sticks, which made local elites more responsive to the wishes and interests of national leaders than local electorates.

The processes that produced this centralized state of affairs also marginalized the role of ethnicity and religion in Indonesian politics. Before transferring sovereignty to Indonesia in 1949, the Netherlands created more than a dozen small states outside Java and required the new republic to adopt a federal system that protected these states. Less than a year later, the national government peacefully eliminated the federal structure and replaced it with a unitary one that reduced the authority of regional governments. During the 1950s, however, several regions outside Java rebelled against the national government. Some demanded that the country become an Islamic state, while others objected to the rising influence of communism on Java. In many regions, however, the reasons were economic. The national government obtained the bulk of its revenues from taxes on trade, most of which was controlled by the export-oriented plantation economies in Sumatra and Sulawesi, and spent most of that money on the densely populated island of Java. By the early 1960s, the army managed to quell these rebellions. Although a system of "de facto federalism" prevailed until the late 1960s, from that point forward the process of political centralization advanced steadily.[5]

Soeharto's ability to achieve a higher level of political centralization than his predecessor, Sukarno (1945–66), was due partly to the achievements of the army before he took power in 1966 and partly to an influx of new financial resources afterward. Through its confrontation with regional rebels in the 1950s, the army became stronger and more united. It strengthened further in the mid-1960s, when it purged left-leaning members from its own ranks and led the massacres of half a million suspected leftists throughout the country, thereby eliminating its chief political rival, the Indonesian Communist Party, and paving Soeharto's way to the presidency. Once Soeharto had taken control of the government, two other factors enabled him to pursue the goal of centralization more aggressively than Sukarno ever had. One was easy access to foreign aid, which anticommunist countries granted him in liberal amounts. Another was the even greater amount of revenues he acquired from oil and natural gas exports once prices began to rise in the early 1970s. These funds enabled him to secure the cooperation, or at least acquiescence, of regional elites as he strengthened the central government's control over regional politics. The result was not just a centralized political and military structure, but also a centralized structure of patronage. After Soeharto's first decade in power, a veteran observer of Indonesian politics concluded that "the essential unity of the political system can [now] be taken for granted."[6]

The centralization of political power affected provinces, districts, and villages on Java as well as on other islands, but people outside Java tended to view the process as synonymous, or nearly so, with Javanization. Several aspects of national government policy provided a strong basis for this view. One was the government sponsored transmigration program mentioned in the introduction above. Although both the Dutch and Sukarno had pursued similar policies, Soeharto was able to do so much more vigorously during the 1970s and early 1980s, when the government was flush with oil revenues. The three million people who left Java between 1970 and 1980 amounted to a very small proportion of that island's population, which now stands at more than 110 million. However, transmigrants from Java usually accounted for a large proportion of the population in regions where they settled. Moreover, people already living in those regions often resented the benefits, meager though they were, that the transmigrants received from the government to begin their lives anew. The chief benefit, of course, was land, and the national government's frequent disregard for traditional land rights added to the resentment of the people who previously used the land on which transmigrants were settled.

Another element of government policy that disrupted societies outside Java also concerned land use. The Indonesian constitution reserves all natural resources to state control. Under Soeharto, as during the 1950s, the national government obtained most of its revenues from sources outside Java. For much of the 1970s and 1980s, this meant oil and natural gas produced in Sumatra and Kalimantan. In addition, however, it used its authority to grant logging permits and to regulate the development of large-scale plantations to benefit investors close to the president and his family. As in the case of transmigration, Jakarta rarely paid heed to traditional forms of land rights when granting permits to well-connected investors.

The national government also treated Java as the country's cultural center. In part, this simply reflected the cultural orientations of Indonesia's first two presidents, Sukarno and Soeharto. Both were Javanese and tended to speak in Javanese idioms. It also reflected the preponderant demographic weight of the Javanese. Javanese officials dominated the civil service and frequently were sent to govern distant regions. Coming from urban areas, they viewed the sparsely populated islands as empty, and transmigration policies seemed eminently reasonable to them. Java's privileged place was also reflected in countless official mottoes, awards, and military commands that were given

Sanskrit-derived names more characteristic of Javanese than other Indonesian societies. As a result, the government's economic and social policies were not perceived outside Java merely as technocratic solutions to commonly recognized challenges, as government officials regularly claimed, but as the assertion of Javanese political supremacy over regional political and economic interests.

Under Soeharto, the government also acted in ways that systematically promoted not just Javanese culture, but Javanese notions of what constitutes culture.[7] In 1945 the authors of Indonesia's constitution recognized that the citizens of the new country had both pan-Indonesian and local or regional cultural identities, and they included a provision calling on the national government "to advance the national culture." Soeharto's government capitalized on that provision. Officially, the department of education and culture conceptualized the national culture not as a monolith but as a mosaic containing aspects of various regional and local cultures. To build a national culture from these regional cultures, it examined and documented a wide range of cultural practices. However, in order to determine which elements were "the best," and therefore deserved to be promoted and incorporated into a pan-Indonesian culture, various cultural practices were compared and measured against standards borrowed from Javanese culture.

The hierarchical ordering of cultural identities was not limited to Javanese over non-Javanese. It extended to the multiplicity of cultural identities found within various administrative regions. Public rituals, such as Independence Day celebrations, required culturally appropriate representatives of each region, and the construction of public buildings in "local" style required choosing among the various styles available. In practice, this often involved the subordination of many locally present cultural forms to another. North Sulawesi was represented far more by Christian Minahasans than Muslim Gorontalese, North Sumatra by Muslim Bataks than Christian Bataks or Muslim Malays. Riau province, to the south of North Sumatra, was associated with Malay culture, disregarding the variety of Malay cultures within the province as well as the strong presence of Minangkabau from neighboring West Sumatra.

To complement its policy of selectively promoting local cultures, the national government also adopted a policy of containment. In particular, it aimed to confine "local" cultures to private, subnational realms, while reserving the national, public realm to pan-Indonesian culture and identity. The tensions inherent in such a policy required constant management, and have left an ominous legacy to the post-Soeharto era. Until recently, subnational societies were permitted to celebrate their cultures in art, architecture, and music, but were denied the right to express political interests in those terms. After three decades, these restrictions have generated grievances among many groups. In some places, these are directed at groups within the same territory, as in Maluku and West Kalimantan. In other places, they are directed primarily at the national government, as in Aceh, East Timor, and Irian Jaya.

Major Cases of Violent Social Conflict since 1997

THE DAYAK-MADURESE CONFLICT IN WEST KALIMANTAN

Prior to 1997, violence between Dayaks and Madurese in the province of West Kalimantan was common but infrequent and limited. The Madurese are mostly Muslim and have been migrating to West Kalimantan (as well as other parts of Borneo) since the 1930s, and in large numbers since the early 1970s. The Dayaks, most of whom profess Christianity, are indigenous to Borneo. During January and February 1997, as many as five hundred people, mostly Madurese, were killed, and twenty-five thousand driven from their homes by Dayaks. The violence was remarkable for its savagery. Press accounts featured dismemberment and other forms of torture as well as cannibalism. In early 1999, Dayaks, now assisted by indigenous Muslim Malays, again attacked Madurese and over the course of four months about two hundred people on both sides were killed and thirty thousand Madurese displaced.[8]

Initially, the deep and readily observed cultural differences between the groups encouraged many to interpret the violence as mainly a function of ethnic differences. Common stereotypes hold that the Dayaks and Madurese are prone to certain forms of violence. The Madurese are famously hot-tempered, while the Dayaks are said to practice headhunting. On these grounds, Indonesian and foreign journalistic accounts often portrayed the violence as the result of inevitably clashing cultures or the enactment of traditional rites. However, even though the violence could be associated with some stereotypes, it defied many others. For instance, conflict did not follow religious lines: while the principal divide ran between Christian Dayak and Muslim Madurese, in the 1999 violence, the Muslim Malays allied themselves with the Dayaks against the Madurese. And while local Chinese communities often become targets during social conflicts elsewhere in Indonesia, the violence in West Kalimantan did not follow this pattern either.

As one of Soeharto's former transmigration ministers acknowledged in 1999, the conflict is best understood as a local response to the imposition of central control over three decades.[9] In the late 1960s, as part of the military's effort to eliminate communism, local army units mobilized Dayaks against rural-dwelling Chinese, who were suspected of communist sympathies. As a result of their participation in this effort, the Dayaks gained possession of prime agricultural land that the Chinese had tilled. Over the next three decades, however, an influx of migrants from Java, but especially Madura, eroded their control of these lands. In addition, the national government's centralization of political control over West Kalimantan diminished Dayaks' role in government and allowed the national government to open the province to large-scale logging of forests on which many Dayaks depended for their own livelihoods. Rivalry between the Dayaks and Madurese resulted in many conflicts since the 1970s, but while the national government remained strong it was able to limit the violence. In 1997, as Soeharto weakened, and in 1999, when the transition to a new regime was underway but incomplete, the national government no longer possessed the capacity to contain violence between these groups.

Since January 1999, violence between Christian and Muslim groups in the Maluku islands has claimed several thousand lives and turned more than half a million people into refugees. In the process, it has destroyed hundreds of villages and devastated the capital city of Maluku province, Ambon, where the violence began. As in the case of West Kalimantan, this violence has been remarkable for its savagery. Neighbors have fought each other, entire villages have been attacked and destroyed, and heads, severed from their bodies, displayed prominently.[10]

Initially, this conflict seemed primarily a sectarian one. It began in the city of Ambon with a Christian attack against Muslims on the holy day that celebrates the end of the Muslim fasting month, Ramadan. And it followed a string of incidents elsewhere in the country in which Christians and Muslims fought one another. In November 1998, a riot broke out in Jakarta in which Muslim youths killed several Christians from Ambon and destroyed thirteen churches after they heard a rumor that Ambonese Christians had destroyed a mosque. A week later, Christian youths in Kupang, the capital of West Nusatenggara province, responded by attacking Muslim immigrants from South Sulawesi, as well as their businesses, homes, and places of worship. And less than a week after that, apparently in response to the Kupang violence, Muslims torched a church in Makassar, the capital of South Sulawesi.

Since the incidents in Jakarta, Kupang, and Makassar were followed by two years of intense Christian-Muslim violence in Maluku, but not in other parts of the country where people of both faiths live, a deeper explanation of Maluku's trouble is needed. As in the case of West Kalimantan, the principal elements include immigration, as well as economic and political competition between the immigrant and native communities. Since colonial times, Christians dominated the region's major urban center, Ambon, as well as the bureaucracy. However, Christians' numerical superiority has eroded over the past thirty years as Muslims from Sulawesi migrated to Ambon and surrounding islands. Most of these migrants came on their own, drawn by economic opportunities in Maluku. As Muslims became more numerous and acquired a dominant role in the local economy, they also entered the local bureaucracy. In 1992, Soeharto appointed the first Muslim as governor of Maluku province, threatening the Christian community's political influence and its continued access to the patronage that Jakarta controlled. In 1997 the appointment of another Muslim governor from the same clan was followed by rumors that he had replaced dozens of Christian officials with Muslims. Amid the country's worsening political and economic crisis in 1997–98, tensions between the two communities also deteriorated. Still, it is widely believed that large-scale violence began only in January 1999 after powerful local and national politicians conspired to provoke it, in part to displace Muslim politicians and in part to demonstrate that the new civilian government in Jakarta was unable to maintain order, thereby creating an excuse for the old regime to return.[11]

While violence continued in Ambon, similar conflicts erupted in the northern Maluku islands. On the island of Halmahera, Muslim Makianese immigrants fought violently with native, mostly Christian Kao people. Relations between the two groups had been tense and occasionally violent ever since the national government resettled several thousand Makianese near the Kao in 1975, when a volcano threatened the Makianese. The island of Halmahera is predominantly Muslim, but Muslims are concentrated in the south and Christians in the north. Rather than resettle the Muslim Makianese with other Muslims, the national government placed them along the narrow isthmus that connects the Muslim and Christian parts of the island. Christians interpreted this as an effort to contain them and their religion. In August 1999 the district government acceded to a long-standing Makianese request that they be granted their own subdistrict. However, the new subdistrict was planned to include predominantly Christian villages too, and this incited Christian natives to violence against Muslim immigrants. Subsequently, the national government separated Halmahera and nearby islands from Maluku province to create a new province of North Maluku. This policy exacerbated local conflicts by creating new positions of political power over which warring factions could struggle. Conflicts in the northern and southern Maluku islands continued throughout 1999 and 2000.

EAST TIMOR'S VIOLENT ROUTE TO INDEPENDENCE

In May 1999 Indonesia's transitional president, B. J. Habibie, reached agreement with the United Nations to allow a UN-supervised referendum on the future status of East Timor. Although the ballot was conducted peacefully at the end of August, horrific violence followed in September. After nearly 80 percent of East Timorese voted in favor of independence, pro-Indonesia militias killed at least a thousand East Timorese and drove about one-third of the tiny territory's eight hundred and fifty thousand people out of their homes and across the border into Indonesian West Timor.[12]

In contrast to conflicts in West Kalimantan and Maluku, the violence that wracked East Timor in 1999 did not pit Christians against Muslims. For the most part, Roman Catholic East Timorese fought among themselves. Still, many observers viewed it as yet another instance of ethnic and religious conflict. The main reason was the sharp religious divide between the East Timorese and Indonesia's Muslim majority. However, although religion provided East Timorese with a common identity, the religious difference between them and the majority of Indonesians was certainly not the most important reason for their opposition to Indonesian rule.

Unlike all other territories incorporated into Indonesia, East Timor remained under Portuguese rule until the mid-1970s. Consequently, the people of East Timor did not participate in the same nationalist and anticolonial movements against Dutch colonialism, and never came to imagine themselves as part of a broader Indonesian nation. Likewise, prior to Portugal's precipitous decision in 1974 to decolonize the territory, few Indonesians imagined East Timor as properly a part of their country. However, fearful that leftist movements in the territory would gain power and turn it into a Southeast Asian Cuba, the staunchly anticommunist regime in Jakarta invaded the half-island in 1975. By the 1980s, it had crushed the East Timorese resistance, but in the process nearly a third of the small territory's population died of war-induced famine and disease. In 1976, Indonesia organized a "representative council" of East Timorese who requested Indonesia to accept the territory as its newest province. Despite widespread East Timorese collaboration with Indonesian rule, the United Nations continued to consider the territory as separate from Indonesia. And in the minds of most East Timorese, they remained a nation separate from Indonesia.

During the 1990s a new generation of East Timorese revitalized opposition to Indonesian rule. This generation resented Indonesia's rule for many reasons other than the brutality of its military during the 1970s. Most important were the lack of economic opportunity and continued repression. Indonesian bureaucrats filled many of the region's most important political posts, and migrants from Sulawesi and other islands dominated the marketplaces that the Indonesian government constructed. In 1995 violence between merchants from East Timor and Sulawesi led several thousand immigrants to flee to Sulawesi and Java. After Soeharto resigned the presidency in 1998, Indonesia's hold on East Timor weakened, people began to speak more openly of independence, and many more Indonesian migrants left the territory.

The Indonesian army considered its conquest of the territory one of its greatest achievements and strongly opposed its independence. To that end, it organized militias among East Timorese groups whose collaboration had enabled Indonesia to rule the territory. Fear of reprisals they might suffer if Indonesia surrendered its control, combined with logistical support from Indonesian army units, enabled these militias to conduct the scorched-earth policy described above. While this policy did not enable them to maintain their own positions of influence, it did allow the Indonesian armed forces to obtain revenge against an enemy they had been unable to defeat despite a quarter century of war and occupation.

ACEH'S REINVIGORATED REBELLION

In mid-1999, while attention was focused on the organization of a referendum on East Timorese independence, violence flared in Aceh between the Indonesian army and the pro-independence Free Aceh Movement. In addition to approximately five thousand people who were killed in the conflict between 1989 and 1998, nearly three hundred died during 1999 and, as fighting intensified, more than eight hundred during 2000. Tens of thousands more became refugees.[13]

The origins of Aceh's violent separatist movement are deep.[14] In the late 1940s the region played a leading role in Indonesia's revolution against Dutch colonialism but afterward did not enjoy as much autonomy from the national government as its leaders had expected. In their view the region was clearly unique and entitled to special treatment. It had been one of the last to submit to Dutch rule and did so only after three decades of bloody war. During the Japanese occupation in the early 1940s, it regained substantial autonomy. Although Dutch troops managed to regain control over much of their colony after Japan withdrew, they never did so in Aceh. In addition, the Acehnese believed then, as they continue to believe today, that they are more religiously devout than most other Indonesian Muslims, a view that most non-Acehnese Indonesians share.

Disappointed at their status within the Indonesian republic, Acehnese mounted a rebellion against the national government in the 1950s and won the status of a special region, as opposed to an ordinary province. President Sukarno agreed that Aceh's government would have authority over educational and religious matters, but during the next few decades the central government circumscribed this autonomy so tightly as to make it meaningless. In the Soeharto era, the region developed a new grievance against Jakarta. During the 1970s, the national authorities began to develop Aceh's rich natural gas reserves into a major export industry and revenue earner. In 1997 liquefied natural gas exports amounted to about $2 billion annually and accounted for nearly one-fifth of the country's total oil and gas exports. Nearly all this money went to the national government, the state oil and gas company, and foreign contractors.[15] The development, production, and export of natural gas from Aceh is conducted from an enclave in the territory that appears to most Acehnese as exclusive, wealthy, and largely non-Acehnese. Resentment fostered a short-lived rebellion in the late 1970s and a much more serious one in the late 1980s. By 1993, however, a brutal Indonesian military campaign was able to suppress most rebel activity.[16]

Following Soeharto's resignation, the Acehnese took advantage of Jakarta's weakening grip to publicize the atrocities Indonesian troops committed during their counterinsurgency operation in the early 1990s. Most prominently, they identified and uncovered mass graves into which Indonesian troops had thrown their victims several years earlier.[17] These revelations inflamed relations between Aceh and the national government and seem to have been a principal factor in keeping voter turnout in Aceh in the June 1999 general election below 70 percent, in contrast to a national figure slightly above 90 percent.[18] Jakarta's weakness also emboldened the Free Aceh Movement to recruit, train, and organize new members. The movement's leaders quickly managed to gain control over much of the countryside and stage attacks on Indonesian offices and personnel. A nonviolent movement also emerged in 1999 to demand Jakarta's approval of an East Timor–style referendum. In November it demonstrated the strength of opposition to Indonesian rule by organizing a rally in the provincial capital city that attracted nearly one-quarter of the province's four million people.[19] In contrast to the East Timorese, the Acehnese have much in common with the majority of Indonesians. They share a common religion and a common history of resistance to colonialism. For much of the past century, they have found ways to reconcile their Acehneseness with a sense of Indonesianness. Their principal grievances over the past fifty years have concerned Jakarta's excessive centralization of power. However, the harsh treatment that Indonesian armed forced meted out to Acehnese during the 1990s has made it more difficult to resolve the conflict simply by granting Aceh more autonomy over its religious and educational affairs and by granting it more control over local economic resources. Half a century of broken promises and continual exploitation have severely eroded Jakarta's credibility and reduced the opportunities for compromise and reconciliation.

Since Soeharto's fall, separatists in Irian Jaya, which they call Papua, have stepped up their efforts to achieve independence. As in Aceh, a nonviolent civilian movement has formed alongside an established military force, the Free Papua Organization. In contrast to Aceh, however, there has been relatively little violence. Most incidents have occurred when peaceful demonstrators attempted to raise the independence movement's flag. In mid-1998, under the transitional government of President B. J. Habibie, Indonesian army troops gunned down dozens of Papuans. Even after democratically elected President Abdurrahman Wahid took office in October 1999, similar incidents continued to occur. Wahid himself, in contrast to security forces in the province, adopted a soft line toward Papuan separatists. In February 2000, his government did nothing to prevent a gathering of five hundred Papuan leaders who called themselves the Papua Presidium and promised to form a transitional government. Indeed, in May, Wahid donated more than $120,000 to support a Papuan People's Congress that presidium leaders convened to chart a course toward full independence from Indonesia.[20] In the aftermath of that meeting, which nearly three thousand delegates attended, the government toughened its position and the level of violence increased. From January through November, more than eighty people died in clashes over the flying of the Papuan flag, including more than two dozen Indonesian immigrants whom Papuans attacked.[21]

Papuan grievances are similar to those of the Acehnese and East Timorese. As in East Timor, only a minute share of the indigenous population is Muslim. In addition, Irian Jaya was not actively involved in the Indonesian nationalist movement, did not join the republic with the rest of the Dutch East Indies in 1949, and was unable to achieve independence on its own. The Netherlands retained control of Irian Jaya until 1962, when it ceded the territory to United Nations administration. In 1963 the United Nations transferred the territory to Indonesia, and in 1969 Indonesia staged an Act of Free Choice in which it selected a group of about one thousand elders to vote in favor of joining the Indonesian republic. The United Nations chose not to endorse the outcome of the vote, but merely to "note" it. However, the Papuans, unlike the East Timorese, were not able to engage the Indonesians in a long military struggle. The Free Papua Organization mounted some significant military operations in the 1970s, but managed only intermittent attacks on Indonesian targets in the 1980s. Compared to East Timorese and Acehnese rebel armies, it posed a small threat to Indonesian forces in the 1990s. With only 2.5 million people spread over mountainous terrain that accounts for one-fifth of the entire country's land area, the indigent Papuans lack the logistical and financial means to confront the Indonesian military effectively.

Like Aceh, Irian Jaya is home to rich lodes of natural resources that the national government has exploited intensively over the past three decades, and like the Acehnese, the Papuans believe that they have benefited very little from these resources. Business analysts consider the province's copper and gold mines "the greatest . . . in the world." Freeport-McMoRan, the U.S. company that owns more than 80 percent of the Indonesian company that operates the mines, earned revenues of $1.8 billion in 1998 and $1.9 billion in 1999, almost entirely on production in its Irian Jayan mines.[22] In addition to this project, Jakarta has moved hundreds of thousands of transmigrants from Java to Irian Jaya, granted logging permits to well-connected investors in Jakarta, and staffed much of the local bureaucracy with officials from other parts of the country. Despite the wealth that the province's natural resources has generated, Papuans' living standards remain far below those of nearly all other parts of the country.

Conclusion

On closer examination, the simultaneous occurrence of violent conflicts in many parts of Indonesia is due much more to political and economic conflicts than simple religious or ethnic differences. Such differences are real, observable markers of everyday social life in Indonesia, but on their own they have not caused Indonesians to engage in violence. Recent conflicts appear to stem from a combination of at least three important factors. One is certainly the existence of commonly recognized religious or ethnic differences that divide various societies. None of the conflicts has occurred in ethnically or religiously homogeneous settings. Second, and more important, is the ability of one group to attribute to another group a material disadvantage that it feels it is suffering. In each case, a strong, readily observable empirical basis underpins the beliefs aggrieved groups hold about their rivals. Whether the group on which economic problems are blamed is a community of immigrants or the national government seems to determine whether the aggrieved group seeks independence or revenge. And third, violence has increased as the opportunity for aggrieved groups to attack their rivals has grown. There is no doubt that the state's declining capacity to regulate conflict in society has declined since Soeharto's fall and that the level of violence since then is higher than during the previous period.

Grouping recent conflicts according to the target of the violence leads to two additional observations. One is that the level of violence, measured in terms of the number of people killed and displaced during recent conflicts, is lower in cases of vertical conflict—that is, where groups seek independence. In part, of course, this is because the national government has not sought to resolve these challenges through full-scale warfare. In addition, however, it reflects the principal focus of separatist movements' anger—the central government, not immigrants. A second observation is that vertical conflicts are motivated in part by factors that are not present in cases of horizontal conflict. In Irian Jaya and Aceh, the national government has backed massive projects to exploit natural resources over the course of three decades. East Timor and Irian Jaya can claim never to have chosen union with Indonesia, as other provinces did. And all three regions can claim to have suffered serious human rights abuses at the hands of the Indonesian military.

Notes

For their generous comments on earlier drafts of this chapter, I thank Symeon

Giannakos and William Liddle. Liddle incorporated some of the comments he delivered orally at the Interethnic and Religious Conflicts in Cross-Cultural Perspective conference in a published commentary on political change in Indonesia. See R. William Liddle, "Menjawab Tantangan Reformasi." [Answering the challenge of reform], *Kompas,* June 8, 2000.

1. Hildred Geertz, "Indonesian Cultures and Communities," in *Indonesia,* ed. Ruth T. McVey (New Haven: Yale University Press, by arrangement with HRAF Press, 1963), 24.

2. Graeme Hugo, "Indonesia," in *Southeast Asia: Diversity and Development,* ed. Thomas R. Leinbach and Richard Ulack (Upper Saddle River, N.J.: Prentice Hall, 2000), 321.

3. Hal Hill and J. A. C. Mackie, introduction to *Indonesia's New Order: The Dynamics of Socio-Economic Transformation,* ed. Hal Hill (St. Leonard's, NSW: Allen and Unwin, 1994), xxviii.

4. For a fuller discussion of these issues, see Michael Malley, "Regions: Centralization and Resistance," in *Indonesia beyond Suharto: Polity, Economy, Society, Transition,* ed. Donald K. Emmerson (Armonk, N.Y.: M. E. Sharpe, 1999).

5. Herbert Feith, "Dynamics of Guided Democracy," in *Indonesia,* ed. Ruth T. McVey (New Haven: Yale University Press, by arrangement with HRAF Press, 1963), 382

6. A. C. Mackie, "Integrating and Centrifugal Factors in Indonesian Politics since 1945," in *Indonesia: The Making of a Nation. Indonesia: Australian Perspectives,* ed. J. A. C. Mackie (Canberra: Research School of Pacific Studies, Australian National University, 1980), 669–84.

7. On Soeharto-era cultural policies, see Patrick Guinness, "Local Society and Culture," in *Indonesia's New Order: The Dynamics of Socio-Economic Transformation,* ed. Hal Hill (St. Leonard's, NSW: Allen and Unwin, 1994).

8. Though they had lived in Kalimantan for over twenty years, thousands returned to Madera or portions of nearby East Java. However, as of early 2000, at least fourteen thousand Madurese remained in refugee camps, and the number continued to grow as many who had returned to Java and Madura came back to West Kalimantan after failing to find work. John McBeth and Margot Cohen, "Dayak Destruction: New Ethnic Violence Erupts in Kalimantan," *Far Eastern Economic Review,* April 1, 1999; Human Rights Watch, *Communal Violence in West Kalimantan* (New York: Human Rights Watch, 1997); "Pengungsi Sambas Ancam Rusuh." [Sambas refugees threaten riot], *Suara Pembaruan,* March 6, 2000.

9. Maggie Ford, "Rule of the Headhunters," *Newsweek,* April 5, 1999.

10. Detailed reports on the conflict have been issued by Human Rights Watch, *The Violence in Ambon* (New York: Human Rights Watch, 1999);

International Crisis Group, *Indonesia's Maluku Crisis: The Issues* (Jakarta: ICG Briefing, July 19, 2000); and Van Zorge Report, "War in the Malukus," *Van Zorge Report* 2 (12) (July 18, 2000).

11. John McBeth and Dini Djalal, "Tragic Island: Ambon Violence May Have Its Origins in Jakarta," *Far Eastern Economic Review,* March 25, 1999.

12. For a history of the conflict, see John G. Taylor, *Indonesia's Forgotten War: The Hidden History of East Timor* (London: Zed, 1991); Jose Manuel Tesoro and Dewi Loveard, 1991, "Aceh: Jakarta's Big Headache," *Asiaweek,* November 26, 1999. On human rights abuses see Amnesty International, *East Timor Violations of Human Rights: Extrajudicial Executions, Disappearances, Torture and Political Imprisonment, 1975–1984* (London: Amnesty International, 1985); Human Rights Watch, *Deteriorating Human Rights in East Timor* (New York: Human Rights Watch, 1995). On events in 1999, see Donald K. Emmerson, "Voting and Violence: Indonesia and East Timor in 1999," in *Indonesia beyond Suharto: Polity, Economy, Society, Transition,* ed. D. Emmerson (Armonk, N.Y.: M. E. Sharpe, 1999); Richard Tanter, Mark Selden, and Stephen R. Shalom, eds., *East Timor, Indonesia, and the World Community: Resistance, Repression, and Responsibility,* special issue of *Bulletin of Concerned Asian Scholars* 32 (1–2) (January–June, 2000).

13. "Selama Februari, 115 Orang Tewas di Aceh" [Through February, 115 killed in Aceh], *Kompas,* March 4, 2000; "Forum Data Shows 841 People Killed in Aceh This Year," *Jakarta Post,* December 9, 2000.

14. Tim Kell, *The Roots of Acehnese Rebellion, 1989–1992* (Ithaca, N.Y.: Cornell Modern Indonesia Project, 1995).

15. Tesoro and Loveard, "Aceh."

16. Amnesty International, *Indonesia: "Shock Therapy": Restoring Order in Aceh, 1989–1993* (London: Amnesty International, 1993).

17. See, for instance, "Aceh Barat Menangis, 51 Mayat Korban Operasi Militer Ditemukan." [West Aceh cities, bodies of 51 victims of military operations are found], *Kompas,* July 30, 1999.

18. Donald K. Emmerson, "Voting and Violence: Indonesia and East Timor in 1999," in *Indonesia beyond Suharto: Polity, Economy, Society, Transition,* ed. D. Emmerson (Armonk, N.Y.: M. E. Sharpe, 1999), 348.

19. Edward Aspinall, "Whither Aceh?" *Inside Indonesia,* no. 62 (April–June, 2000).

20. "Old Paradigms, New Beginnings: The Papuan National Congress," *Van Zorge Report* 2 (9) (June 5, 2000).

21. "Penduduk Sipil Tewas Karena Bintang Kejora." [Civilian killed because of morning star], *Kompas,* December 6, 2000.

22. Stewart Yerton, "Hot Metal," *Times-Picayune* (New Orleans), February 13, 2000.

9

Sources of and Responses to Violent Conflict in South Asia

Chetan Kumar

As a region, South Asia consists of India, Pakistan, Bangladesh, Sri Lanka, Nepal, Bhutan, Maldives, Afghanistan, and Myanmar. Apart from being home to nearly a fourth of the world's population, it is also the locale for the world's most tense nuclear flash point, for a plethora of apparently ethnic and religious conflicts, and for two of the world's longest-lasting civil wars (in Sri Lanka and Afghanistan). With the notable exception of India, democracy has only a tenuous foothold in the region, and both political and economic development have been stunted by the region's numerous conflicts.

Although they involve different actors and resources, conflicts in the region share some common characteristics. Over time, unresolved domestic and regional conflicts tend to interconnect, reinforce each other, and thus acquire the appearance of intractability. Even outside actors that may be the best equipped to resolve them might themselves become entangled. The cost of managing them, in both human and material resources, may become prohibitively expensive. At the core of all the region's conflicts lie instances of massive political failure; successful political leadership holds the key to preventing, managing, and resolving the region's disputes.

Types of Violent Conflict in South Asia

Manifestations of violent conflict in the region can be divided into seven discrete categories:[1]

1. *Localized sectarian violence:* interreligious or intercommunal violence, common to all South Asian states.

2. *Localized sectarian violence resulting from demographic shifts:*[2] violence resulting from demographic shifts within localities; violence resulting from tension between migrants and the local population; and violence resulting from population movements across borders.

3. *Localized insurgencies:* violence generated by organized separatist movements.

4. *Insurgencies with external networks of support:* violence generated by organized separatist movements with the direct or indirect political and economic involvement of nonlocal actors.

5. *Internal conflicts at the nexus of interstate disputes:* large-scale domestic conflicts that turn into interstate war.

6. *Interstate conflicts:* conflict along international borders between at least two countries.

7. *The nuclear standoff:* the direct or indirect threat of the use of nuclear weapons in relation to interstate disputes or conflicts.

Two points are especially important in this regard:

- The emergence of India and Pakistan from the nuclear closet has institutionalized categories 5 and 6 above. This means that these conflicts are deterred from rising to the level of all-out war. However, to the extent that the risk of an all-out conventional war with heavy casualties is no longer as high, the incentive for India and Pakistan to continue deterring each other with nuclear weapons instead of negotiating to resolve the conflict is also greater. Hence, India and Pakistan at least may continue in a nuclear stalemate for a while.

- Nuclear weaponization in South Asia is a symptom of deeper pathologies, rather than a cause of conflict itself, and should therefore not be the primary focus of conflict management in the region. Rather, the deeper political causes of conflicts (detailed below) must be targeted.

Causes of Violent Internal Conflict in South Asia

Violent internal conflicts in the region include violence in Assam, India, between migrants from Bangladesh and the longer-term ethnic Assamese residents; violence along the India-Nepal border due to population movements across the border; tensions in Bhutan from demographic shifts; the Naxalite separatist movements in the Andhra Pradesh and Bihar provinces of India; organized separatist violence in the Sind and Northwest Frontier provinces in Pakistan; the civil war between the Liberation Tigers of Tamil Eelam (LTTE) and the Sri Lankan government in the Jaffna peninsula of Sri Lanka; minor insurgent movements in India's northeastern states (Assam, Nagaland, Manipur, and Tripura); the Chakma insurgency in Bangladesh; and the Shan and Karen insurgencies in Myanmar.

To varying degrees, these violent conflicts appear to be correlated with factors such as poverty, environmental degradation or catastrophe, religious[3] and ethnic schisms, transboundary population movements, or external networks of support for insurgent groups. But no matter how diverse these conflicts appear to be, they share fundamental causes that, as will be seen below, point toward similar policy prescriptions. They have all resulted from *political failure to resolve disputes before they turn violent.* These political failures can be divided into four types:

- Failure of political leadership to anticipate and resolve disputes before they turn violent.
- Absence of skills, mechanisms, and aptitude for resolving disputes peacefully.
- Exploitation of existing religious, social, and other group differences for short-term political gain by local or national leaders.
- Deliberate exclusion or marginalization of particular communities for short-term political gain by local or national leaders.

Causes of Violent Interstate Conflict in South Asia

Examples of these conflicts include four brief wars between India and Pakistan[4] (including the most recent episode at Kargil) and one between India and China; and, border skirmishes occurring intermittently between Indian and Pakistani troops along the international border between the two countries, and along the Line of Control, which separates the Indian and Pakistani areas in Kashmir.[5] These conflicts manifest themselves in three general typologies: disputes over territory, geopolitical concerns, and identity concerns.

DISPUTES OVER TERRITORY

These disputes include those between India and Pakistan over Kashmir, Siachen, and Rann of Kutch; and between China and India over parts of Kashmir and India's northeast.

GEOPOLITICAL CONCERNS

Among the secular considerations for the Pakistani support for the Taliban has been the need for greater strategic depth vis-à-vis India that Afghanistan provides. India, Russia, and the Central Asian states have supported the Northern Alliance in Afghanistan because of the perceived threat of the spread of religious extremism. In the 1980s, the Afghan civil war was a subset of the Cold War.

IDENTITY CONCERNS

Iran and Uzbekistan have supported the Northern Alliance in Afghanistan because of links with Shias (Iran) and Uzbeks and Tajiks (Uzbekistan). Similarly, Pakistan has been a close supporter of the Taliban because of long-term links with the majority Pashtun community. Both Pakistan and India have used issues pertaining to their respective national identities to bolster claims to Kashmir with their own populations. India claims that separation of Muslim-majority Kashmir would render obsolete its identity as a haven for all democracy-loving South

Asians regardless of religion. Pakistan claims that letting Muslim-majority Kashmir remain in India would be an affront to its identity as a refuge for Muslim brethren oppressed in Hindu-dominated India (this argument formed the basis for the demand by some Muslim leaders in the first half of the twentieth century for the creation of a Muslim state separate from British-ruled India). Of course, both claims of threats to identity are themselves rendered obsolete by the fact that Pakistan's founder, Mohammad Ali Jinnah, had proudly declared it a secular state (thereby launching the national schizophrenia that separates the cosmopolitan urban Pakistanis from their antediluvian rural brethren), and that even without Kashmir, India would have the third largest number of Muslims in the world, after Indonesia and Pakistan.

Causes of Internal Conflicts at the Nexus of Interstate Disputes

Examples of internal conflicts at the nexus of interstate disputes include the Pakistani civil war, which turned into the Indo-Pakistani war of 1971, the Afghan civil war, which started in 1979 with the Soviet intrusion into Afghanistan and continues, and the insurgency in Indian Kashmir that started in 1990.

Instances of intrastate conflict have been acquiring interstate parameters in South Asia largely as a result of political failure. Leaders assailed by domestic pressures have sought to cohere national causes around opposition to "evil" neighbors. In most instances, they have sought to reinforce their own power, and the structures supporting it, by presenting themselves as the last defense against their neighbor's plots. Once again, while the apparent causes of the region's interstate conflicts have been varied, these conflicts have been fanned and sustained by leaders in search of political advantage. Short-lived wars and deliberately fanned border crises have helped to win elections for politicians and legitimize coups d'état for militaries.

While internal conflict in Nepal, Myanmar, Bhutan, Sri Lanka, and Bangladesh has threatened only the tranquility of these countries, such conflict in India and Pakistan has carried strategic implications for the region. In Pakistan, continued domination of political and economic life, including of the military, by Punjabis has alienated Sindhis, Pashtuns, and Baluchis to the point of creating low-level, simmering, and constant states of insurgency in Sind and the regions bordering Afghanistan. In the latter areas particularly, the control of the Pakistani state is tenuous and fleeting. Growing anarchy, compounded by the numerous failures of the state in providing good governance, is the order of the day.

The backing provided by Pakistan to the Taliban militia in Afghanistan in a search for strategic depth, and to the Kashmiri insurgents for reasons described above, has rebounded on Pakistan, with guns, drugs, and money flowing across the borders of Pakistan into the hands of insurgents of all stripes across the region, including in Pakistan itself. The growing radicalization of Pakistani army and society, avidly fanned by military dictator General Zia-ul-Haq in the 1980s to rally Pakistanis for holy war in Afghanistan, and in support of his regime, has now led to sectarian strife within the country, as Pakistanis who are not ready for jihad clash with those with more strident views. Domestic and interstate conflict can thus be linked to the same set of bad political choices.

In India, decades of corruption and mismanagement in Kashmir had created a fertile breeding ground for insurgency.[6] Unlike in the rest of the country, elections in the province—a sinkhole forever increasing federal development assistance—were often a charade, and the polity and the economy continued to be dominated by a few corrupt families. Whereas the federal government had successfully contained or eliminated ethnically grounded insurgencies in Punjab, Assam, and the northeastern provinces, the violence in Kashmir continued to spiral out of control. India's attempts to continue a façade of political normalcy in the province through elections and elected bodies had only further alienated the population and reified the control of the traditional leadership. Real political influence in the province had long shifted to an umbrella body of outlawed organizations—Hurriyat—whose members advocated positions ranging from extreme autonomy for Kashmir to secession from India followed by either union with Pakistan or outright independence for both parts of Kashmir held by India and Pakistan. While most of the fighting against the Indian army was carried out by two rabidly extremist and pro-Pakistan militias—the Hizb-ul-Mujahideen and the Lashkar-e-Toiba—which were both on the U.S. State Department's list of terrorist organizations, the mainstream of Kashmiri nationalism was represented by the Jammu and Kashmir Liberation Front, which wanted a Kashmir independent of both India and Pakistan.

The popular mood had also been complicated by the Indian military's ham-handed approach to counterinsurgency, which left almost as many civilians as insurgents brutalized and resentful, particularly after Indian soldiers would rough up entire villages or carry out random arrests in order to weed out militants or information regarding their whereabouts. On the part of the Indian government, there appeared to be a profound dearth of creative ideas with which to resolve this imbroglio, other than ratcheting up the military presence in Kashmir and routinely denouncing Pakistan. Indian policy planners continued to insist that they would not accept third-party mediation on Kashmir and that Pakistan had to stop all military support for Kashmiri insurgents (which Pakistan denied giving) as a precondition for negotiations. However, given pressure from religious extremists within Pakistan itself, no Pakistani government could hope to survive in power if it stopped support for Kashmiri militants.

External Actors and the Strategic Landscape of South Asia

Outside intervention in South Asia has only occasionally been directed toward resolving the conflicts described above. Certainly, in most instances, it has complicated the particular conflicts to an even greater extent than before. Non–South Asian countries that are involved in the security dynamics of the region include China, Iran, and the Russian Federation, to the extent of its engagement in Central Asia. Of the developed states, the United States is the key actor.

U.S. involvement first emerged during the Cold War, when Pakistan, starting in the mid-1950s, was seen as a key bulwark against

Soviet expansion, and also as a counterpoint to India's suspect friendship with the Soviet Union. In the 1980s, Pakistan provided a platform to U.S. intelligence to launch a covert counteroffensive against the Soviet presence in Afghanistan. Armed with U.S.-supplied weapons, Afghan mujahideen, or holy warriors, provided a nadir for the Soviet military machine. Having driven the foreigners from Afghanistan by early 1990s, they then fell upon each other, generating a disastrous civil war that continues at the time of writing. Meanwhile the backwash of drugs, Islamic extremism, and small arms left by the Cold War struggle has, at the beginning of the new millennium, made Afghanistan one of the primary global hot spots. In addition, the conservative Islamic military government of Pakistan, which had allied itself with the United States during the 1980s, paved the way, in its own aftermath, for a Pakistani state that is increasingly buffeted by this backwash and by elements of the Pakistani state which see Pakistan—particularly since it is the only nuclear-armed Islamic state—as a champion for the Islamic cause. Pakistani military and intelligence are reportedly closely involved in supporting a swath of holy warriors that range across much of the region, but whose actions are particularly evident in Afghanistan and the Indian part of Kashmir.

These warriors originated in two interrelated phenomena. The Afghan civil war had drawn in many idealistic and unemployed young Arabs who, flush with weapons supplied by the CIA through Pakistan and paid for with Saudi cash, had joined the jihad against the Soviet Union in droves. For many conservative Arab states, this served the convenient purpose of directing the energies of their young radicals away from their faulty monarchies and onto external enemies. Once the Soviets had withdrawn from Afghanistan, these warriors, rather than return home, took on a number of additional causes, including fighting for allegedly oppressed Muslims in places as diverse as Bosnia, Chechnya, Tajikistan, and Kashmir. In some instances, their Saudi financiers fell out with their own government and formed their own independent networks to wage jihad against all and sundry, including the United States and the conservative Arab monarchies. Most prominent among these was Osama bin Laden, the former Saudi financier who is a major supporter of jihad. Joining the ranks of these itinerant Arabs were thousands of Afghans who had few skills but the ability to fight and who faced a destroyed economy and infrastructure in their own country. When they were not fighting in the country's civil war, they were fighting abroad. Also joining their ranks were tens of thousands of young and unemployed Pakistanis, trained in ostensibly religious schools, or madrasas, armed with only the ability to recite the Qur'an and use light weapons, and deployed away from Pakistan and against external enemies so that their energies would not be directed against a Pakistani state that had failed to provide them with alternate employment or livelihood.

This spreading jihad has had two prominent consequences—the United States and the Russian Federation often now find themselves on the same side in combating drugs and terrorism. Meanwhile India, the former Cold War irritant, finds itself enjoying an increasingly closer relationship with the United States and its allies. Driven primarily by the growing clout of Indian infotech entrepreneurs in the world economy and in American political fund-raising, this reorientation has seen phenomena as diverse as Israeli experts providing advice on internal security matters to the Indians and a Hindu priest being invited to deliver the invocation of a joint session of the U.S. Congress to hear the visiting Indian prime minister. India recently joined the United States in hosting a global democracy summit and was the only country that was not a NATO ally or traditional U.S. friend to be among the first to join a U.S.-led "democracy caucus" at the United Nations.

Indian, Russian, and U.S. interests have also converged in opposition to the Taliban, the most well-knit and extreme of Afghanistan's warring factions, which, with Pakistani support, had acquired control of over 95 percent of the country's territory at the time of writing.[7] In addition to implementing a harsh version of Islam that made all its Islamic neighbors blanch in embarrassment,[8] the Taliban also used drug cultivation and profits to bolster its military fortunes. While denying that it prosecuted a worldwide campaign of jihad, it provided refuge to Osama bin Laden. The close relationship between Pakistani intelligence and the Taliban, and also between the former and the host of Pakistan-based religious schools that churned out human fodder for jihad from Chechnya to Kashmir, had brought Pakistan close to being considered a worldwide sponsor of terrorism. More damagingly, it had created an extremist colossus that an increasingly beleaguered Pakistani state—still clinging to vestiges of moderation—found increasingly hard to withstand.[9]

Two recent events brought the strategic cauldron to boil. In 1998 a nationalist Indian government overthrew nearly two decades of a policy of restraint and brought India's nuclear capacity, first demonstrated through a "peaceful" nuclear explosion at Pokhran in 1974, into the open with a series of well-publicized tests. Pakistan responded with tests of its own, and both countries found themselves in an overt nuclear standoff with none of the restraints that had characterized the U.S.-Soviet standoff during the Cold War.[10] This situation was further complicated by the fact that while India had developed its capacity overtly and indigenously, and had scrupulously shied away from proliferating its know-how in any form, Pakistan had covertly obtained its capacity reportedly through assistance from China, Iran, and North Korea, and had violated a number of proliferation regimes in doing so. These violations had brought U.S. sanctions to bear on Pakistan in 1990 and had consequently limited the U.S. role in staying Pakistan's nuclear hand.

While nuclear optimists hoped that mutual deterrence would prevent India and Pakistan from undertaking more frequent conventional warfare, the pitfalls of this reasoning were revealed in 1999, when Kashmiri mujahideen ventured across the Line of Control (LOC) that separates Indian from Pakistani Kashmir and, with the backing of Pakistani army regulars, established a bridgehead at Kargil overlooking a critical Indian military supply route. The Indian army retaliated with all it had, but failed to rapidly dislodge the intruders. With the conflict looking as if it might snowball into a nuclear exchange, U.S. president Bill Clinton personally intervened with Pakistani prime minister Nawaz Sharif to withdraw the Pakistani element of the intrusion. In return, he promised to use his personal influence to promote movement on the long-standing dispute between India and Pakistan over Kashmir.[11]

While Pakistan had won a tactical victory by establishing a bridgehead in Indian territory and holding on against superior Indian forces, India won the political battle. Early on in the battle, evidence emerged of the presence of Pakistani army troops and equipment among intruders that were allegedly only Kashmiri mujahideen (whom Pakistan claims to support politically but not militarily). Furthermore, India responded to this provocation by restraining from crossing the LOC itself in order to encircle the intruders, even though not doing so led to a greater loss of Indian lives. Through this maneuver, India acquired the moral and diplomatic high ground as a model of restraint, whereas Pakistan came across as incapable of exercising the responsibility that came with being a nuclear power. To complicate matters further, tensions between Prime Minister Sharif and the army chief, General Pervez Musharraf—who had reportedly plotted and executed the Kargil misadventure without informing the civilian leadership—led to a coup in which Musharraf assumed power as the new "chief executive" of Pakistan. Compared with India's resolute democracy, Pakistan now looked like a throwback. To give India's nationalist government credit, it had made two significant overtures that had both been thwarted by Pakistan. A historic bus ride by Indian prime minister A. B. Vajpayee to Lahore in 1999 seemed to presage a new era in Indo-Pakistani relations despite nuclear complications;[12] hopes generated by this initiative were soon dissipated, however, by the Kargil misadventure. In 2000, India seriously took up a call by a leading Kashmiri insurgency group for a cease-fire and negotiations. However, pressure from other insurgent groups and reportedly from Pakistan soon caused the group to revert to more extreme positions.

Complicating this bleak strategic picture were two elements. The first was China, which traditionally sees India as an enemy and Pakistan as an ally and which fought a brief war with India in 1963, laid claims to parts of Kashmir and India's northeast. While India's nuclear capability was minuscule compared to China's, the latter saw a nuclear-armed India with a credible space program as a potential strategic threat, and India harbored similar perceptions of China. When India had acquired an undeclared weapons capability with its nuclear explosion at Pokhran, an alliance with Pakistan had become logical for China. The Sino-American rapprochement under Nixon had further facilitated a partnership with the then U.S.-allied Pakistan, particularly since India appeared to be close to the Soviet Union, no friend of either China or the United States.

In the aftermath of the Cold War, many of these relations went into high flux. On the one hand, China found itself on closer terms with the Russian Federation, successor to the former Soviet Union, in opposing a U.S.-led unipolar world. On the other hand, both Russia and China, despite many ups and downs in their relations with the United States, sought investment and at times partnership with the latter on key issues. All three collaborated in many instances, particularly at the UN Security Council, in maintaining international peace and security. India, while it had retained its close friendship with Russia, clearly sought a similar friendship with the United States. Pakistan, always seen as a threat by Russia, now came to be perceived as being even more so as an exporter of jihad. The one constant in all this was that India and China still saw each other as a potential nuclear threat, despite assiduous diplomacy by both sides aimed at countering these perceptions. To counter India, China therefore provided Pakistan with most of the wherewithal for developing its own nuclear option. By 2000, however, China had begun to rethink this policy. Jihad had begun to wash up on its borders with incidents of terrorism rising among the Uighur population in its Muslim-majority Xinjiang province. Also, balancing India increasingly seemed less of a strategic concern than lessening irritants in relations with the United States, which had maintained military sanctions against Pakistan since 1990 for seeking to acquire a nuclear capacity through underground means.

The tensions and the conflict scenarios discussed above point to the urgency of addressing the political factors that have generated these tensions, before full-scale wars engulf the region. War that the region has seen so far have been limited engagements, fought for limited objectives rather than millenarian reasons. But this could change. In several instances in the recent past, leaders of key states have managed to limit or manage brief instances of armed conflict that could led to wider eruptions. There is no guarantee that they will be able to do so the next time. The rest of the chapter makes the argument that the key to peace in the region lies in preventing future conflicts by addressing underlying factors. Practical measures and steps for doing so are identified.

Recent Instances of Conflict Management in South Asia

The three instances described below highlight the risks inherent in managing the conflicts that may occasionally erupt as ongoing tensions boil over.[13] In each instance, the particular instance almost led to a wider conflict and occurred because of circumstances that can arise again at any time in the future.

THE BRASS TACKS EPISODE

A border crisis between India and Pakistan in 1988 that originated in a military exercise called "Operation Brass Tacks" conducted by the former,[14] and that could have led to a full-scale war since the latter saw its nearness to the India-Pakistan border as presaging an invasion and hence as a threat, was averted as a result of personalized "cricket diplomacy" between Prime Minister Rajiv Gandhi and President Zia-ul-Haq. Contacts between the directors-general of military operations of the two armies over a special hot line reportedly also eased tensions.

THE 1990 CRISIS

For reasons never fully understood, India and Pakistan reportedly came close to a nuclear clash in 1990 (on India's side, the cause was perceptions of the rising levels of Pakistani-sponsored violence in Kashmir). The director of the U.S. Central Intelligence Agency reportedly averted the crisis thought informal diplomacy.

THE KARGIL EPISODE

As described earlier, overt Pakistani backing for a significant intrusion by militants across the LOC in Kashmir brought India and Pakistan to the brink of full-scale war. However, India exercised restraint in the limited military engagement fought at Kargil between Indian troops and the militants. Subsequent escalation of the conflict was avoided because of informal diplomacy by President Clinton.

ALL THREE OF these episodes, while good examples of conflict management, also reflect ongoing tensions that could lead to more such episodes. To the extent that the remedies applied in each case reflect idiosyncratic factors (including the personalities of the individual leaders involved), there is no guarantee that such remedies will also be available in the future. A more sustainable way of dealing with these episodes will be to prevent them from occurring instead of preparing to manage them once they have occurred. Some systematic mechanisms and procedures, as well as initiatives targeted at improving the quality of political leadership in the region, could go a long way toward ensuring such prevention.

Past Instances of Conflict Prevention in South Asia

The adage—prevention is better than cure—certainly applies to South Asia. With better leadership, the region's numerous disputes can be arrested when they are still at the stage of general tension. In fact, there exist several examples of both internal and interstate disputes that have been arrested through timely intervention before they lead to widespread violent conflict. The following examples are worth noting.

THE INDUS RIVER WATER-SHARING AGREEMENT

Perhaps the most successful conflict prevention measure in South Asia, this agreement negotiated between India and Pakistan in the 1960s dealt with what was potentially a major source of violent conflict between the two countries. Mediated with the assistance of the World Bank, the agreement formed a joint commission to manage the sharing of the waters of the Indus River and its tributaries, all of which flow from India to Pakistan, and to cooperatively resolve dis-putes thereof. Interestingly, this arrangement has continued to work relatively smoothly despite the other difficulties in Indo-Pakistani relations.

In the mid- to late 1980s, as Bangladesh stood on the brink due to po-litical ineptitude in the face of massive internal turmoil and ecologi-cal and economic crises, a network of international and domestic nongovernmental organizations (NGOs) launched a series of activi-ties focused on women's education and empowerment, local govern-ment, and sustainable development. The impact of these activities on Bangladesh's political life has been tremendous. Although the coun-try remains crisis ridden, the existing system of governance, despite all its shortcomings, has ensured a civilian system for government, without the military coups of the past, for a little over a decade.

ECONOMIC AND POLITICAL LIBERALIZATION IN INDIA

In 1991, shortly after its election, the government of Prime Minister P. V. Narasimha Rao launched a series of reforms aimed at decentraliz-ing political decision making, giving more power to the states, and handing the reins of the economy to the private sector. Over the next five years, as the impact of the reforms spread throughout the coun-try (albeit differentially), separatist insurgencies in Punjab and Assam were significantly reduced in scale, as were violent (although minor) uprisings in Andhra Pradesh (as a result of new progressive state leadership) and Uttar Pradesh (as a result of the central govern-ment's agreement to create the new state of Uttarakhand). The northeast, however, continues to see separatist violence, and similar violence in Kashmir grew into a full-blown insurgency. Chronic problems of mismanagement and corruption among state govern-ments in these regions, combined with the heavy-handedness of the federal government when intervening in what are seen as insecure border regions, has meant that impact of the nationwide reform process has been felt only marginally, or not at all, in the northeast and Kashmir.

Future Measures for the Prevention and Management of Conflict in South Asia

Past instances of successful conflict prevention and management in the region point toward future strategies that center primarily on developing political resources for addressing concerns and managing tensions before they lead to widespread violence. Such strategies could incorporate the following elements:

DISPERSAL OF CONFLICT RESOLUTION AND MANAGEMENT SKILLS AMONG POLITICAL LEADERSHIPS AT STATE AND COMMUNITY LEVELS

While South Asian states jealously guard their sovereignty and will not welcome any international intervention aimed at conflict resolution, private initiatives by NGOs and policy institutes to inculcate a culture of nonviolent conflict management at various levels of political leadership—through seminars, workshops, and multisector dialogues, particularly in those areas of India, Pakistan, Bangladesh, and Nepal that suffer from bouts of communal violence—could be welcomed by the central governments in these countries.

ENCOURAGEMENT FOR REGIONAL PHILANTHROPY IN CONFLICT MANAGEMENT

A network of endowments and think tanks with the ability to sponsor and foster strategic thinking aimed at conflict management at all levels of governance in the states of South Asia is critically needed. Major international foundations, such as the Ford and Rockefeller Foundations, have taken some key steps in this direction. Much more needs to be done, particularly in terms of establishing such institutes outside capital cities at regional universities, which have a greater capacity for reaching out to local levels of leadership than elite schools. Also, the work of existing institutes, particularly in New Delhi, Islamabad, Dacca, and Colombo, should be oriented more toward training, outreach, seminars, and workshops than only toward research and networking among elite scholars.

PUBLIC EDUCATION

In practically all the South Asian states, public awareness of key foreign policy and security issues, and of the dynamics of internal conflicts, is abysmally low. The population is easily manipulated by politicians who exploit intergroup or communal differences or national chauvinism for political gain. A series of privately supported mass media initiatives (e.g., Voice of Peace radio stations) that blend religion, popular culture, and news to convey the message of peaceful coexistence should constitute an important measure toward the prevention of violent conflict. Paid for by NGOs and private foundations, and produced and directed on a charitable basis by sympathetic media figures, such programming could avail of the growing pervasiveness of cable and satellite television in the region, even in areas where it is banned.

LOCAL PEACEBUILDING IN AFGHANISTAN

In the 1990s, both Afghanistan and Somalia became bywords for state collapse and anarchy. Recently, local peacebuilding processes culminated in the partial revival of a legitimate and national state in Somalia. These processes bypassed the quarrelsome warlords. They were launched by local leaders and continued on their own steam in the aftermath of the disastrous UN intervention without significant international support. The UN mission in Afghanistan should be also be supported in reviving local peacebuilding processes, particularly on isues relating to the coexistence of the minority Uzbeks and Tajiks with the majority Pashtuns.

While the current interests of the Central Asian states support some of the factions in the Afghan civil war, and this has not changed despite several UN-led efforts, the situation is amenable to long-term change. A key element here is the growing insecurity of the Central Asian states because of a swath of jihad-variety extremism that now stretches from the Caucasus to Kashmir and Xinjiang. In the medium term, this insecurity can be partially addressed through a concerted international effort that targets the political economy of this extremism (as opposed to more visible but far less effective manhunts for specific individuals). A long-term effort by several international organizations to promote sustainable development in the Ferghana Valley has borne limited but positive fruits, in that it has given economic alternatives to local population, and thus reduced the fodder available to shortsighted leaders. In Afghanistan, efforts to provide alternatives to poppy cultivation to local farmers have also had very limited, but nevertheless positive, outcomes. However, the quality of political leadership in the region still leaves much to be desired.

LEARNING FROM INDUS VALLEY COOPERATION

The mechanisms through which this lasting arrangement for dispute resolution on the sharing of Indus waters between India and Pakistan was negotiated, sustained, and continues to function should be carefully examined to determine the factors that made it possible.[15] Perhaps a number of these factors could be applied to other issues. Scholars of the region could apply themselves to eliciting these factors and making them available to international and regional policy makers.

THE SRI LANKAN CIVIL WAR

This conflict appears to have become one of the world's most intractable over a period of nearly two decades. Various initiatives by the Sri Lankan government to decentralize power or to address the issues that led to the conflict in the first place have all failed. Only a two-pronged strategy will provide a medium-to-long-term chance of resolving this conflict. First, the LTTE's international resource base needs to be severely constricted in order to convince it of the need to sit in good faith at the negotiating table. In particular, international restrictions, preferably levied by the UN Security Council, should be placed on the transnational flows of arms and finances that support the LTTE. The sanctions placed on UNITA in Angola by the UN Security Council should provide a very good example of how this can be done. Second, a serious, nonpartisan national dialogue is needed among all concerned to reach an agreement on the type of autonomy that could be offered to Jaffna in return for peace. Various proposals generated to date have fallen victim to the country's turbulent electoral dynamics. Such proposals should encompass not just substantial autonomy for Jaffna, but also adequate power sharing with the Tamil minority at the national level in Colombo. Recently, in the aftermath of Kumaratunga's reelection as president of Sri Lanka, the country's political parties have appeared to converge around autonomy for Jaffna. The LTTE should now be coerced or induced into taking advantage of this moment.

KASHMIR—THE LINKAGE FACTOR

Two sets of linkages continue to bedevil the prospects of negotiations between India and Pakistan over Kashmir. First, the Kargil episode has ruined the trust between the two countries, with India expressing particular ire toward the current Pakistani head of state, General Pervez Musharraf, for his role in that misadventure. Indian leaders now link the end of explicit Pakistani support for the Kashmiri militants with the revival of the negotiations. Pakistan—which has been more willing to negotiate given the upper tactical hand enjoyed by its proxies in Kashmir—has said that such withdrawal of support would preempt what should be a negotiated outcome, particularly since, by its own insistence, it is providing only political and not military support to the Kashmiri mujahideen. One possible method of breaking this impasse could for an influential third party to simultaneously declare that it has seen a decline in separatist violence in Kashmir (thus allowing India to claim that its policies have successfully forced Pakistan to reduce backing for Kashmiri militants) simultaneously with the lessening of the overt Indian military footprint in the province (thus allowing Pakistan to claim that it has won breathing space for its Muslim brethren from being oppressed by an infidel government). Both sides may then be able to claim that pre-conditions for restarting negotiations have been met.

Another important linkage that has bedeviled negotiations between India and Pakistan has been the linking of the Kashmir issue with the other issues that the two countries need to negotiate over. India has argued that negotiations over other, less urgent, issues should pave the way for a better set of negotiations on Kashmir, apropos of the beleaguered Middle East peace process. Pakistan has argued that a focus on lesser issues could only mean that India is not serious about negotiating on Kashmir. According to the Pakistani viewpoint, Kashmir is the central issue, and its prior resolution will let everything else fall into place. What is common to both positions is that both link the Kashmir negotiations with the remaining set of issues. This linkage needs to be broken. A formula that could accomplish this, provided the decision to restart negotiations is made, could involve the following steps (drawing upon the methodology of synchronized moves used by former U.S. Senator George Mitchell in Northern Ireland):

- India and Pakistan both agree that Kashmir is a significant issue that needs immediate resolution (without saying that Kashmir is *the* issue, as Pakistani hard-liners would have it, or that Kashmir is only as, or even less, important than trade, as Indian hard-liners would have it).

- Next, India and Pakistan both agree to negotiate on number of issues through the formula used in developing the Indus water-sharing arrangement, and using the arrangement itself as a precedent for negotiations on these issues.

- Simultaneously, India and Pakistan create a joint high-powered commission to examine all aspects of the Kashmir issue. To satisfy India, the commission is given an extended time frame in which to submit its report. To satisfy Pakistan, the work of the commission is marked with clear benchmarks which, if not met, could allow either side to withdraw from the commission.

- The work of the commission, as well as the negotiations on other issues, could be housed and reported on by a secretariat established under the auspices of an influential third party (the best here would be a nonregional multilateral organization, such as the Association of South-East Asian Nations [ASEAN] or the European Union) that could also perform basic facilitation functions.

KASHMIR—THE LOC QUESTION

Many top thinkers in both India and Pakistan agree that the only practicable solution to the Kashmir issue is to make the Line of Control (LOC) that divides Indian and Pakistani portions of Kashmir the international boundary between the two countries.[16] The two key problems here are:

- Nationalists on both sides will not want to renounce their claim on the entire province.
- Many Kashmiris now associate themselves with an identity that transcends the LOC. They see themselves less as Pakistanis or Indians and more as Kashmiris.

Both these issues could be addressed by a formula that

- accepts the LOC as a lasting de facto international boundary in Kashmir, thus making it possible for each side to retain its claims for perpetuity;
- makes it possible for Kashmiris to move across the LOC without visas, thus recognizing the common identity of the province;
- divides administrative functions on each side of the LOC between India and Pakistan respectively, as well as an elected trans-Kashmiri council that deals with functions such as cross-LOC travel, cultural preservation, opening observer offices abroad, and so on.

In addition:

- On each side of the LOC, Indian and Pakistani administrative control can continue to be expressed through elected provincial governments, as it currently is.

- If all sides are willing, the international status of Kashmir could be defined as a joint Indo-Pakistani condominium.

In order for this formula to be accepted, a significant change in public attitude may be required in both countries. For this, an active engagement between the civil societies on both sides is needed. A number of admirable initiatives to promote such engagement have been launched in the past decade with the assistance of primarily U.S. foundations and think tanks like the Rockefeller Foundation, the Ford Foundation, and the Stimson Center. The burden of funding such activities should also be taken up by other donors who have expressed interest in the peaceful resolution of this issue (including Canada and the European Union), and they could be significantly expanded.

A POLITICAL HOT LINE

While a hot line exists between the directors-general of military operations of India and Pakistan, it is not used in times of crisis if there are political obstructions from higher up in the hierarchy. The most critical offices in the two countries in times of crisis are the Prime Minister's Office in India and the Military Chiefs of Staff Headquarters in Pakistan. Multiple and layered hot line connections should be established between these offices. In addition, privately sponsored conferences in neutral locations such as Kathmandu or Dacca should attempt to bring together officials from both offices so that personal connections and links are formed, and can subsequently be sustained through e-mail and other electronic means.

STABILIZING THE NUCLEAR EQUATION

While India and Pakistan have emerged from the nuclear closet, their nuclear establishments still lurk in the shadows.[17] Nuclear debate in the two countries is largely rhetorical, and neither side has the ability to manage a stable nuclear deterrent. To this end, private foundations abroad (primarily those that have supported track-two initiatives) could support the formation of a high-level private commission with access to the relevant levels of government, and which could also include nuclear experts from the West participating in an informal capacity. Perhaps, given the fact that China is an important part of India's nuclear calculations, eminent Chinese persons should also participate in such a commission. The commission's objective should be to submit a detailed report on techniques and strategies for maintaining a stable nuclear equation at the both the strategic and tactical levels between India, Pakistan, and China.

ECONOMIC INTEGRATION

Well-integrated economic activity, while not forming the core of political decisions (particularly those relating to the quality or style of leadership), nevertheless often has a visible and consequential political impact.[18] While no systematic correlation of this nature has been identified yet for South Asia (partly because of a lack of detailed research on this issue), there is some suggestive anecdotal evidence. The Sensex at the Bombay Stock Exchange plunged at the start of the Kargil crisis and remained jittery throughout. While diplomatic considerations were obviously the primary factor behind Indian restraint, the flight of foreign investment portfolios, which constitute a significant bottom line for India's foreign exchange stability, would certainly have been a consideration for any Indian planners about to launch a full-scale war on Pakistan. If this anecdotal correlation has some larger significance (and more research is needed here), then an increased pace for the advent of the global economy in the region, and for the comprehensive launch of the South Asian Preferential Trading Area, will certainly be conducive to long-term peace in the region.

Conclusion

The proposals offered above represent policy choices that have to be made by the political leadership in the region in order to sustainably manage the region's numerous tensions before violent conflict erupts. The leaders have to choose to acquire better conflict management skills, learn to apply these skills, and adhere to the results of that application.[19] There is nothing intrinsic to the current, or even any impending, crop of leadership that will make them more amenable to such application. A difference could be made, though, if an increasingly aware population demands that its leaders make better political decisions on their behalf. The dissemination among the general population of the basic understanding that disputes at all levels—communal, provincial, national, or interstate—do not necessarily have to be resolved by violence is therefore as key as the dissemination of dispute resolution skills among the leadership. The central point underlying all this, of course, is that violent conflicts in South Asia or anywhere else are not the result of historical inevitability, but of clear and identifiable choices made by political leaders for specific reasons. These conflicts can hence be prevented and managed and their impact reversed.

Notes

The views expressed in this chapter are strictly those of the author and do not represent the views of the United Nations.

1. For wide-ranging analyses of the interplay of diverse factors in causing conflicts in the region, see Marvin Weinbaum and Chetan Kumar, eds., *South Asia Approaches the Millennium: Reexamining National Security* (Boulder, Colo.: Westview Press, 1995).

2. In this context, see Partha S. Ghosh, "Regional Security and Cross-Border Population Movements in South Asia," in *Regional Security, Ethnicity, and Governance: The Challenges for South Asia,* ed. Justus Richter and Christian Wagner (New Delhi: Manohar, 1998).

3. In this context, see Douglas Allen, ed., *Religion and Political Conflict in South Asia: India, Pakistan, and Sri Lanka* (Westport, Conn.: Greenwood Press, 1992).

4. For a detailed historical analysis of the first three episodes, see Sumit Ganguly, *The Origins of War in South Asia: Indo-Pakistani Conflicts since 1947* (Lahore: Vanguard Books, 1988).

5. In 1948, Pakistan challenged the accession to India by the Hindu ruler of a largely Muslim Kashmir, and before Indian rule over the province could be consolidated, invaded the province and took control of a third of its area before Indian troops moved in. The UN mediated a cease-fire, and called for a referendum among the Kashmiris to determine whether they wanted to join India or Pakistan. However, with both countries laying claim to the entire Kashmir, no referendum has been held, and Indian and Pakistani troops have since faced each other across the cease-fire line, also known as the Line of Control.

6. See Salman Rushdie, "Kashmir, the Imperiled Paradise," *New York Times,* June 3, 1999.

7. For a comprehensive account of the Afghan civil war and the rise of the Taliban, see Barnett R. Rubin, "Afghanistan: The Forgotten Crisis," *Writenet country paper*, February 1996, <http://www.unhcr.ch/refworld/country/writenet/wriafg.htm>.

8. See *Amnesty International Report 1997: Afghanistan.* Also see Amnesty International, testimony before the Senate Foreign Relations Committee, Subcommittee on Near East and South Asia, "Afghanistan: The Crisis Continues," by T. Kumar, Advocacy Director for Asia and Pacific, Amnesty International USA, April 14, 1999.

9. See Amin Saikal, "The Enhanced Dangers of a Clash Over Kashmir," *International Herald Tribune,* May 29, 1999.

10. For a comprehensive analysis of the causes and implications of these events, see Stephen P. Cohen, "Nuclear Weapons and Conflict in South Asia" (paper presented at Harvard/MIT Transnational Security Project Seminar, November 23, 1998).

11. See "Kargil: What Does It Mean?" *CSIS South Asia Monitor,* no. 12, July 19, 1999.

12. See Eqbal Ahmad, "The BUS Can Bring a Nobel Prize," *Dawn,* February 21, 1999.

13. On recent conflict management in South Asia, see Chetan Kumar, "A Chronology of Indo-Pak Cooperation, 1947–1995," in *Brasstacks and Beyond: Perception and Management of Crisis in South Asia,* Kanti Bajpai et al. (New Delhi: Manohar; Urbana: Program in Arms Control, Disarmament, and International Security, University of Illinois, 1995).

14. For more on this crisis, see Kanti P. Bajpai et al., *Brasstacks and Beyond: Perception and Management of Crisis in South Asia* (New Delhi: Manohar, 1995).

15. For the role of the World Bank in facilitating this critical agreement, see S. Kirmany and G. LeMoigne, *Fostering Riparian Cooperation in International River Basins,* World Bank Technical Paper (1996).

16. See Amitabh Mattoo, "Need to Make Line of Control the International Border," *India Abroad,* July 9, 1999.

17. See Neil Joeck, *Maintaining Nuclear Stability in South Asia,* Adelphi Papers, no. 312 (Oxford: Oxford University Press for International Institute for Strategic Studies, 1998).

18. On economic integration, see Vineeta Kumar, "Only Economics Can Bury South Asia's Ghosts," *Wall Street Journal,* July 21, 1999.

19. For arguments relating to the role of political institutions in this matter, see Subrata K. Mitra and Dietmar Rothermund, *Legitimacy and Conflict in South Asia* (New Delhi: Manohar, 1998).

10

International Organizations and the Prevention of Ethnic Conflicts

Searching for an Effective Formula
Albrecht Schnabel

THERE IS NOW ample evidence of more and, usually, less successful attempts by international organizations to prevent internal, often ethnically motivated conflicts. An effective formula (based on a mixture of general and case-specific approaches and effective collaboration between international, state, and nonstate actors) needs to be developed for addressing successfully the challenge of potential and impending internal conflicts. This requires the international community to agree both on a new consensus on intervention and on full commitment to the difficult and unpopular task of conflict prevention.

This chapter examines the roots, challenges, and consequences of internal conflict. It offers an assessment of the art of conflict prevention and international organizations' recent efforts in developing and applying conflict prevention mechanisms in their work. Since the brunt of the work of international organizations (both the UN and regional organizations) has concentrated on conflict management, after conflicts have broken out, with little or no systematic efforts to prevent conflicts from erupting (particularly within states), much has to be done to sensitize the world community (i.e., states and their intergovernmental organizations) to develop more effective steps toward effective prevention of ethnic and other internal conflicts.

The Challenges and Consequences of Ethnic Conflict

Since the end of the Cold War the world's attention has been focused on violent conflicts within states. Intrastate conflicts were brought to the attention of public, official, and intergovernmental circles and thus received much more attention than before. The growing awareness of internal conflict has naturally attracted the attention of the scholarly community. Numerous Sovietologists reinvented (and trained) themselves by focusing on the successor states and their tribulations of transition, or studying minority struggles. Also, the United Nations and regional organizations refocused their attention from superpower competition, defense, and deterrence, to the many nontraditional security threats that now became fashionable to study—environmental threats, human security threats, and ethnic conflicts or refugee movements. Some organizations that were initially invented because and for the Cold War competition between East and West also reinvented themselves to stay in existence. The North Atlantic Treaty Organization is probably the most prominent among them. Created as a Cold War defensive alliance against the Soviet Union, NATO ended up attacking a sovereign nonmember state in defense of an oppressed ethnic minority (Kosovo, 1999). Many regional organizations, originally created to facilitate economic and possibly political cooperation, have assumed or are in the process of assuming a new role as regional (cooperative) security provider (including the OAU, OAS, EU, or ASEAN).

At the same time, many domestic conflicts are indeed the direct result of the collapse of the Soviet system. In eastern and southeastern Europe and in the former Soviet Union, the political and economic transitions left many or most of the successor and former Soviet Bloc states structurally weak and vulnerable to internal and external political and economic pressures. As established political elites began to compete for power with newly emerging elites, most of these countries struggled through their first-ever experience with democracy and free political and economic competition. In short, what emerged after the fall of the Iron Curtain were political entities that had been created under dictatorial force—now without stable and legitimate governments—plenty of opportunistic contestants for political power, and in poor economic conditions. Populations throughout the postcommunist camp experienced a drop in wealth, personal security, and living standards. A combination of political vacuums, economic collapse, and opportunities and demands for political strongmen caused the eruption of internal conflict and war. The former Yugoslavia, the southern Caucasus, and Central Asia have suffered the most from this development.

In the meanwhile, internal conflicts, often with significant involvement from neighboring states, have continued to rage in Africa, Asia, and Latin America. From Somalia to Rwanda, from Cambodia to East Timor, and from El Salvador to Haiti, internal conflicts have continued to destabilize their regions and to cause immense human suffering. Since the end of the Cold War, due to diminished concerns that local and regional conflicts could escalate into international ones, local boiling points were left more or less unchecked by major powers. Instead emphasis was put on (and opportunity created for) international responses through the UN, but without providing the UN with the means to embrace that role.

Finally, the end of the Cold War has seen a surge of newly acknowledged security threats—a development that has created greater awareness of the great variety of potential roots of conflict and insecurity. International organizations have been champions of this awareness. It gave them new purposes and tasks. It also changed their mandates and brought them into conflict with some of their core principles, such as respect for and protection of their member states' sovereignty.

The Roots of Ethnic Conflict

One of the great tragedies of the post–Cold War period has been the ease with which conflicts have been dubbed ethnic conflicts. A good many conflicts could have been either prevented or managed at an early stage of violence if the international community had not taken this approach. In most if not all cases of "ethnic" conflict, the roots of disputes and escalating violence have not been and are not of an ethnic nature. The roots of these conflicts lie in poor or absent governance, failed states, competition over resources and political power, elite politics, and general economic or environmental degradation. In other words, though many conflicts are fought along ethnic lines, ethnicity is not the root of intergroup violence. Interethnic violence is the eventual manifestation of an elite-driven process to use the lowest common denominators—race and ethnicity—as the means for political mobilization; and of the tendency of oppressed, marginalized, or starving people to identify themselves with ethnic identities in the absence of legitimate governmental authorities. Therefore, while most domestic conflicts begin as disputes over access to power and resources, eventual battle camps are created around ethnic groups. Unfortunately, many of these conflicts are seen as insoluble due to the supposed primordial ethnic nature of violence. As mentioned in earlier chapters, in the former Yugoslavia, intergroup struggles were considered the result of deep-seated ethnic hatreds with their roots in historic antagonisms and violence. Therefore the assumption has been that little can be done to solve historic animosities from outside. Moreover, such conflicts were considered to be part of a natural process to return to pre–communist era power struggles between ethnic groups for control over territory and political power.

This assumption has clearly been a mistake. While it is reasonable to assume that it would be difficult for a third party to resolve historic antagonisms or to prevent the natural course of historic events, these were simply not the reasons responsible for the violence experienced in numerous internal conflicts. Poor governance and distorted democratization processes, breakdown of judicial and economic structures, poverty, and political anarchy—the feeding ground for racial and nationalist polarization and politicization—are all issues that could and should have been addressed by the donor community and so-called regional and international security providers at an early point. Not only did the international community fail to act early to prevent ethnic extremism from determining daily politics, they even accelerated this process with poor policy decisions in the face of emerging crises. The West's ignorance of and indifference to the plight of many postcommunist societies and states accelerated their descent into political and economic anarchy. Thoughtful financial and political programs could have prevented or contained many of the root causes of internal breakdown.

Moreover, the West's naive fancy with self-determination and ethnic liberation movements encouraged secession and secessionist war. It also motivated secessionist groups to present themselves as unique ethnic groups who needed to pursue self-determination as a means of survival. The quest for ethnic self-determination should not by itself serve as the justification to pursue secession with international support. Few ethnic minority communities would ever be viable as independent states, and the recognition of some would most certainly trigger a chain reaction of similar claims and struggles within their home state and elsewhere. The result is the creation of quasi-states—hollow structures recognized by the international community but with no means to provide for their people and little chance of political and economic survival.[1] Moreover, separation does not resolve many of the underlying issues of contention—they could then be pursued further between the former and new states—turning intrastate conflicts into interstate conflicts. Conflicts between Ethiopia and Eritrea, India and Pakistan, or Bosnia and Croatia are cases in point.

Finally, labeling domestic conflicts over power and resources as primordial ethnic conflicts, conflicts that cannot possibly be solved by outsiders, relieves potential security providers of the responsibility of early and even late intervention. Once the roots of a conflict are fully understood and point to relatively simple solutions (such as economic assistance), it becomes more difficult to avoid involvement and ignore the escalation of an evolving crisis. If a conflict seems insoluble, the international community can retreat with a clear conscience. If a conflict appears solvable, there will be pressure (domestic and foreign) to assist in the prevention of further conflict escalation. In other words, as Bruce Jentleson argues, there is little interest on the part of many international actors (IOs and individual states) to explore opportunities for conflict prevention and resolution at the pre-conflict level, as knowledge and information, once gained, commit one to action.[2]

Of course, if conflicts are left untouched until leaders and elites have turned them into ethnic opposition and competition, ethnicity and clashing identities gradually become the basis along which violence is exercised. Then group identity delineates the warring parties, and the main reasons for violence are fear of oppression, physical harm, and extermination based one one's group membership. Intergroup conflicts over power and resources become intergroup conflicts over identity. Once a conflict has evolved from material to ideological and identity fears and threats, once the initial reasons for conflicting interests are replaced with existential fears for group survival, group identity defines the lines of battle. At that stage the stakes are much higher and competition over influence gives way to competition over existence. In addition, it becomes more difficult for third parties (state and nonstate actors) to find effective entry points for conflict containment. While at an earlier conflict stage it would have been sufficient to offer loans to governments to maintain basic social services or to restructure the domestic economy, or to pressure titular nations to offer some degree of political autonomy to politically and economically oppressed or neglected segments of the population, such measures are of little help once they resort to violence.

Moreover, manifesting group identity becomes indispensable in the face of fear for survival. Political elites can play up to group identity manifestations as rallying points around which the necessary support for conflict—and the accompanying sacrifices—can be secured. As the conflict escalates and casualties accumulate, group cohesiveness strengthens. Even those (usually large) parts of the population previously opposed to armed violence will support efforts to step up the means of warfare. As the recent conflict in Kosovo showed, nonviolent resistance between 1991 and 1998, and broad opposition to the use of force to gain (or regain) autonomy and some degree of self-governance, gave way to broad public support for the Kosovo Liberation Army's strategy for armed conflict.

The Costs of Ethnic Conflict

The consequences of ethnic conflict are devastating for the populations involved in the conflict and for those willing to offer assistance in settling and resolving it. Once a conflict has been defined along ethnic lines, it becomes all-encompassing as entire segments of the population are targeted, irrespective of age, occupation, and gender. Victims thus include in equal numbers children, women, the old, and those unable to fight or defend themselves. Targeting civilians moreover becomes a deliberate strategy of attrition. This contributes greatly to the tremendous brutality of ethnic conflicts, which, in turn, contributes to the deep sense of hatred and hostility that is so characteristic of domestic conflicts. Once children have been murdered and women have been raped, hatred and antagonism penetrates the entire society and continues to strengthen the support for violence.

Beyond the initial consequences for the nature and duration of war, violent conflicts are difficult to settle and even more difficult to resolve. They become protracted conflicts. Memories of civilian atrocities permeate societies and make it difficult for present and future generations to develop the level of trust and respect that is necessary for diverse societies to function without frequent resort to violence. This has significant consequences for the international community's attempts to build peace and reestablish a semblance of order.

The international community finds it extremely difficult to assist societies to manage violent conflict and to recover from its consequences. Nongovernmental organizations (NGOs) and humanitarian aid organizations have often been present in societies of transition for many years, or have set up their operations after the first signs of social, economic, political, or environmental degeneration in efforts to assist suffering populations. Once fighting begins, their work becomes increasingly risky: they get caught in the crossfire of warring groups, or they are targeted out of suspicion that their assistance aids the war effort of the adversary. Since civilians become strategic targets, assistance and humanitarian relief for the opposing group becomes a threat to one's own war efforts.

International organizations are limited even further—first by the principle of sovereignty, which does not allow for intervention in another state's domestic affairs; by the high level of violence, which poses great risks to intervening parties; and by the protracted nature of domestic conflicts, which require long-term commitment to peace operations. Without a clear exit strategy and hopes for an eventual solution to a conflict, few countries and organizations are willing to accept great risks in attempting to resolve violent domestic conflicts. The resolution of domestic conflicts depends to a large degree on the willingness of conflicting parties to engage in negotiations toward ending the violence. Only when such commitment to peace is present will there be enough support from member states to allow IOs to participate in peace operations. The international community's experiences in various conflicts of the post-Cold War years, particularly in Somalia and Bosnia (and now in Sierra Leone), have shown that peace operations deployed into ongoing wars are dangerous, ineffective, and often counterproductive to the eventual resolution of conflict.

In summary, letting domestic conflicts take on an ethnic dimension spells disaster for both conflicting parties and potential conflict managers and security providers. Unless the international community wants to continue to live with the humanitarian consequences of ethnic conflict, it has two options: it can intervene forcefully in domestic conflicts and accept the risks of warfare, or it can prevent the escalation of domestic disputes before they take on an ethnic dimension. It is doubtful that the UN, regional organizations, or alliances of willing states will intervene in domestic conflicts on a principled basis (whenever and wherever intervention would be necessary). The human, economic, and political risks are too great to allow for systematic military intervention in ongoing conflicts. The best strategy is to prevent those conflicts from taking place.

The Challenges of Conflict Prevention

Conflict prevention is not a utopian notion. The management of emerging conflicts, with clearly identifiable entry points for outside intervention (in the form of mediation, negotiation, facilitation, sanctions, or even military deployment) is feasible. As discussed above, in many cases ethnic conflicts are avoidable if addressed at an early stage. The rationale for conflict prevention is simple: It is easier and less costly to prevent a conflict from emerging than to deal with the many human and other costs after violence has begun. Since the current international system favors conflict management over conflict prevention, a new consensus needs to emerge, allowing humanitarian intervention before the outbreak of armed violence. This consensus has to be reached primarily between the member states of regional and international organizations.

Conflict prevention (before, during, and after violent conflict) is emerging as an important alternative to the management and resolution of violence. However, if conflicts are to be prevented successfully and systematically, ideally with the help or guidance of the United Nations, the only multipurpose and universal international organization, a concrete operational definition needs to be developed for all who become involved in creating, providing, and applying early warning mechanisms to detect the emergence of a potential conflict. This would also apply to those who respond to an escalating conflict in efforts to contain or stop a conflict from developing into all-out violence.

Former UN secretary-general Boutros Boutros-Ghali has offered a sweeping definition of conflict prevention that has often been used by governments and regional organizations. For him, preventive diplomacy is "action to prevent disputes from arising between parties, to prevent existing disputes from escalating into conflicts and to limit the spread of the latter when they occur." He further argues that "the most desirable and efficient employment of diplomacy is to ease tensions before they result in conflict—or, if conflict breaks out, to act swiftly to contain it and resolve its underlying causes. . . . Preventive diplomacy requires measures to create confidence; it needs early warning based on information gathering and informal or formal fact-finding; it may also involve preventive deployment and, in some situations, demilitarized zones."[3] However, such a broad approach to preventive action, virtually circumscribing all perceivable stages of conflict, from prevention to resolution, is of limited help and does not allow us to distinguish preventive action from conflict management or resolution. As Michael Lund notes, "Defining conflict prevention as actions taken at virtually any conflict stage—from the causes of disagreements through many possible thresholds of bloodshed—is too inclusive and . . . blurs important operational distinctions among the interventions made at different stages of conflict."[4]

In response to what he describes as the "Life History of a Conflict," Lund provides a more useful approach to conflict prevention. He envisions peace enforcement (or conflict mitigation) as the appropriate response to war situations and peacekeeping (or conflict termination) as a means to defuse war and conflict, followed by postconflict peace building (or conflict resolution).[5] Each of these stages requires different operational and institutional responses, while conflict prevention as such is only effective during a situation of unstable peace—when the signs for an emerging conflict become obvious to the informed local and external observers. According to Lund, conflict prevention can be understood as peacetime diplomacy (or politics) during eras of durable and stable peace, preventive diplomacy (or conflict prevention) during eras of unstable peace, crisis diplomacy (or crisis management) during a crisis situation, and peacemaking (or conflict management) during war.[6] Bruce Jentleson echoes this more subtle interpretation of conflict prevention by distinguishing between normal diplomacy, developmentalist diplomacy, preventive diplomacy, and war diplomacy, an approach which seems more fitting to explain the wide range of external involvement in zones of instability.[7]

Of course, the most effective approach to conflict prevention would be to create an environment of stability, prosperity, and opportunity with constitutionally regulated competition over land, resources, and political access and control. This is highly unlikely to happen in many parts of the world. However, steps in that direction should and can be taken. Addressing structural causes of conflict and strengthening institutions that can foster democracy, development, human rights, and peaceful relations between groups and states are important components of a long-term, early approach to conflict prevention. For this task, the role of IOs is indispensable. This approach also targets the root causes of what might develop into ethnic conflict at a later stage and, thus, is particularly crucial to the discussion in this chapter. In the absence of intergroup conflict, identity—its defense and preservation—plays only a small role in domestic and foreign policy. Peaceful, safe, and prosperous relations within multiethnic societies are the best recipe for the prevention of armed conflict and violence.

The Difficult Task of Conflict Prevention

Rhetoric and policy in conflict prevention are two different issues. While there is much talk by many governments, IOs, and scholars about the utility of and necessity for conflict prevention, little is done to give this concept a leading role in foreign policy. Partly, this is because the international community is already busy containing the flames of existing conflicts, and few resources and political commitment will be invested in those conflicts that have not yet emerged. On the other hand, conflict prevention is a daunting challenge that quickly meets the resistance of governments and IOs who show little willingness to invest in the future of potentially unstable societies. Then, one needs to consider the nature of IOs. Their primary clients are their member states. The United Nations as well as regional organizations can only do as much as their member states allow them to do. Moreover, even if there is agreement to pursue a certain course of action, participation by member states is voluntary. IOs cannot enforce their decisions beyond the use of moral power, economic sanctions, or political pressure. In addition, IOs have often been created to protect and defend, not to challenge and undermine, state sovereignty. Despite its usefulness in some cases, intervention can go wrong (it can be abused by one or more states), or a more relaxed policy of intervention can at some point backfire, offering the pretext for other countries' intervention in one's own internal affairs. Finally, few interventions are followed up with matching postsettlement commitments. Rebuilding war-torn societies, especially after ethnic conflicts have divided societies for years to come, requires long-term commitment to political, economic, and cultural peace-building. However, once a conflict has receded, headlines have moved from title pages, and other emerging and raging conflicts have captured the attention of international public opinion, then crucially necessary monies, troops, and other assistance are shifted away from postconflict environments.

Still, there are a few structures in place that allow the international community to intervene in a potentially destabilizing situation and provide the good governance necessary to avoid an escalation of fear and violence. The international community engages in conflict prevention—in both the long and the short term—through the UN and regional organizations, interested states, interested groups of states, NGOs (both public and private), and individuals. The European Union's high commissioner for national minorities is an example of a successful conflict prevention tool used by a regional organization. With their various activities, on smaller local or larger national, regional, or even global scales, these actors stabilize societies, offer social services not provided by the state, provide economic and environmental assistance, or organize intergroup mediation of disputes.

However, few of the existing conflict-preventive activities are systematically organized and coordinated. They are left as small and isolated steps. Nonstate, state, and interstate actors pursue their own policies, activities, and security projects, with little or no coordination with each other. The voice of the so-called international community is in fact a multitude of voices, each pursuing its goals and interests, driven by its own mandates and motivations. Competition and turf fights between them are not rare. There is much overlap, and the many responses by the various representatives of the international community are an uncoordinated mess—certainly not a suitable response to societies in risk of blowing up into violence.

Put together and coordinated with each other, they may easily add up to a powerful strategy, a division of labor based on the comparative advantage of each actor. Interorganizational collaboration requires that each organization can speak as a single voice, that each organization works effectively, within its purpose and mandate, and that this collaboration can be maintained for some time. Since every organization has its special expertise, its particular comparative advantage, coordination and collaboration between them will result in none of them being overburdened. In such an arrangement, organizations would complement each other's involvement and become more efficient and effective.

For example, the United Nations can draw on its role as the only global organization with a virtually complete membership of the world's nations. It has a certain degree of moral power and, if the Security Council and the major states agree, its political weight is unmatched. Its various programs have worldwide representation and support. The UN Development Program, the UN Environment Program, the UN High Commissioner for Refugees, the UN Office of the High Commissioner for Human Rights, and the UN International Children's Emergency Fund (UNICEF) are closely engaged in what we could call long-term conflict-prevention tasks. The many conventions ranging from child soldiers to land mines contribute to the same cause. The Security Council and the secretary-general address emergency situations; they engage in preventive diplomacy and conflict management tasks—ranging from sanctions to the deployment of preventive, peacekeeping, or peace-enforcing troops.

Regional organizations are involved in many activities similar to those of the UN—from economic to technical assistance, political pressure, human rights advocacy, high-level preventive diplomacy, and the deployment of military personnel. However, regional organizations operate within their sphere of influence, usually within the territories of their member states. Thus, they are often better equipped to prevent conflicts. They are highly motivated, they possess greater local knowledge and understanding, they are able to offer carrots and sticks either to enhance membership privileges (when disputes are resolved) or to withhold these privileges (when disputes continue). In some cases regional organizations possess greater financial resources, and all members of the organization are directly affected by the consequences of conflict. This cannot be said about the United Nations. On the other hand, not all regional organizations are as well funded and equipped as, for instance, the European Union (EU) or the Organization for Cooperation and Security in Europe (OSCE). Moreover, the EU in particular is the closest that international society has come to creating a "security community." The combination of internal stability and economic prosperity put these organizations in an excellent position to pursue long-term conflict prevention and peacebuilding policies. The Organization of American States (OAS) has a very good track record in the promotion of human rights and democratization throughout its region. Nevertheless, regional organizations in developing countries need the support of the UN or of regional organizations in the North in their efforts to advance their own and member states' capacity for conflict prevention. [8]

Individual member states are important actors in preventive and crisis diplomacy. Close contacts between high-ranking officials of neighboring countries can be more effective than high-ranking delegations sent from faraway places and organizations. For interests usually related to their own national security, interested states or groups of states (such as the Contact Group in southeastern Europe, the role of Liberia in Sierra Leone, the role of Russia in the southern Caucasus and Central Asia, or Australia in East Timor) are willing to become involved in the provision of short- or long-term security in neighboring states. This may be useful to conflicts that would not otherwise attract outside involvement, but it also raises the danger of abuse. While Australia's involvement in East Timor has been laudable, Russia's involvement in conflicts in its own sphere of interest has been less than evenhanded and stabilizing. As long as UN standards and rules of engagement are followed, regional organizations and groups of states or single states have a crucial role to play in the provision of security. If those actors follow their own moral and legal justification, less and not more order will likely be the consequence. NATO's decision to wage an air war against Yugoslavia to assist the Albanian population of Kosovo has been just such a questionable operation—but it also points to the weakness of the UN to respond adequately to crises and to let regional alliances take matters into their own hands.[9]

Civil-society actors are involved at all stages of instability and conflict, often providing the services and assistance failed governments cannot or do not want to provide. Business communities, often part of the cause of conflict, can also serve to stabilize a society and local economy. Although they can be a blessing or a curse, usually they are the latter. There is moreover very little coordination between NGOs—who have to compete with each other for scarce funds and the justification for their existence.

Collaboration on conflict prevention is based on a division of labor in which the UN offers international legitimacy, and regional organizations and neighboring states or interested groups of states possess both regional and local knowledge as well as the political will necessary to pursue the quick settlement of a conflict that may destabilize the entire region. Local actors—NGOs from within and outside society—know local circumstances; they know what works and what does not work on a local level. Every attempt by the international community to prevent or manage a conflict, particularly in the case of ethnic conflicts, requires international legitimacy, regional resources, and local expertise. Collaboration and coordination between international, regional, and local actors is thus essential to utilize the various actors in the best way possible. Little collaboration and coordination has thus far been accomplished.

What needs to be done by IOs to effectively promote collaboration toward conflict prevention?[10] Meaningful research on conflict prevention and resulting prescriptions for effective training and application need to be grounded in thorough situational analysis. Emphasis should be put on multilateral and multitrack applications of applied conflict prevention strategies. These strategies must be sustainable in order to be effective. They also need to converge and be harmonized in order to facilitate coordination between different actors. Such convergence requires information exchange and joint activities. Harmonization and mainstreaming could take place through policy coordination that is both formal and informal. Moreover, harmonization requires identification of key stakeholders and an inventory of needs and security providers.

None of these activities, from basic research to capacity building and training, can be achieved without adequate funding. Thus, donors need to be included in this process at all stages—not only as funders, but also as stakeholders who are keenly interested in participating in research and training activities. Donors can act as catalysts for the process of coordination and cooperation between actors.

Conflict prevention needs to be "sold" effectively. This persuasion should be based on thorough impact assessments—of potential projects and of concluded projects. Different approaches work in different cultural, political, and social contexts—and at different stages of intervention. Thus, lessons have to be thoroughly based on local experience and impact. Although it is true that it is hard to measure counterfactuals (and, thus, the potential success of conflict prevention measures), the evidence that does exist needs to be publicized effectively among various internal and external stakeholders. Lessons learned from previous collaboration between the UN, regional organizations, and civil-society actors need to be analyzed and shared. Very little has been done in that regard, particularly when it comes to the sharing of experience. "Lessons-learned" exercises undertaken by various regional organizations and UN institutions need to be thoroughly evaluated by all actors involved in conflict prevention activities.

Finally, conflict prevention strategies need to be congruent with local experiences, circumstances, and expertise. Local ownership has to be a priority, as only local projects, managed locally (with external assistance and input, if invited) are bound to be successful in the long term. Sustainability, one of the key requirements for successful conflict prevention, could be best achieved through self-ownership and the development of indigenous capacities. An engaged civil society may be the best route to achieve grassroots multitrack conflict prevention at the local level.

A number of very specific challenges need to be addressed if conflict prevention is to be successful and effective: working relationships have to be forged between regional organizations and the UN; among regional organizations; and between programs, departments, and institutions of the UN. Where such relationships exist at rudimentary levels, they need to be improved dramatically. Conflict prevention has to move closer to the local level, or, at the very least, national and international efforts have to be well tuned in to local needs and must invest in local capacity building. Conflict prevention, at all levels, has to be sustainable (and has to be sustained) to assure meaningful results. Regional organizations and the UN should have at their disposal standby expert groups (with theoretical, practical, and regional expertise on conflict prevention) for urgent advice on early warning and preventive measures. Academics and policymakers alike need to develop successful approaches to sell conflict prevention to decision makers and opinion makers. Too much rhetoric that has not been followed up has made conflict prevention a hollow concept and exercise for many stakeholders. Thus, "smaller steps, based on pragmatic assessments of what can and cannot be done, along with honest efforts to engage in long-term human development, conflict avoidance and peace management, can go a long way in re-instilling confidence in the ability of intergovernmental, state and non-state actors to prevent or minimize violent conflict and human suffering."[11]

In summary, preventive measures have to be timely. Entries have to be as early as possible, and exit strategies have to be flexible to respond adequately and not too hastily to changing local conditions. In potential ethnic conflicts, entry has to be secured before a conflict takes on an intergroup and ethnic character. This requires the effective use of existing information on early warning and societal dynamics. Once a conflict is being translated and waged on ethnic terms, it is often too late to forge peaceful settlements. There needs to be an international consensus on the concept of failed states. There needs to be agreement on the point at which a state can be considered to be a failed state, one that is unable to meet the basic security needs of all parts of its population.

The focus of international responses to failed states needs to rest on the concept of human security—the provision of which should be attempted quickly, with broad international support and with long-term commitment by a variety of international actors—states, regional organizations, and the United Nations. Competing justifications for intervention, driven by competing interests and interpretation of international legal principles, need to be avoided. The international community needs to speak and act in collaboration—if such collaboration cannot be forged in general terms, it needs to be forged in each individual case. The initiative can best be taken by a state or group of states with a direct interest in the resolution of an evolving conflict.

Conclusion

The simple categorization *ethnic conflict* has now long been reassessed and revised, and numerous so-called ethnic conflicts have been traced to basic inequalities and the absence of adequate human needs provision. Similarly, conflict prevention needs to focus on political and economic stabilization, to prevent the escalation of basically economic and political disputes into violent conflict along ethnic lines.

We need to acknowledge that most societies—both homogeneous and heterogeneous—do live in peace. What has been hailed as a culture of peace already does exist. Most societies manage to resolve disputes peacefully. Stability is normal, as is the nonviolent resolution of social conflict. While most domestic disputes are ably addressed by responsible governments, poor governance leads to the breakdown of societal order and security and to escalation to violent conflict. What steps are necessary to move conflict prevention beyond rhetoric and create broadly supported policies that allow us to mitigate ethnic conflicts? Can there be a new formula for successful ethnic conflict prevention?

What we need are mechanisms that allow for an early entry into the domestic politics of unstable societies by regional organizations and the United Nations—in a concerted effort that includes nongovernmental and civil-society actors representing society in a failed state. The uniqueness and potential effectiveness of this formula is a coordinated early entry into a failed state. This has to be based on very clearly defined rules and regulations, supported by the vast majority of states.

Who should take the initiative in this endeavor? Is the UN able to provide the necessary leadership? The UN can initiate an effective approach to conflict prevention only if it is willing to cooperate internally. For this to happen the United Nations needs to coordinate its own departments, programs, and agencies in the development and application of long- and short-term conflict prevention tasks. The UN needs to act as one actor, with one voice. First steps in that direction have been taken, including the Strategic Framework for Analysis at the UN Secretariat and the UN Staff College's innovative training course on Early Warning and Preventive Measures.[12] Once the UN has accomplished this task, it will be able to reach out and incorporate regional organizations in its efforts. Then the partnership can be expanded to integrate civil society actors.

Such a prospect, however, requires the vision of committed leaders within the UN, regional organizations, and NGOs, as well as the continuous support of these organizations' members. This is a tall order and may be neither realistic nor feasible. But we do not have a choice if we are serious about effective conflict prevention. We should agree on global standards that prohibit states from allowing disputes to become violent ethnic conflicts. This requires that we replace the sanctity of state sovereignty with the sanctity of human security as the guiding principle of international and global order. This is an agenda that has been promoted by a number of enlightened governments (among them the Scandinavian governments, Canada, or Japan) and that may be successful in the long run. Promoting these ideas is part of an overall effort to make greater use of international organizations to serve peace, security, justice, and dignity in international and global politics.

Notes

The opinions expressed in this chapter are the author's and do not necessarily reflect the views of the United Nations University.

1. See Robert H. Jackson, *Quasi-States: Sovereignty, International Relations, and the Third World* (Cambridge: Cambridge University Press, 1993).

2. Bruce Jentleson, *Preventive Diplomacy and Ethnic Conflict: Possible, Difficult, Necessary,* IGCC Policy Paper no. 27 (San Diego: Institute on Global Conflict and Cooperation, June 1996).

3. Boutros Boutros-Ghali, *An Agenda for Peace* (New York: United Nations, 1992), pars. 20, 23.

4. Michael Lund, "Early Warning and Preventive Diplomacy," in *Managing*

Global Chaos, ed. Chester A. Crocker, Fen Osler Hampson, with Pamela Aall (Washington, D.C.: U.S. Institute of Peace Press, 1996), 382–83.

5. Ibid., 386; Michael Lund, *Preventing Violent Conflict: A Strategy for Preventive Diplomacy* (Washington, D.C.: USIP Press, 1996), 38.

6. Lund, "Early Warning and Preventive Diplomacy," 386.

7. Jentleson, "Preventive Diplomacy and Ethnic Conflict," 7.

8. For a number of examinations of the success and failures of the UN and regional organizations, see David Carment and Albrecht Schnabel, eds., *Conflict Prevention: Path to Peace or Grand Illusion?* (Tokyo: United Nations University Press, 2001).

9. For an extensive examination of the Kosovo conflict, see Albrecht Schnabel and Ramesh Thakur, eds., *Kosovo and the Challenge of Humanitarian Intervention: Selective Indignation, Collective Action, and International Citizenship* (Tokyo: United Nations University Press, 2000).

10. Some of the following lessons are drawn from David Carment and Albrecht Schnabel, "Conflict Prevention: Naked Emperor, Path to Peace, Grand Illusion, or Just Plain Difficult?" (paper presented at the forty-first Annual Convention of the International Studies Association, Los Angeles, March 14–18, 2000).

11. David Carment, Abdul-Rasheed Draman, and Albrecht Schnabel, *From Rhetoric to Policy: Towards Workable Conflict Prevention at the Regional and Global Levels,* occasional paper no. 23 (Ottawa: Centre for Security and Defense Studies, Carleton University, 2000), 38.

12. See Carment and Schnabel, *Conflict Prevention,* esp. the contributions by Derek Boothby and George D'Angelo, by John Cockell, and by Connie Peck.

Contributors

Walker Connor is currently Distinguished Visiting Professor of Political Science at Middlebury College. He has held resident appointments at, inter alia, Harvard, Dartmouth, the London School of Economics, the Woodrow Wilson International Center for Scholars, Oxford, Cambridge, Bellagio, Warsaw, Singapore, and Budapest. The University of Nevada named him Distinguished Humanist of 1991–92 and the University of Vermont named him Distinguished American Political Scientist of 1997. He has published over fifty articles and five books dealing with the comparative study of nationalism.

S. A. Giannakos is Visiting Assistant Professor of Political Science at Ohio University. He received his Ph.D. in foreign affairs from the University of Virginia and he teaches courses on international relations and comparative politics with a concentration on nationalism and ethnic conflict, conflict resolution, and ethics and international affairs. His research focuses on national identity and conflict as well as on Balkan and eastern Mediterranean affairs. His articles on those topics appear in edited volumes and regional journals such as the *Mediterranean Quarterly* and the *Journal of Southeast Europe and the Balkans*. He spent nearly five years (1993–1998) overseas, conducting research and offering courses on Balkan politics at the American University in Bulgaria. He has also taught at Norwich University in Vermont and at Washington and Lee University in Virginia.

George Khutsishvili is founder, chair of the board, and Director of the International Center on Conflict and Negotiation in Tbilisi, Georgia, and Professor of Conflict and Peace Studies at Tbilisi State University. In 1993–94 he was Research Fellow at the Center for International

Security and Arms Control at Stanford University (IREX Program in International Security Studies). In 1996 he initiated the first Georgian/Abkhaz non-governmental group interactions, which evolved into the current program of confidence-building measures (CBMs) in Georgia/Abkhazia. He has published over seventy academic articles and essays in Georgian, Russian, and English publications and he is the editor of *Understanding Conflict* (1998).

Chetan Kumar is Program Officer with the Office of the Special Representative of the Secretary-General for Children and Armed Con-flict at the United Nations Headquarters in New York. He joined this office in October 1999. Between 1995 and 1999 he was Senior Associate at the International Peace Academy (IPA), an independent, nonpartisan, international institution located in New York dedicated to promoting the prevention and settlement of armed conflicts between and within states. Dr. Kumar's research interests include the politics of peacekeeping and peacemaking operations, the building and sustaining of peace in conflicted societies, conflict resolution in general, and the impact of the information technology revolution on international politics. His articles on these subjects have been published as occasional papers, book chapters, reports, and articles in journals such as *Bulletin of Peace Proposals* (now *Security Dialogue*) and *Review of International Studies*. He is the editor, with Marvin Weinbaum, of a volume on new aspects of security in South Asia, *South Asia Approaches the Millennium: Reexamining National Security* (1995), and author of *Building Peace in Haiti* (1998).

Neil MacFarlane is the Lester B. Pearson Professor of International Relations at Oxford University and Director of the Centre for International Studies, St. Anne's College, Oxford. He is well known for his book *Superpower Rivalry and Third World Radicalism: The Idea of National Liberation* (1985). His numerous articles and edited volumes deal with international and regional security. Currently he is the European Commission's advisor on European Union policy toward the Caucasus region.

Michael Malley is Assistant Professor of political science at Ohio University, where he specializes in Southeast Asian politics. He earned M.A. and Ph.D. degrees in political science at the University of Wisconsin, an M.A. in Asian Studies at Cornell University, and a B.S. from the School of Foreign Service at Georgetown University. Since the late 1980s, he has conducted extensive field research in Indonesia. Part of that research has been published as "Regions: Centralization and Resistance," in Donald K. Emmerson, ed., *Indonesia beyond Suharto* (1999). In addition, he has devoted attention to Indonesia's ongoing process of political reform in "Beyond Democratic Elections: Indonesia Embarks on a Protracted Transition," *Democratization* 7, no. 3 (Autumn 2000).

Steven Miner is Professor and Chair of the Department of History at Ohio University. He is the author of *Between Churchill and Stalin: The Soviet Union, Great Britain, and the Origins of the Grand Alliance* (1988), winner of the George Louis Beer Prize awarded by the American Historical Association. His forthcoming book is *Stalin's Holy War: Religion, Nationalism and the Alliance, 1939–1945.*

Muna Ndulo is Professor of Law at Cornell Law School. He has been educated in Zambia and at Harvard and Oxford Universities. Prior to coming to Cornell, he was Professor of Law and Dean of the School of Law at the University of Zambia and the editor of *Zambia Law Reports* and *Zambia Law Journal.* He has served as legal advisor to numerous international institutions, including being the Senior Political Adviser to the Special Representative of the United Nations Secretary-General for South Africa from 1992 to 1994. He is the editor of *Law in Zambia* (1984) and the coauthor, with Kwaku Osei-Hwedie, of *Issues in Zambian Development* (1985) and *Studies in Youth and Development* (1989) and, with John Hatchard, of *The Law of Evidence in Zambia: Cases and Materials* (1991) and *Readings in Criminal Law and Criminology in Zambia* (1992). Currently his research focuses on elections and human rights, common law and the African legal system, and trade and investment.

Albrecht Schnabel is Academic Officer in the Peace and Governance

Program of the United Nations University, Tokyo. He was educated at the University of Munich, the University of Nevada, and Queen's University, Canada, where he received his Ph.D. in Political Studies in 1995. Previously he taught at Queen's University (1994), the American University in Bulgaria (1995–96), and the Central European University (1996–98). In 1997 he was a research fellow at the Institute for Peace Research and Security Policy at the University of Hamburg and served on OSCE election monitoring missions in Bosnia-Herzegovina. He serves as a Trainer in Early Warning and Preventive Measures for the UN Staff College in Turin and as current president of the International Association of Peacekeeping Training Centers. His publications have focused on ethnic conflict, refugee policy, peacekeeping, conflict prevention and management, and humanitarian intervention. Among his most recent pieces are *The Southeast European Challenge: Ethnic Conflict and the International Response*, coedited with Hans-Georg Ehrhart (1999), *Kosovo and the Challenge of Humanitarian Intervention: Selective Indignation, Collective Action, and International Citizenship*, coedited with Ramesh Thakur (2000), and *Conflict Prevention: Path to Peace or Grand Illusion?* with David Carment (2001).

Paula Worby has been working with displaced persons and refugees from Guatemala since 1985. She lived in Guatemala for over twelve years, first as a researcher with the Asociación para el Avance de las Ciencias Sociales en Guatemala (Association for the Advancement of the Social Sciences in Guatemala, AVANCSO), and then as a UNHCR staff member from 1992 to 1999. With UNHCR, she specialized in the areas of conflict negotiation, land access, and economic reintegration for returning refugees. In 1998 she collaborated as an UN expert on the Guatemala Truth Commission report and aided in drafting Guatemalan legislation to improve women's land rights. Initial research for her chapter was conducted on behalf of UNHCR. The United States Institute of Peace (USIP) supported further research during the author's 1999–2000 affiliation with Yale University's Program in Agrarian Studies. The content was enriched by ongoing discussion with many colleagues from UNHCR, Guatemalan refugee women's organizations, and the research team working with returnee women supported in 1999–2000 by Project Counseling Services.

Index

Abdurrahman Wahid, 185
Abkhazia. *See* Autonomous Republic of
    Abkhazia.
Aceh, 182–84
Afghanistan. *See also* South Asian con-
    flict.
    bin Laden, Osama, 197–99
    civil war, 197
    conflict prevention and management,
        206
    jihad, 197–99, 201
    Taliban, 193, 195
African conflict
    causes of
        authoritarian governments, 145
        colonial rule, 141–42
        ethnically based parties, 143
        external intervention, 143–44
        nature of political power, 143
        presidents *vs.* colonial governors,
            142–43
        rural-urban divide, 142
        winner-take-all politics, 143, 150,
            156
        worldwide perceptions, 144–45
    governance
        centralization of power, 148
        citizen participation, 152
        constitutional democracy, prin-
            ciples of, 153–54
        democracy, definition, 151
        dos Santos, José Eduardo, 156
        economic backwardness, 155
        electoral process, 148–50, 156–57
        Eritrea, 157
        ethnicity, effects of, 154–55
        financial centralization, 148
        freedom of speech, 154
        good governance, definition,
            150–51
        inequality of the sexes, 155

Lissouba, Pascal, 156
Namibia, 157, 159
Nigeria, 156
presidents, negative traits, 155–56
Republic of the Congo, 156
Sasso-Nguesso, Denis, 156
Savimbi, Jonas, 156
social backwardness, 155
South Africa, 157
traditional leaders, 152–53
UNDP (United Nations Develop-
    ment Program), 150–51
winner-take-all politics, 143, 150,
    156
Zambia, 146, 149
governance, constitutions
    adoption process, 157–59
    bill of rights, 159
    commission method, 146–47
    drafts, 157–58
    European models, 147
    national, 153, 157
Mandela, Nelson, on African wars,
    144
Aland Islanders, autonomy *vs.* indepen-
    dence, 32
Ambon, 179–80
Anarchical Society, 9
Anderson, Benedict
    definition of group identity, 4
    view of group identity, 2–3
Antigone, 10
Aristotle, criticism of Platonic forms, 2
Aromanians, 52
Athenians, Balkan history, 50
Austrians, Balkan conflict, 60
authoritarian governments, Africa, 145
Autonomous Republic of Abkhazia
    cease-fire, July 1993, 112
    CIS (Commonwealth of Independent
        States), 113

CISPKF (CIS Peacekeeping Forces),
114
civil war, 112
exclusion from supreme soviet elections, 110
fall of, 112
Gamsakhurdia, Zviad, overthrow of,
111
Gamsakhurdia, Zviad, return of, 113
Kavsadze, Sandro, kidnapping of, 111
Kitovani, Tengiz, 111
Kutaisi, assault on, 113
peace talks stall, 113–14
population distribution, 116
rebellion in Mingrelia, 113
repatriation to the Gali region, 112, 114
retaliation against repatriates, 114–15
Round Table/Free Georgia coalition,
111
Sukhumi, fall of, 112
supreme soviet dissolved, 112
Tbilisi, assault on, 113
autonomy *vs.* independence
Aland Islanders, 32
Baltic nations, 33
Basques, 31, 33–34
Corsicans, 31
division of power, 36
factors in choosing, 33–34
Georgians, 33
loyalty to country, 33–34
meaningful autonomy, 34
movement of people, 36–37
Okinawans, 32
problems with, 35–37
Québécois, 31–34
Scots, 31–33
secession, 34
Slovaks, 31
Soviet Union, 33
Switzerland, 34–35
Tamils, 32
Welsh, 32
Avars, Balkan history, 53

Balkan conflict
actors, 47–48
Balkanization, 63
Bosporus strait, 55
communication networks, 65
Danubian Plains, 55
Dardanelles strait, 55
Dniester River, 55

Dragoman Pass, 55
Drava River, 54–55
empirical manifestations
Aromanians, 52
Athenians, 50
Avars, 53
Byzantine Empire, 52
during the crusades, 54
Greek city-states, liberation of, 51
Greek city-states, wars between,
49–50, 55
Macedonians, 50–51, 52
Minoans, 49
Ostrogoths, 52–53
papal involvement, 53–54
piracy, 50
Romans, 51–52, 55
Russian influence, 54
Slavs, 53
Thucydides' account of, 48–49
Venice, 53–54
Visigoths, 52
Vlachs, 52
geopolitical conflicts
Austrian influence, 60
British influence, 60–61, 62
Byzantine Empire, defeat by the
Turks, 56–57
Constantinople, downfall of, 56
Dushan, Stephan, 57
ethnic nature, 57
feudalism, 55, 57–58, 60, 63
French influence, 60–61
human rights, 61–62
Hungarian defeat at Mohacs, 58
Italian influence, 61
Manzikert, battle of, 56
Marathon, battle of, 56
Muslims *vs.* Christians, 59
national nature, 57
the Ottomans, 58–62
Russian influence, 54, 60–61, 62
Salamis, battle of, 56
Sigismund, King of Hungary, 58
Simeon, 57
Thermopylae, battle of, 56
Yugoslavia, 62–63
geopolitical patterns
BBA (Belgrade-Bucharest-
Athens) triangle, 44–46
central European pressure point,
45–47
Eurasian pressure point, 45–47

extraregional, 46–47
Mediterranean pressure point, 45–47
Near Eastern pressure point, 45–47
pressure points, 45–47
regional, 44–46
ZTI (Zagreb-Tiranë-Istanbul) triangle, 44–46
Maritsa Valley, 55
Morava Valley, 55
Prut River, 55
Sava River, 54–55
Shipka Pass, 55
strategic importance, 54
topography, effects of, 48, 54–55, 63
Balkan Ghosts: A Journey Through History, 22
Balkanization, 63
Baltic nations, autonomy *vs.* independence, 33
Bangladesh, 204. *See also* South Asian conflict.
Basques, autonomy *vs.* independence, 31, 33–34
BBA (Belgrade-Bucharest-Athens) triangle, 44–46
Belgrade-Bucharest-Athens (BBA) triangle, 44–46
bill of rights, African constitutions, 159
bin Laden, Osama, 197–99
Bolsheviks, and religion, 94–96
Bosnia: A Short History, 22
Bosnian Peace Agreement, 26
Bosporus strait, 55
Boutros Boutros-Ghali, 224
Brass Tacks, Operation, 202
Breuilly, John, 4
Bull, Hedley, 9
bytovoi natsionalizm, 124
Byzantine Empire, 52, 56–57

Carey, John, 155–56
Caucasus region. *See* Georgian conflict.
causes of conflict
Africa. *See* African conflict.
the Balkans. *See* Balkan conflict.
ethnic self-determination, 220
fear for survival, 221
Georgia. *See* Georgian conflict.
Indonesia. *See* Indonesian conflict.
material *vs.* ideological conflict, 221
misdiagnosis, 219

power, access to, 219–20
quasi-states, 220
resources, access to, 219–20
South Asia. *See* South Asian conflict.
central European pressure point, 45–47
Chamberlain, Joseph, 25–26
chameleon analogy, 4, 7
Chazon, Naomi, 149
China, in South Asia, 200–201
Christians *vs.* Muslims
Balkans, 59
Indonesia, 179–80
Christie, Agatha, 52
CIS (Commonwealth of Independent States), 113
CIS Peacekeeping Forces (CISPKF), 114
CISPKF (CIS Peacekeeping Forces), 114
city-states. *See* Greek city-states.
civic nationalism, 24
civic nationalists, 4–5
Clinton, Bill, in South Asia, 199
Clinton administration, and Yugoslavia, 22
collective identity. *See* group identity.
colonial rule, Africa, 141–42
Commonwealth of Independent States (CIS), 113
communication networks, the Balkans, 65
conflict. *See* ethnic conflict.
Congo, 156
Connor, Walker, 16
Constantinople, downfall of, 56
Constantius, Emperor of Rome, 52
constitutional democracy, principles of, 153–54
constitutions, African. *See* African conflict, governance.
Coptic Christians *vs.* Muslims, 26
Corsicans, autonomy *vs.* independence, 31
culture-based identity, 2

Danubian Plains, 55
Dardanelles strait, 55
Dayaks *vs.* Madurese, 177–78
de-Stalinization, Georgian conflict, 122–24
democracy
constitutional, principles of, 153–54
definition, 151
Deutsch, Karl, 2–3
Dniester River, 55

dos Santos, José Eduardo, 156
Dragoman Pass, 55
Drava River, 54–55
Durant, Will, 51
Dushan, Stephan, 57

East Timor, 181–82
economic development, Georgian conflict, 121–22
economic functional identity, 13–14
economic integration, South Asia, 212–13
economic liberalization, South Asia, 204–5
education
    conflict prevention and management, 206
    control of group identity, 3
    Guatemalan women refugees, 73–74
Egypt, 26
electoral process, Africa, 148–50, 156–57
endowments, South Asia, 205–6
environment, role in group identity, 16
environmental identity, 13
Eritrea, 157
ethnic conflict. *See also* African conflict; Balkan conflict; ethnonational conflict; Georgian conflict; Guatemalan women refugees; Indonesian conflict; South Asian conflict.
    causes. *See* causes of conflict.
    costs of, 222–23
    end of the Cold War, 217–18
    managing. *See* prevention and management.
    preventing. *See* international organizations; prevention and management.
ethnic nationalism, 24
ethnicity. *See also* group identity.
    African governance, 143, 154–55
    Georgian conflict, politicization of, 118
    Indonesian conflict
        cause of conflicts, 172, 187
        containment of local cultures, 177
        demographics, 171
        hierarchy of cultural identities, 176–77
        in politics, 173–74
ethnonational conflict. *See also* African conflict; Georgian conflict; Guatemalan women refugees; Indonesian conflict; South Asian conflict.
    economic causes, 22
    immutable hatreds, 22
    manipulation by elites, 22
    prevention. *See* international organizations.
    Romania, 39–40
    Yugoslavia, 21–22
ethnonational movements
    definition, 24
    failure to recognize
        Bosnian Peace Agreement, 26
        Egypt, 26
        Muslims *vs.* Coptic Christians, 26
        Northern Ireland, 25–26
    familial words and metaphors, 24–25
    use of language, 24–25
ethnonationalism. *See also* homelands, psychology of.
    civic nationalism, 24
    definition, 23
    ethnic nationalism, 24
    heterogeneity, accommodating, 40
    heterogeneous states, 27
    homogeneous states, 27
    loyalty to the nation, 24
    loyalty to the state, 24
    multiethnic states, 27
    nation, definition, 23
    nationalism *vs.* patriotism, 23, 26
    vs. nationalism, 23
ethnonationalists, 4–5
EU (European Union), 229
Eurasian pressure point, 45–47
European Union (EU), 229
Europeanizers, 4–5
everyday nationalism, 124

familial words and metaphors, 24–25
federalization of the Soviet state, 120–21
feudalism, the Balkans, 55, 57–58, 60, 63
Free Aceh Movement *vs.* Indonesian army, 182–84
Free Papua Organization, 185–86
freedom of speech, Africa, 154
French influence, Balkan conflict, 60–61

Gali region, repatriation, 112, 114–15
Gamsakhurdia, Zviad
    Georgian ethnic conflict, 123
    overthrow of, 111
    return of, 113

Gamsakhurdia government, Georgian independence, 129–31
Gandhi, Rajiv, 202
Geertz, Clifford, 2
Geertz, Hildred, 171
Gellner, Ernest, on group identity, 2–4
genocide, Mayan Indians, 69–70
geography. *See* topography, effects on the Balkans.
geopolitical patterns, the Balkans
    BBA (Belgrade-Bucharest-Athens) triangle, 44–46
    central European pressure point, 45–47
    Eurasian pressure point, 45–47
    extraregional, 46–47
    Mediterranean pressure point, 45–47
    Near Eastern pressure point, 45–47
    pressure points, 45–47
    regional, 44–46
    ZTI (Zagreb-Tiranë-Istanbul) triangle, 44–46
Georgian conflict
    Autonomous Republic of Abkhazia cease-fire, July, 1993, 112
    CIS (Commonwealth of Independent States), 113
    CISPKF (CIS Peacekeeping Forces), 114
    civil war, 112
    exclusion from supreme soviet elections, 110
    fall of, 112
    Gamsakhurdia, Zviad, overthrow of, 111
    Gamsakhurdia, Zviad, return of, 113
    Kavsadze, Sandro, kidnapping of, 111
    Kitovani, Tengiz, 111
    Kutaisi, assault on, 113
    peace talks stall, 113–14
    population distribution, 116
    rebellion in Mingrelia, 113
    repatriation to the Gali region, 112, 114
    retaliation against repatriates, 114–15
    Round Table/Free Georgia coalition, 111
    Sukhumi, fall of, 112
    supreme soviet dissolved, 112
    Tbilisi, assault on, 113

autonomy *vs.* independence, 33
casualties, 109
causes, pre-Soviet era
    collapse of tsarism, 119–20
    Georgian independence, 120
    Georgian nobility, 118–19
    language differences, 116, 118
    Marxism, 119
    miscegenation, 116, 117
    Osset rebellion, 120
    politicization of ethnicity, 118
    RSDLP (Russian Social Democratic Labor Party), 119
    Russian occupation, 118
    social democratic movement, 119
    Tsereteli, Irakli, 119
    Zhordania, Noe, 119
causes, Soviet era
    bytovoi natsionalizm, 124
    de-Stalinization, 122–24
    economic development, 121–22
    everyday nationalism, 124
    federalization of the Soviet state, 120–21
    Gamsakhurdia, Zviad, 123
    Helsinki Watch Committee, 123
    Human Rights Defense Group, 123
    Kostava, Merab, 123
    modernization, 120–21
    organized dissent groups, 123
    Soviet nationality policy, 121
cease-fires
    July 1993, 112, 131–32
    June 1992, 109–10
ethnodemographic profile, 115–17
independence
    cause of conflict, 120
    cease-fire, July 1993, 131–32
    Gamsakhurdia government, role of, 129–31
    Russia, role of, 130–31
    Russian military observers, 131–32
    Russian weaponry, 131
    weakness of central authority, 130
Ossets, 109–10, 116
perestroika and nationalism
    economic reform failure, 125
    factors involved, 125–26
    influence of elites, 126–27
    mass receptivity, 125
    nationalist agenda, 126
    populist demagoguery, 125

violence in Tbilisi, 127–28
Shida Kartli conflict, 109–10
size of groups in conflict, 116
Sochi Accord, 109–10
South Ossetian autonomous oblast,
    109–10
South Ossetian Soviet Democratic
    Republic, 109–10
German reunification, 37–38
Giannakos, S. A., 16
Gluckman, Max, 140–41
governance, African. *See* African conflict,
    governance.
governance, good, 150–51
Great Britain, Balkan conflict, 60–61, 62
Greek city-states, Balkan history
    liberation of, 51
    wars between, 49–50, 55
group identity. *See also* ethnicity.
    as an end itself, 1–2, 7, 15
    benefits of, 2, 7
    chameleon analogy, 4, 7
    changing
        under force, 14–15
        willingly, 10–11
    civic nationalists, 4–5
    control by education, 3
    culture-based identity, 2
    definition, 4
    economic functional identity, 13–14
    environment, role of, 16
    environmental identity, 13
    ethnonationalists, 4–5
    Europeanizers, 4–5
    group manifestations, 11
    Guatemalan women refugees, 70–71
    imposed on the group, 3
    individual manifestations, 11
    as a means to an end, 2–5, 7
    modernists, 4–5
    nationalizers, 4–5
    nature of, 10
    Plato's definition of justice, 6–7
    primordial attachments, 2
    primordialists, 4–5
    prioritizing, 8–9, 11–14
    role of the individual, 3
    security of the group, 11–12, 15
    security of the individual
        failure of, 15
        and group loyalty, 9
        and individual identity, 11–12
        psychological need for, 16

shape *vs.* substance, 9
social structure as defense, 7–8
spiritual identity, 13
transcending time and generations, 12
violence, and forced change, 15
Guatemalan Truth Commission, 69
Guatemalan women refugees
    deserted by partners, 76
    displacement of, 69–71
    education, 73–74
    equality with men, 76
    genocide, 69–70
    group identity, development of, 70–71
    Guatemalan Truth Commission, 69
    human rights violations, 69
    land rights
        credit responsibility, 76–77, 85
        direct ownership, 68
        distribution of land, 69
        the future, 86–87
        institutional obstacles, 84–86
        joint ownership, 78–79
        losing ground, 81–86
        male opposition, 82–84
        proof of ownership, 75
        spiritual value of land, 75–76
        theory *vs.* practice, 78–79, 81–86
    literacy, 72
    Mamá Maquin organization, 72
    Permanent Commissions of
        Guatemalan Refugees, 71
    public speaking, 74
    repatriation, 79–81
    roles
        post-repatriation, 72–75
        pre-refugee, 71–72
    self-confidence, 74
    sexuality and reproductive health, 74
    support organizations, 72–73
    UNHCR (United Nations High Com-
        missioner for Refugees), 67, 72–73
    violence against, 69–71

Habibie, R. J.
    East Timor, 181
    Papua, 185
Halmahera, 180
Helsinki Watch Committee, 123
Herder, Johann Gottfried von, 2
heterogeneity, accommodating, 40
heterogeneous states, 27
History of the Peloponnesian War, 15,
    48–49

Hizb-ul-Mujahideen, 196
Ho Chi Minh, 24–25
Hobsbawm, Eric
    definition of group identity, 4
    view of group identity, 2–3
homelands, psychology of. *See also* ethnonationalism.
    autonomy *vs.* independence
        Aland Islanders, 32
        Baltic nations, 33
        Basques, 31, 33–34
        Corsicans, 31
        division of power, 36
        factors in choosing, 33–34
        Georgians, 33
        loyalty to country, 33–34
        meaningful autonomy, 34
        movement of people, 36–37
        Okinawans, 32
        problems with, 35–37
        Québécois, 31–34
        Scots, 31–33
        secession, 34
        Slovaks, 31
        Soviet Union, 33
        Switzerland, 34–35
        Tamils, 32
        Welsh, 32
    facts *vs.* perceptions, 37–40
    German reunification, 37–38
    nonhomeland states, 30–31
    Québécois, 30
    Soviet Union, 30
    unihomeland states, 30
    worldwide number, 29–30
homogeneous states, 27
hot lines, South Asia, 211
human rights
    Balkan conflict, 61–62
    Guatemala, 69
    Indonesia, 187
    UN Office of the High Commissioner
        for Human Rights, 228
Human Rights Defense Group, 123
Hungarian defeat at Mohacs, 58
Hurriyat, 195–96

independence
    Georgia
        cause of conflict, 120
        cease-fire, July 1993, 131–32
        Gamsakhurdia government, role
            of, 129–31

Russia, role of, 130–31
Russian military observers, 131–32
Russian weaponry, 131
weakness of central authority, 130
vs. autonomy. *See* autonomy *vs.* independence.
India. *See also* South Asian conflict.
    Indus River water-sharing agreement,
        203–5
    Kashmir, 195
    prevention and management, past
        efforts, 203–4, 204–5
Indonesian army *vs.* Free Aceh Movement, 182–84
Indonesian conflict
    Aceh, 182–84
    Ambon, 179–80
    Christians *vs.* Muslims, 179–80
    Dayaks *vs.* Madurese, 177–78
    East Timor, 181–82
    economic factors, 174, 183
    ethnicity
        as cause of, 172, 187
        containment of local cultures, 177
        demographics, 171
        hierarchy of cultural identities,
            176–77
        in politics, 173–74
    factors affecting, 187
    Free Papua Organization, 185–86
    Habibie, R. J.
        East Timor, 181
        Papua, 185
    Halmahera, 180
    Indonesian army *vs.* Free Aceh Movement, 182–84
    interisland migrations, 171, 175
    Irian Jaya. *See* Papua.
    Jakarta, 179–80
    Javanese culture, 176
    Javanese language, 175–76
    Javanization, 174–76
    Kupang, 179–80
    land use, 175
    level of violence, 187
    Makassar, 179–80
    Maluku islands, 179–80
    natural resources
        Aceh, 183
        Papua, 186
        state control of, 175
    Papua, 185–86
    Papua Presidium, 185

Papuan People's Congress, 185
political centralization, 173–74
religions
    cause of conflicts, 187
    demographics, 172
    in politics, 173–74
    Roman Catholic East Timorese,
        181–82
Soeharto
    Aceh rebellion, 183
    Javanization, 174–76
    political centralization, 173–74
    resignation of, 170
Sukarno, Aceh rebellion, 183
vertical conflicts, 187
Wahid, Abdurrahman, 185
West Kalimantan, 177–78
Indus River water-sharing agreement,
    203–5
Indus Valley water-sharing agreement,
    207
international organizations. *See also*
    NGOs (nongovernmental organi-
    zations).
    EU (European Union), 229
    NATO (North Atlantic Treaty Orga-
        nization), 217
    OAS (Organization of American
        States), 229
    OSCE (Organization for Cooperation
        and Security in Europe), 229
    preventing conflicts, 226–28
    UN Development Program, 228
    UN Environment Program, 228
    UN High Commissioner for
        Refugees, 228
    UN Office of the High Commissioner
        for Human Rights, 228
    UNDP (United Nations Development
        Program), 150–51
    UNHCR (United Nations High Com-
        missioner for Refugees), 67, 72–73
    UNICEF (United Nations Interna-
        tional Children's Emergency
        Fund), 228
Italian influence, Balkan conflict, 61

Jakarta, 179–80
Javanese culture, 176
Javanese language, 175–76
Javanization, 174–76
Jentleson, Bruce, 225
jihad, 197–99, 201

Jinnah, Mohammed Ali, 194

Kaplan, Robert, 22
Kargil episode, 203
Kashmir
    India, 195
    linkage factor, 208–10
    LOC (Line of Control), 210–11
Kavsadze, Sandro, kidnapping of, 111
Khrushchev, Nikita, 104
Kingdom of the Serbs, Croats, and
        Slovenes, 21
Kitovani, Tengiz, 111
Kohl, Helmut, 37
Kostava, Merab, 123
Kupang, 179–80
Kutaisi, assault on, 113

land rights, Guatemala
    credit responsibility, 76–77, 85
    desertion by partners, 76
    direct ownership, 68
    distribution of land, 69
    the future, 86–87
    institutional obstacles, 84–86
    joint ownership, 78–79
    losing ground, 81–86
    male opposition, 82–84
    proof of ownership, 75
    spiritual value of land, 75–76
    theory *vs.* practice, 78–79, 81–86
land use, Indonesia, 175
language
    in ethnonational movements, 24–25
    familial words and metaphors, 24–25
    and Georgian conflict, 116, 118
    Guatemala, 67
    Indonesia, 171
    literacy of Guatemalan women
        refugees, 72
    as measure of ethnicity, 171
Lashkar-e-Toiba, 196
life history of a conflict, 225
Line of Control (LOC), Kashmir, 210–11
linkage factor, Kashmir, 208–10
Lissouba, Pascal, 156
literacy, Guatemalan women refugees, 72
Living (Renovationist) Church, 96
LOC (Line of Control), Kashmir, 210–11
Lund, 225

Macedonians, Balkan history, 50–51, 52
Madurese *vs.* Dayaks, 177–78

Magnus Magnentius, Emperor of Rome, 52
Maîtres Chez Nous, 30, 34
Makassar, 179–80
Malcolm, Noel, 22
Malenkov, Georgii, 96
Maluku islands, 179–80
Mamá Maquin organization, 72
managing conflict. *See* prevention and management.
Mandela, Nelson, on African wars, 144
Manzikert, battle of, 56
Mao Tse-tung, 24
Marathon, battle of, 56
Maritsa Valley, 55
Marxism, Georgian conflict, 119
Mayan Indians. *See* Guatemalan women refugees.
meaningful autonomy, 34
Mediterranean pressure point, 45–47
migrations. *See also* Guatemalan women refugees.
    and autonomy, 36–37
    interisland, Indonesia, 171, 175
Mill, John Stuart, 155
Milosevic, Slobodan, 25
Mingrelia, rebellion in, 113
Minoans, Balkan history, 49
miscegenation, Georgian conflict, 116, 117
Mitchell, George, 209–10
modernists, 4–5
modernization, Georgian conflict, 120–21
Morava Valley, 55
multiethnic states, 27
Murder on the Orient Express, 52
Musharraf, Pervez, 200
Muslims
    vs. Christians
        Balkans, 59
        Indonesia, 179–80
    vs. Coptic Christians, 26

Namibia, 157, 159
nation, definition, 23
National Identity, 2
nationalism
    and perestroika. *See* perestroika and nationalism.
    vs. ethnonationalism, 23
    vs. patriotism, 23, 26
nationalizers, 4–5
NATO (North Atlantic Treaty Organization), 217

Near Eastern pressure point, 45–47
NGOs (nongovernmental organizations), 204–5. *See also* international organizations.
Nigeria, 156
nongovernmental organizations (NGOs), 204–5. *See also* international organizations.
nonhomeland states, 30–31
North Atlantic Treaty Organization (NATO), 217
Northern Alliance, 193–94
Northern Ireland
    applied to South Asia, 209–10
    ethnonational movement, 25–26
    ethnonational movements, 25–26
    religious conflict, 6
nuclear stabilization, South Asia, 211–12
nuclear weaponization, South Asia, 191–92, 199
Nwabueze, B. O., 149–50

OAS (Organization of American States), 229
Okinawans, autonomy *vs.* independence, 32
Operation Brass Tacks, 202
Organization for Cooperation and Security in Europe (OSCE), 229
Organization of American States (OAS), 229
OSCE (Organization for Cooperation and Security in Europe), 229
Osset rebellion, 120
Ossets, 109–10, 116
Ostrogorsky, George, 52
Ostrogoths, Balkan history, 52–53

Pakistan. *See also* South Asian conflict.
    Indus River water-sharing agreement, 203–5
    as a secular state, 194
    support for the Taliban, 193, 195
papal involvement, Balkan history, 53–54
Papua, 185–86
Papua Presidium, 185
Papuan People's Congress, 185
perestroika and nationalism
    economic reform failure, 125
    factors involved, 125–26
    influence of elites, 126–27
    mass receptivity, 125
    nationalist agenda, 126

populist demagoguery, 125
violence in Tbilisi, 127–28
Permanent Commissions of Guatemalan
Refugees, 71
piracy, Balkan history, 50
Plato's definition of justice, 6–7
political centralization, Indonesia, 173–74
political hot lines, South Asia, 211
politicization of ethnicity, Georgian
conflict, 118
presidents, African
negative traits, 155–56
vs. colonial governors, 142–43
pressure points, the Balkans, 45–47
prevention and management. See also international organizations.
civil-society actors, 230
collaborative efforts, 230–231
individual member states, 229
international organizations, 226–28
life history of a conflict, 225
local ownership, 231–32
preventive diplomacy, 224–25
rationale for, 224
regional organizations, 228–29
selling prevention, 231
South Asia
1990 crisis, 202
Afghanistan, 206
Bangladesh, 204
Central Asian dimension, 207
dispersing resolution and management skills, 205
economic integration, 212–13
economic liberalization, 204–5
endowments, 205–6
India, 203–4, 204–5
Indus River water-sharing agreement, 203–5
Indus Valley example, 207
Kargil episode, 203
Kashmir, linkage factor, 208–10
Kashmir, LOC (Line of Control),
210–11
NGOs (nongovernmental organizations), 204–5
nuclear stabilization, 211–12
Operation Brass Tacks, 202
Pakistan, 203–5
political hot lines, 211
political liberalization, 204–5
public education, 206
regional philanthropy, 205–6

Sri Lankan civil war, 207–8
think tanks, 205–6
sustainability, 232
timeliness, 232
preventive diplomacy, 224–25
primordial attachments, 2
primordialists, 4–5
prioritizing group identity, 8–9, 11–14
Prut River, 55
psychology of homelands. See homelands, psychology of.
public education, South Asia, 206

quasi-states, 220
Québécois, autonomy vs. independence,
30–34

Rao, V. Narasimha, 204–5
Regan administration, and Yugoslavia, 21
regional philanthropy, South Asia, 205–6
Reid, Ann, 156
religion
Christians vs. Muslims
Balkans, 59
Indonesia, 179–80
Coptic Christians vs. Muslims, 26
Indonesia
cause of conflicts, 187
demographics, 172
in politics, 173–74
Roman Catholic East Timorese,
181–82
Renovationist (Living) Church, 96
Russian Orthodoxy
extinction of the Greek Catholic
Church, 103
Renovationist (Living) Church,
96
Uniate Church, 103
USSR. See USSR, religion.
West Ukrainian Greek Catholic
Church, 100, 103
Renovationist (Living) Church, 96
repatriation. See also Guatemalan women
refugees.
Autonomous Republic of Abkhazia,
112, 114–15
Republic of the Congo, 156
Reynolds, Andrew, 149
Roman Catholic East Timorese, 181–82
Romania, 39–40
Romans, Balkan history, 51–52, 55
Round Table/Free Georgia coalition, 111

RSDLP (Russian Social Democratic
    Labor Party), 119
Russia. *See also* USSR.
    Balkan history, 54, 60–61, 62
    Georgian independence, 130–32
    occupation of Georgia, 118
Russian Orthodoxy
    attempts to extirpate, 95–96
    divide and conquer, 95–96
    extinction of the Greek Catholic
        Church, 103
    Renovationist (Living) Church, 96
    restoration of, 97–98
    return of Stalinism, 99–100
    Sergii, Archbishop, 98, 101
    Sobor of 1943, 101
    waves of repression, 96
    westward shift, 102
    WW II, after, 103–5
    WW II, during, 98–103
Russian Social Democratic Labor Party
    (RSDLP), 119

Salamis, battle of, 56
Sasso-Nguesso, Denis, 156
Sava River, 54–55
Savimbi, Jonas, 156
Schevill, Ferdinand, 48
Scots, autonomy *vs.* independence, 31–33
Scott, Sir Walter, 28
secession, autonomy as prelude, 34
security
    of the group, 11–12, 15
    of the individual
        failure of, 15
        and group loyalty, 9
        and individual identity, 11–12
        psychological need for, 16
Sergii, Archbishop, 98, 101
Shamir, Yitzhak, 29
Sharif, Nawaz, 199
Shida Kartli conflict, 109–10
Shipka Pass, 55
Shugart, Matthew, 155–56
Sigismund, King of Hungary, 58
Simeon, 57
Slavs, Balkan history, 53
Slovaks, autonomy *vs.* independence, 31
Smith, Anthony D., 2
Sochi Accord, 109–10
social democratic movement, 119
social identity. *See* group identity.
social structure as defense, 7–8

Socrates, 12–13
Soeharto
    Aceh rebellion, 183
    Javanization, 174–76
    political centralization, 173–74
    resignation of, 170
Sophocles, 10
South Africa, 157
South Asian conflict
    Afghanistan
        bin Laden, Osama, 197–99
        civil war, 197
        jihad, 197–99, 201
        prevention and management, fu-
            ture efforts, 206
        Taliban, 193, 195
    causes of
        geopolitical concerns, 193
        identity concerns, 193–94
        political failures, types of, 192
        territorial disputes, 193
    common characteristics, 190
    external intervention
        China, 200–201
        Clinton, Bill, 199
        Soviet Union, 197
        United States, 196–99
    Gandhi, Rajiv, 202
    Hizb-ul-Mujahideen, 196
    Hurriyat, 195–96
    India
        Indus River water-sharing agree-
            ment, 203–5
        Kashmir, 195
        prevention and management, past
            efforts, 203–4, 204–5
    internal conflicts, 194–96
    interstate disputes, 194–96
    Jinnah, Mohammed Ali, 194
    Kashmir
        India, 195
        linkage factor, 208–10
        LOC (Line of Control), 210–11
    Lashkar-e-Toiba, 196
    Musharraf, Pervez, 200
    Northern Alliance, 193–94
    nuclear weaponization, 191–92, 199
    Pakistan
        Indus River water-sharing agree-
            ment, 203–5
        as a secular state, 194
        support for the Taliban, 193, 195
    prevention and management, future

efforts
Afghanistan, 206
Central Asian dimension, 207
dispersing resolution and management skills, 205
economic integration, 212–13
endowments, 205–6
Indus Valley example, 207
Kashmir, linkage factor, 208–10
Kashmir, LOC (Line of Control), 210–11
NGOs (nongovernmental organizations), 205
nuclear stabilization, 211–12
political hot lines, 211
public education, 206
regional philanthropy, 205–6
Sri Lankan civil war, 207–8
think tanks, 205–6
prevention and management, past efforts
1990 crisis, 202
Bangladesh, 204
economic liberalization, 204–5
India, 203–4, 204–5
Indus River water-sharing agreement, 203–5
Kargil episode, 203
NGOs (nongovernmental organizations), 204
Operation Brass Tacks, 202
Pakistan, 203–5
political liberalization, 204–5
Rao, V. Narasimha, 204–5
Sharif, Nawaz, 199
Taliban, 193, 195
terrorist organizations
Hizb-ul-Mujahideen, 196
Lashkar-e-Toiba, 196
Taliban, 193, 195
types of conflict, 191
Zia-ul-Haq, 195, 202
South Ossetian autonomous oblast, 109–10
South Ossetian Soviet Democratic Republic, 109–10
southeastern Europe. See Balkan conflict.
Soviet nationality policy, Georgian conflict, 121
Soviet Union. See USSR.
spiritual identity, 13
Sri Lankan civil war, 207–8. See also South Asian conflict.

Stalin, Joseph
de-Stalinization and Georgian conflict, 122–24
and religion. See USSR, religion.
Stavrianos, Leften, 48
Sukarno, Aceh rebellion, 183
Sukhumi, fall of, 112
Suny, Ronald, 118
Switzerland, autonomy vs. independence, 34–35

Taliban, 193, 195
Tamils, autonomy vs. independence, 32
Tbilisi, Georgian conflict, 113, 127–28
terrorist organizations
Hizb-ul-Mujahideen, 196
Lashkar-e-Toiba, 196
Taliban, 193, 195
the Ottomans, Balkan conflict, 58–62
Thermopylae, battle of, 56
think tanks, South Asia, 205–6
Thucydides, 15, 48–49
topography, effects on the Balkans, 48, 54–55, 63
triangular geopolitical patterns. See geopolitical patterns, the Balkans.
tsarism, collapse of, 119–20
Tsereteli, Irakli, 119

UN Development Program, 228
UN Environment Program, 228
UN High Commissioner for Refugees, 228
UN International Children's Emergency Fund (UNICEF), 228
UN Office of the High Commissioner for Human Rights, 228
UNDP (United Nations Development Program), 150–51
UNHCR (United Nations High Commissioner for Refugees), 67
Uniate Church, 103
UNICEF (UN International Children's Emergency Fund), 228
unihomeland states, 30
United Nations Development Program (UNDP), 150–51
United Nations High Commissioner for Refugees (UNHCR), 67
United States, in South Asia, 196–99
USSR. See also Russia.
autonomy vs. independence, 30, 33
in South Asia, 197

USSR, religion
  anti-Russian religious community, 100
  under the Bolsheviks, 94–96
  hostility towards, 94–96
  Khrushchev, Nikita, 104
  Malenkov, Georgii, 96
  reemergence since 1991, 93–94
  religious revival, 100
  restoration of state control, 101–2
  Russian Orthodoxy
    attempts to extirpate, 95–96
    divide and conquer, 95–96
    extinction of the Greek Catholic Church, 103
    Renovationist (Living) Church, 96
    restoration of, 97–98
    return of Stalinism, 99–100
    Sergii, Archbishop, 98, 101
    Sobor of 1943, 101
    waves of repression, 96
    westward shift, 102
    WW II, after, 103–5
    WW II, during, 98–103
  Uniate Church, 103
  West Ukrainian Greek Catholic Church, 100, 103
  Zhurnal Moskovskoi patriarkhii, 101

Venice, Balkan history, 53–54
vertical conflicts, 187
Via Egnatia highway, 52

violence, and forced change, 15
Visigoths, Balkan history, 52
Vlachs, Balkan history, 52

Wahid, Abdurrahman, 185
Welsh, autonomy vs. independence, 32
West, Rebecca, 50
West Kalimantan, 177–78
West Ukrainian Greek Catholic Church, 100, 103
Westendorp, Carlos, 26
Wilson, Woodrow, 21
winner-take-all politics, 143, 150, 156
women
  and African governance, 155
  Beijing Conference on Women, 155
  Guatemalan refugees. See Guatemalan women refugees.
  inequality of the sexes in Africa, 155
Wyszynski, Stefan Cardinal, 28–29

Yugoslavia
  Balkan conflict, 62–63
  ethnonational conflict, 21–22

Zagreb-Tiranë-Istanbul (ZTI) triangle, 44–46
Zambia, 146, 149
Zhordania, Noe, 119
Zhurnal Moskovskoi patriarkhii, 101
Zia-ul-Haq, 195, 202
ZTI (Zagreb-Tiranë-Istanbul) triangle, 44–46